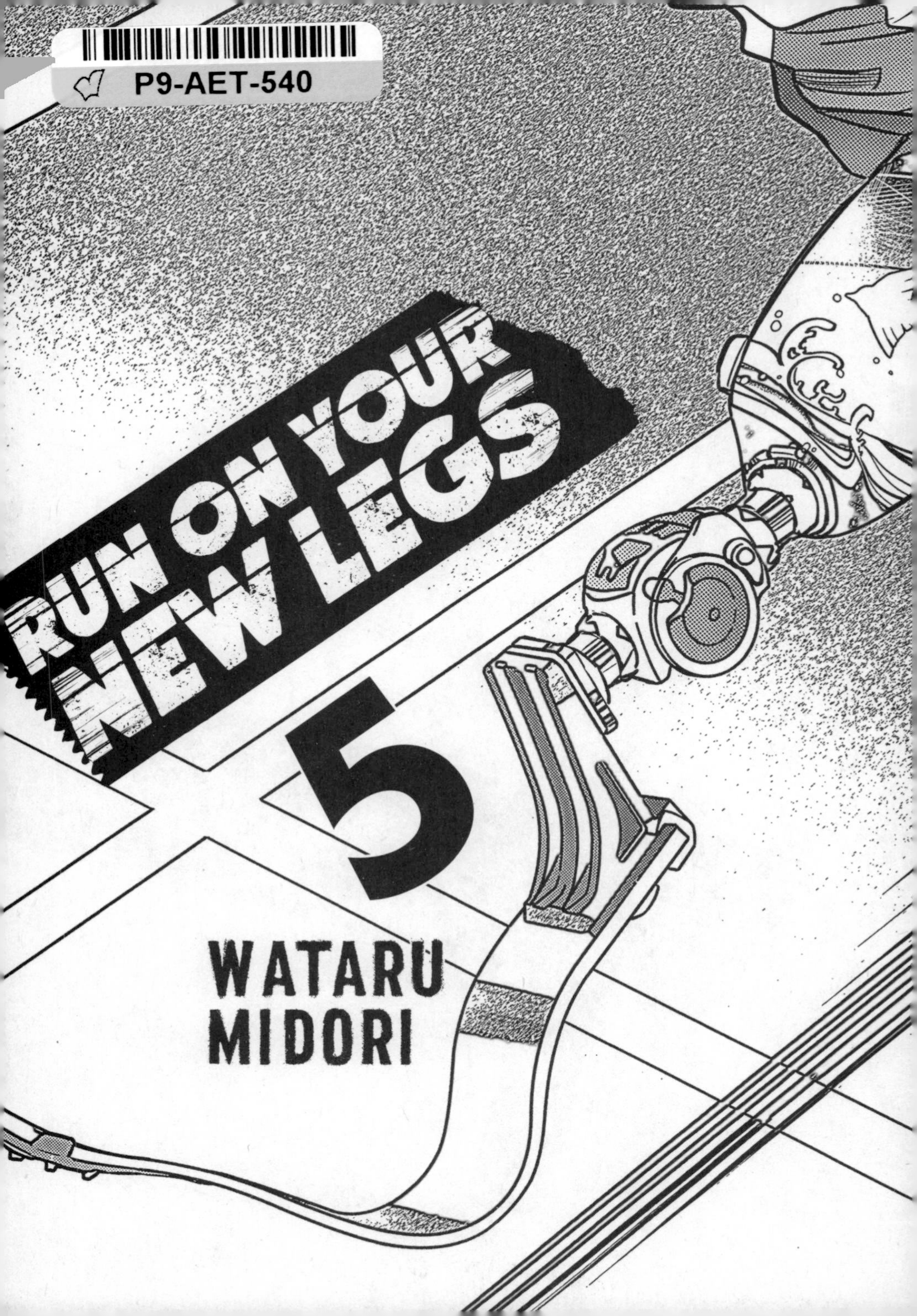
RUN ON YOUR NEW LEGS
5
WATARU MIDORI

TABLE OF CONTENTS

Chapter 31: The Theme of My Summer

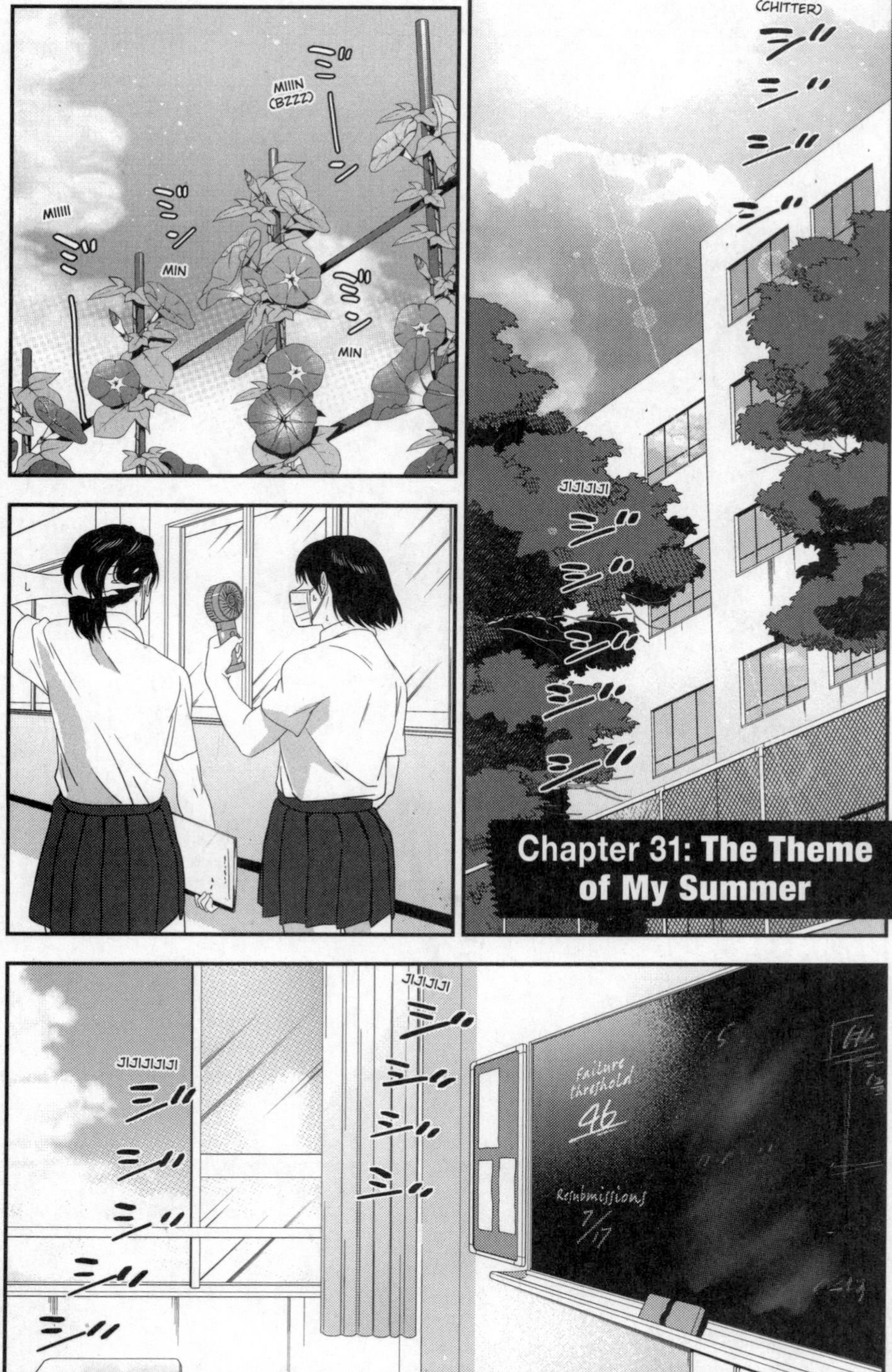
JIJIJIJI
(CHITTER)
JIJIJI
Chapter 31: The Theme of My Summer
MIIIN
(BZZZ)
MIIIII
MIN
MIN
Failure threshold
46
Resubmissions
7/17
JIJIJI
JIJIJIJI

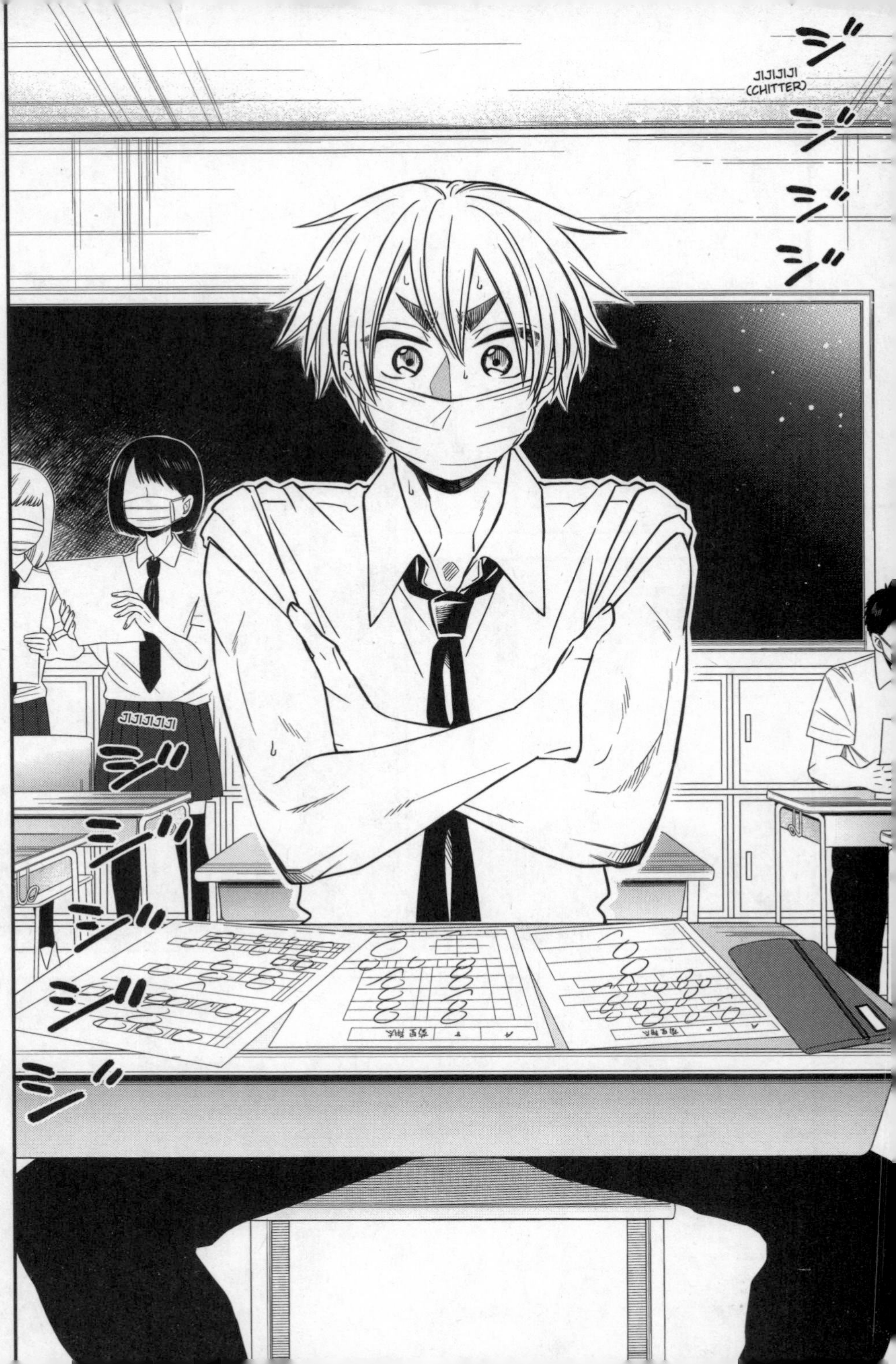
JIJIJIJI (CHITTER)
JIJIJIJI

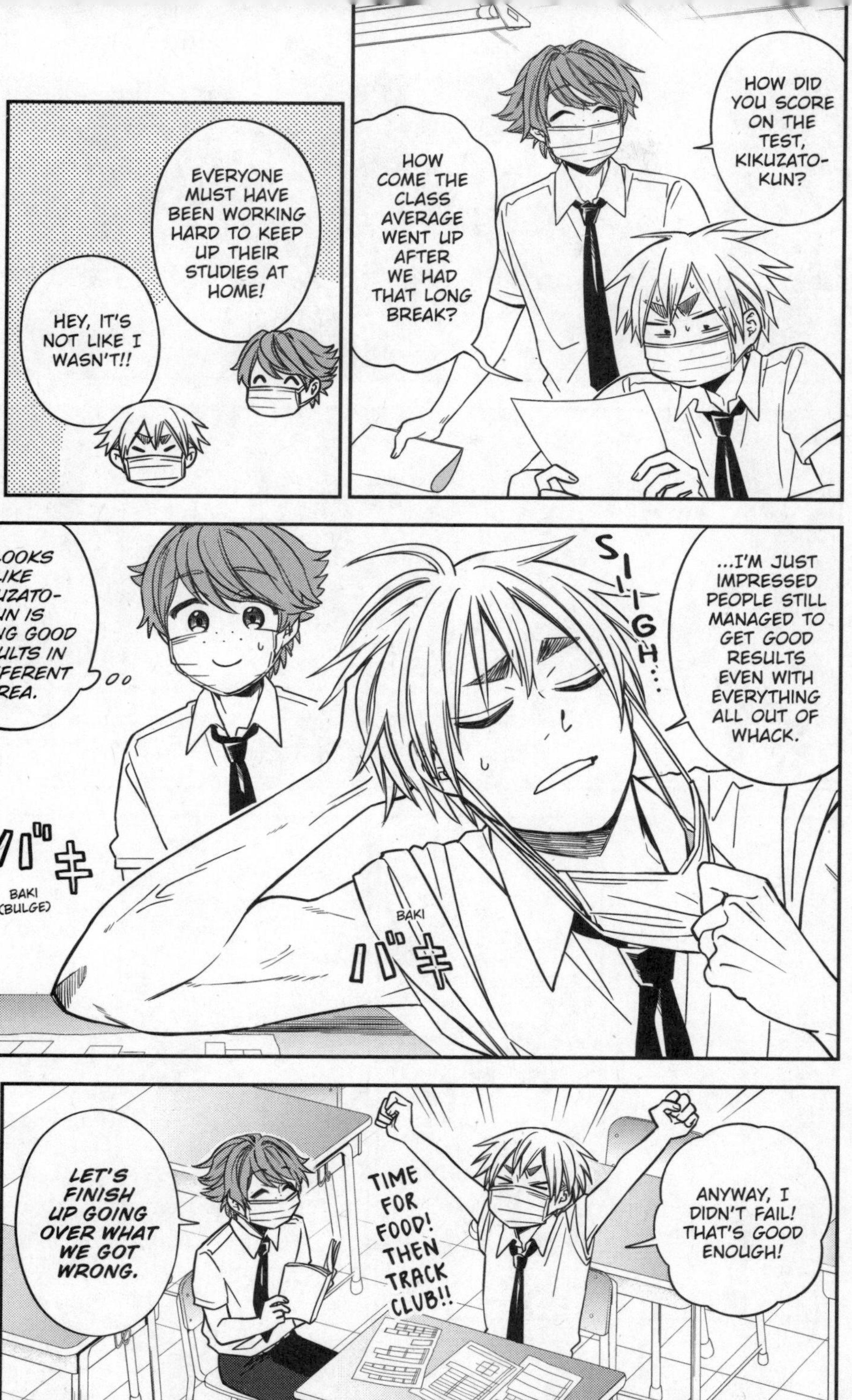
HOW DID YOU SCORE ON THE TEST, KIKUZATO-KUN?
HOW COME THE CLASS AVERAGE WENT UP AFTER WE HAD THAT LONG BREAK?
EVERYONE MUST HAVE BEEN WORKING HARD TO KEEP UP THEIR STUDIES AT HOME!
HEY, IT'S NOT LIKE I WASN'T!!
...I'M JUST IMPRESSED PEOPLE STILL MANAGED TO GET GOOD RESULTS EVEN WITH EVERYTHING ALL OUT OF WHACK.
SIIIGH...
バキ
BAKI
バキ
BAKI (BULGE)
...LOOKS LIKE KIKUZATO-KUN IS SEEING GOOD RESULTS IN A DIFFERENT AREA.
ANYWAY, I DIDN'T FAIL! THAT'S GOOD ENOUGH!
TIME FOR FOOD! THEN TRACK CLUB!!
LET'S FINISH UP GOING OVER WHAT WE GOT WRONG.

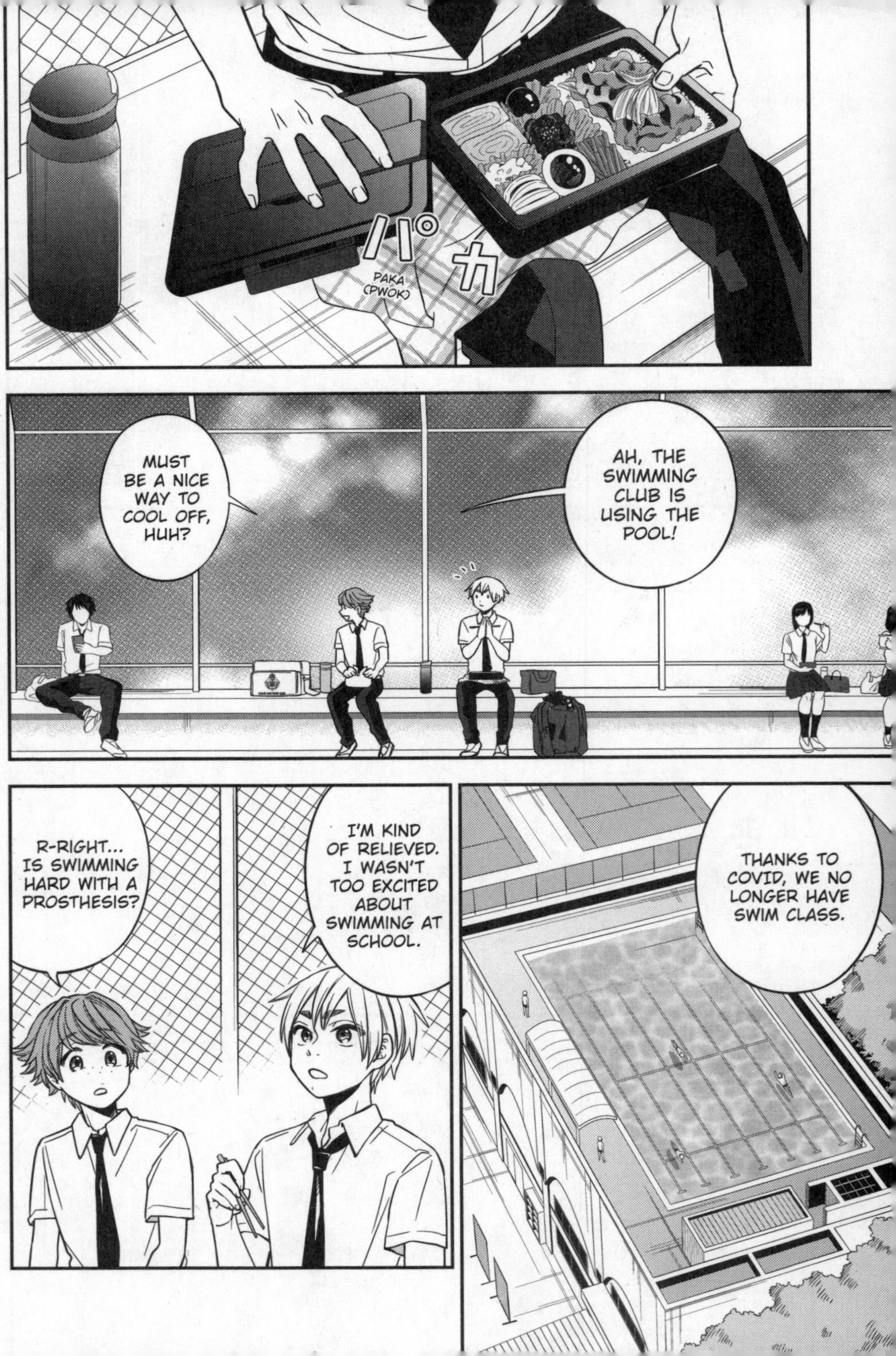
パカ
PAKA (PWOK)
AH, THE SWIMMING CLUB IS USING THE POOL!
MUST BE A NICE WAY TO COOL OFF, HUH?
THANKS TO COVID, WE NO LONGER HAVE SWIM CLASS.
I'M KIND OF RELIEVED. I WASN'T TOO EXCITED ABOUT SWIMMING AT SCHOOL.
R-RIGHT... IS SWIMMING HARD WITH A PROSTHESIS?

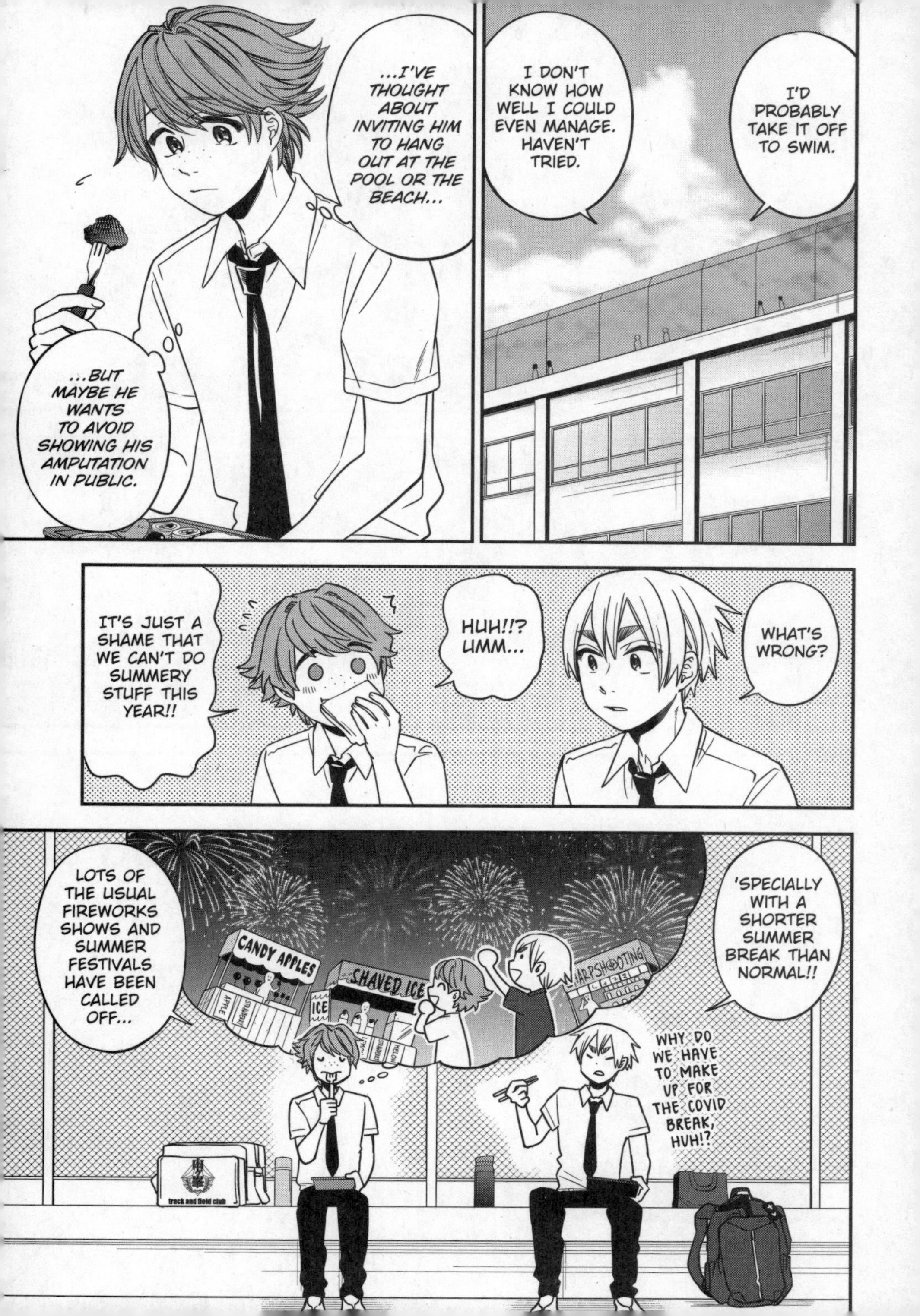

I'D PROBABLY TAKE IT OFF TO SWIM.
I DON'T KNOW HOW WELL I COULD EVEN MANAGE. HAVEN'T TRIED.
...I'VE THOUGHT ABOUT INVITING HIM TO HANG OUT AT THE POOL OR THE BEACH...
...BUT MAYBE HE WANTS TO AVOID SHOWING HIS AMPUTATION IN PUBLIC.
WHAT'S WRONG?
HUH!!? UMM...
IT'S JUST A SHAME THAT WE CAN'T DO SUMMERY STUFF THIS YEAR!!
'SPECIALLY WITH A SHORTER SUMMER BREAK THAN NORMAL!!
LOTS OF THE USUAL FIREWORKS SHOWS AND SUMMER FESTIVALS HAVE BEEN CALLED OFF...
CANDY APPLES
SHAVED ICE
ICE
WHY DO WE HAVE TO MAKE UP FOR THE COVID BREAK, HUH!?
track and field club

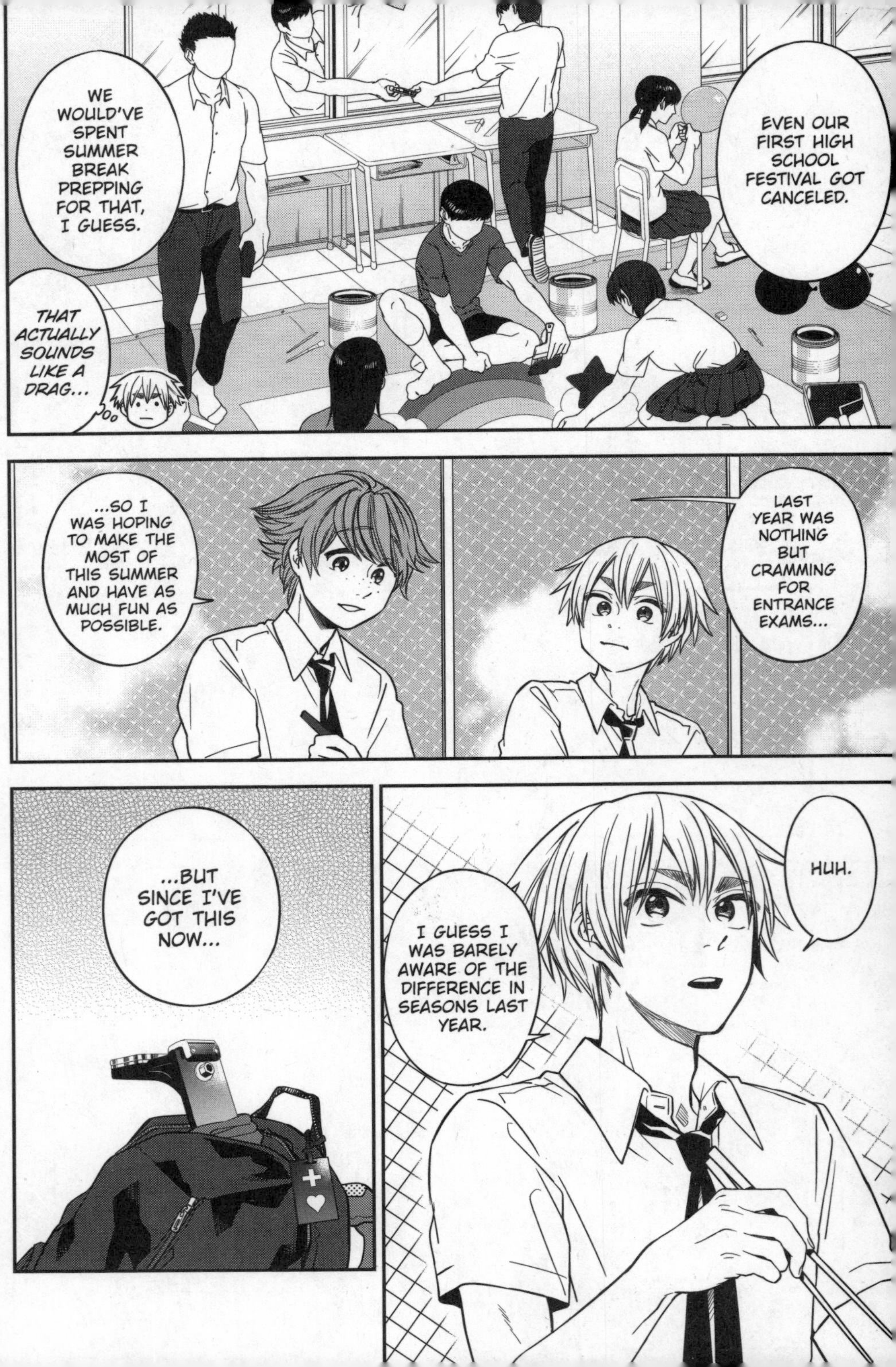
EVEN OUR FIRST HIGH SCHOOL FESTIVAL GOT CANCELED.
WE WOULD'VE SPENT SUMMER BREAK PREPPING FOR THAT, I GUESS.
THAT ACTUALLY SOUNDS LIKE A DRAG...
LAST YEAR WAS NOTHING BUT CRAMMING FOR ENTRANCE EXAMS...
...SO I WAS HOPING TO MAKE THE MOST OF THIS SUMMER AND HAVE AS MUCH FUN AS POSSIBLE.
HUH.
I GUESS I WAS BARELY AWARE OF THE DIFFERENCE IN SEASONS LAST YEAR.
...BUT SINCE I'VE GOT THIS NOW...

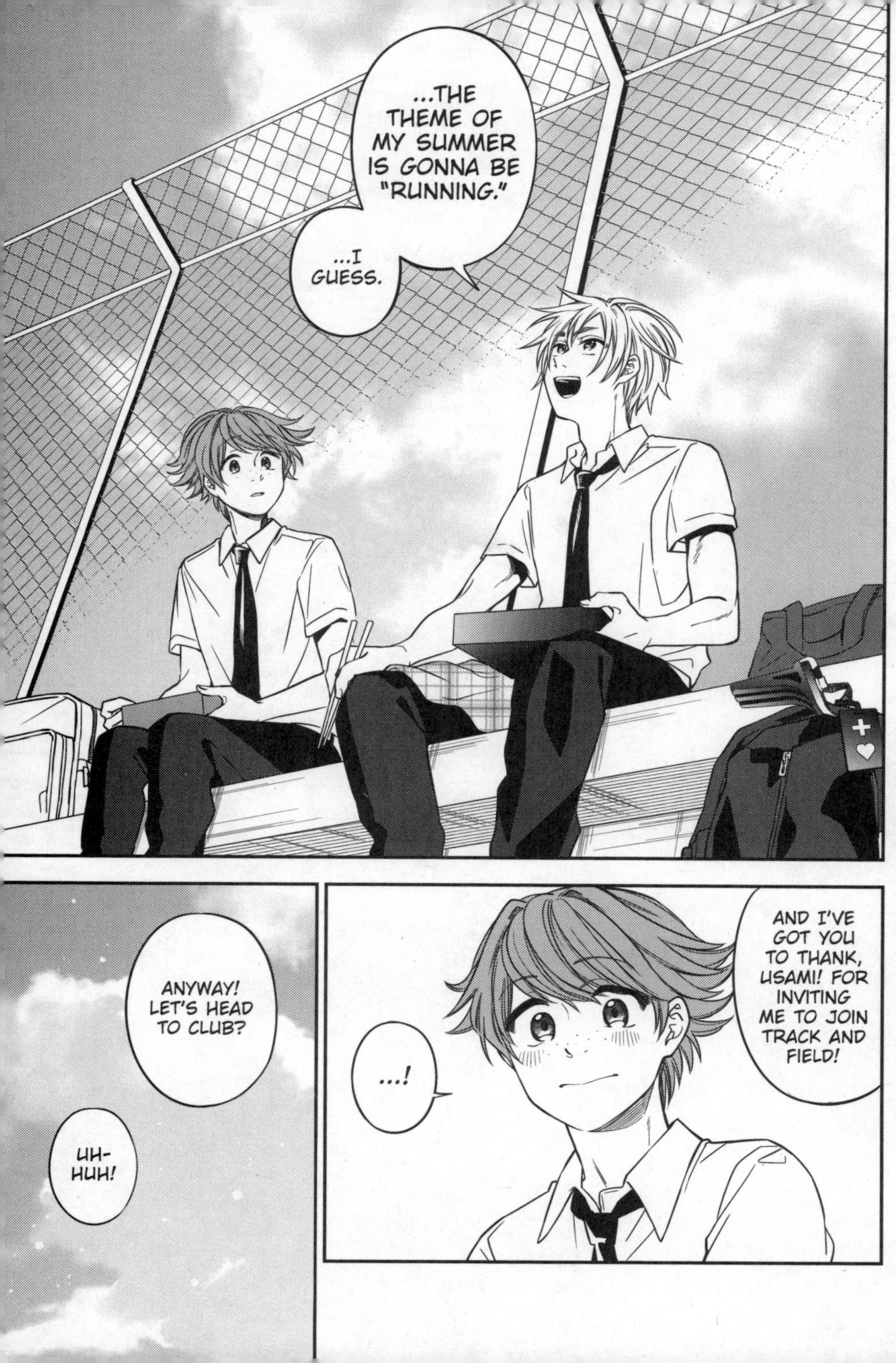
...THE THEME OF MY SUMMER IS GONNA BE "RUNNING."
...I GUESS.
AND I'VE GOT YOU TO THANK, USAMI! FOR INVITING ME TO JOIN TRACK AND FIELD!
...!
ANYWAY! LET'S HEAD TO CLUB?
UH-HUH!

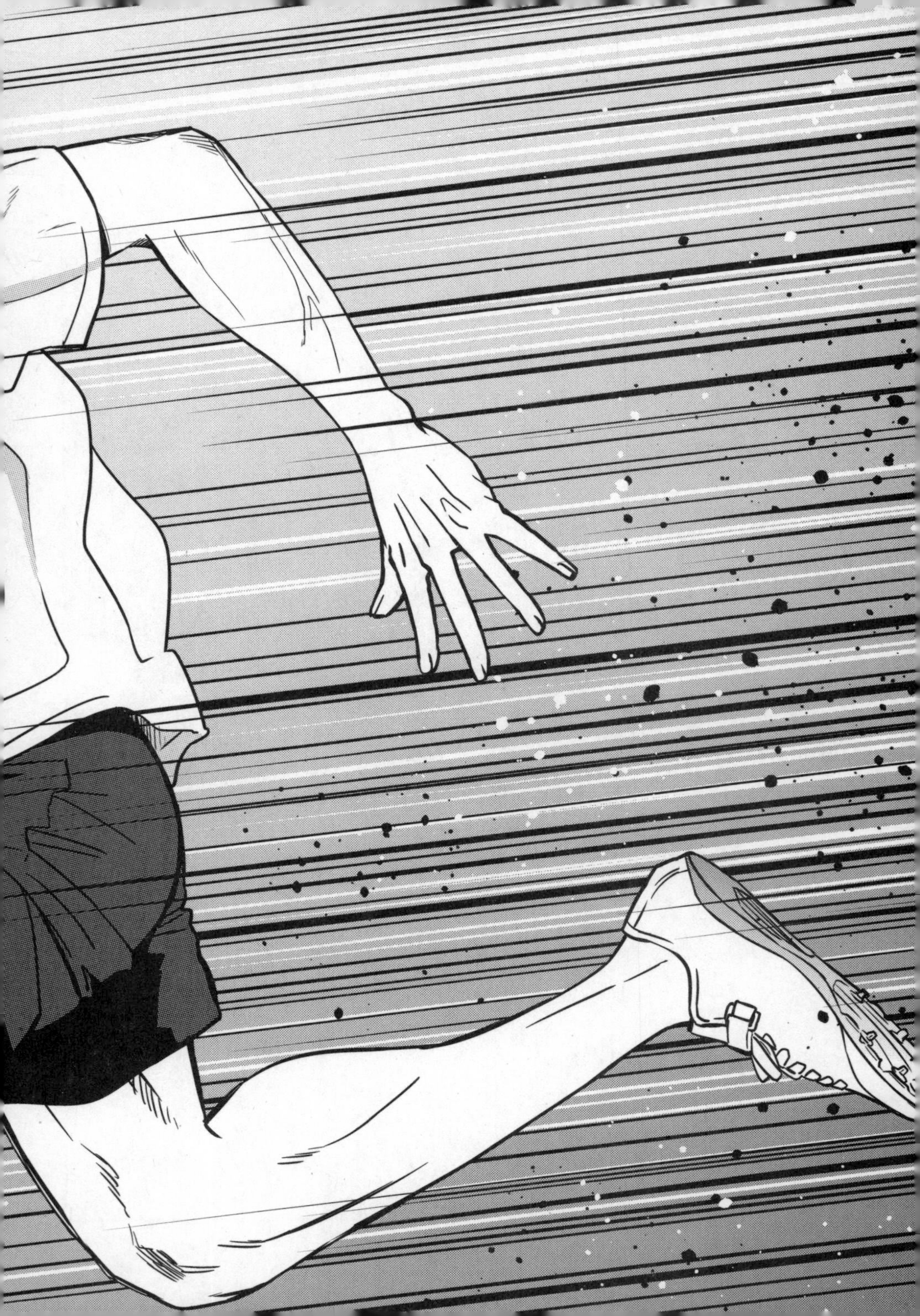

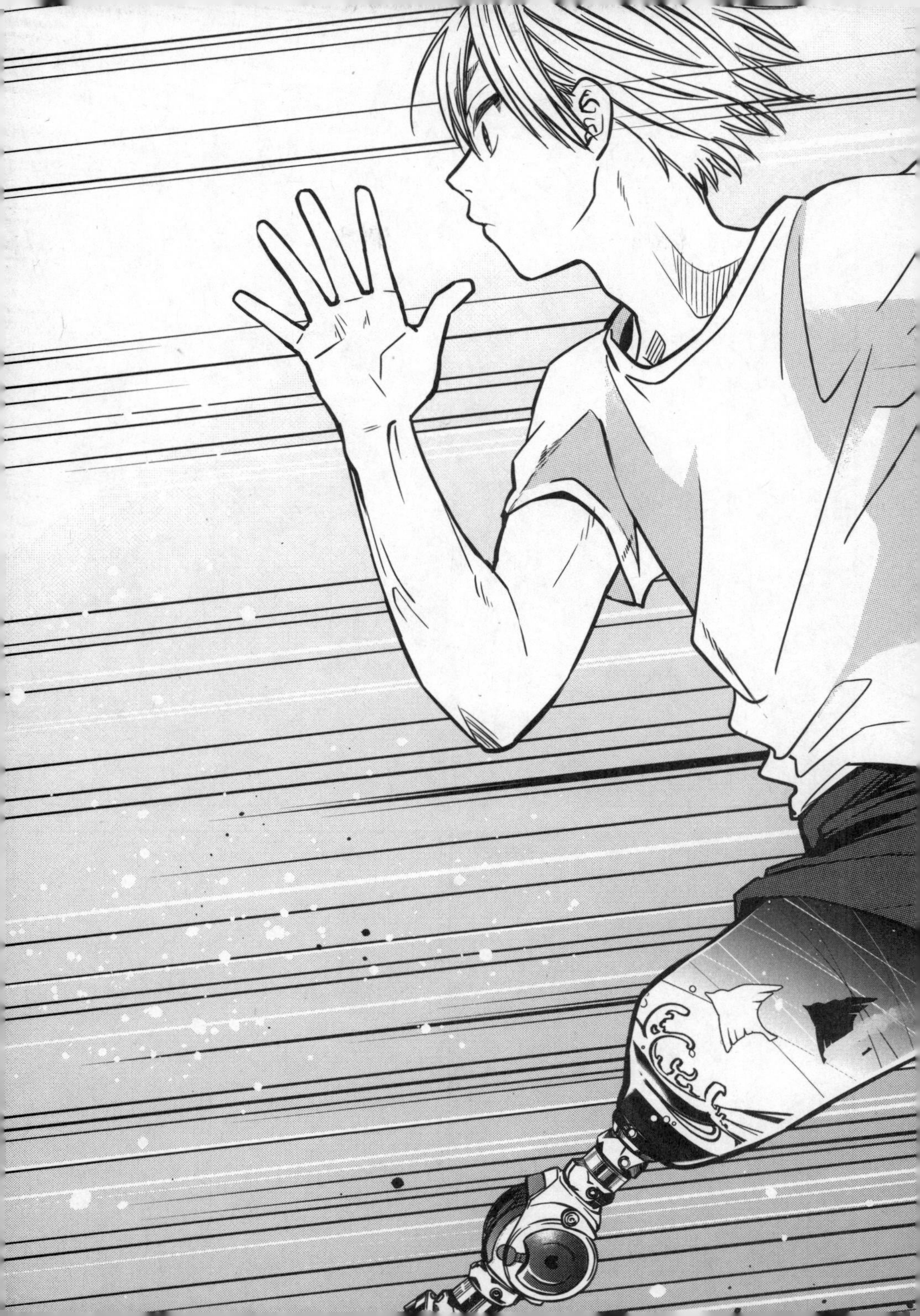

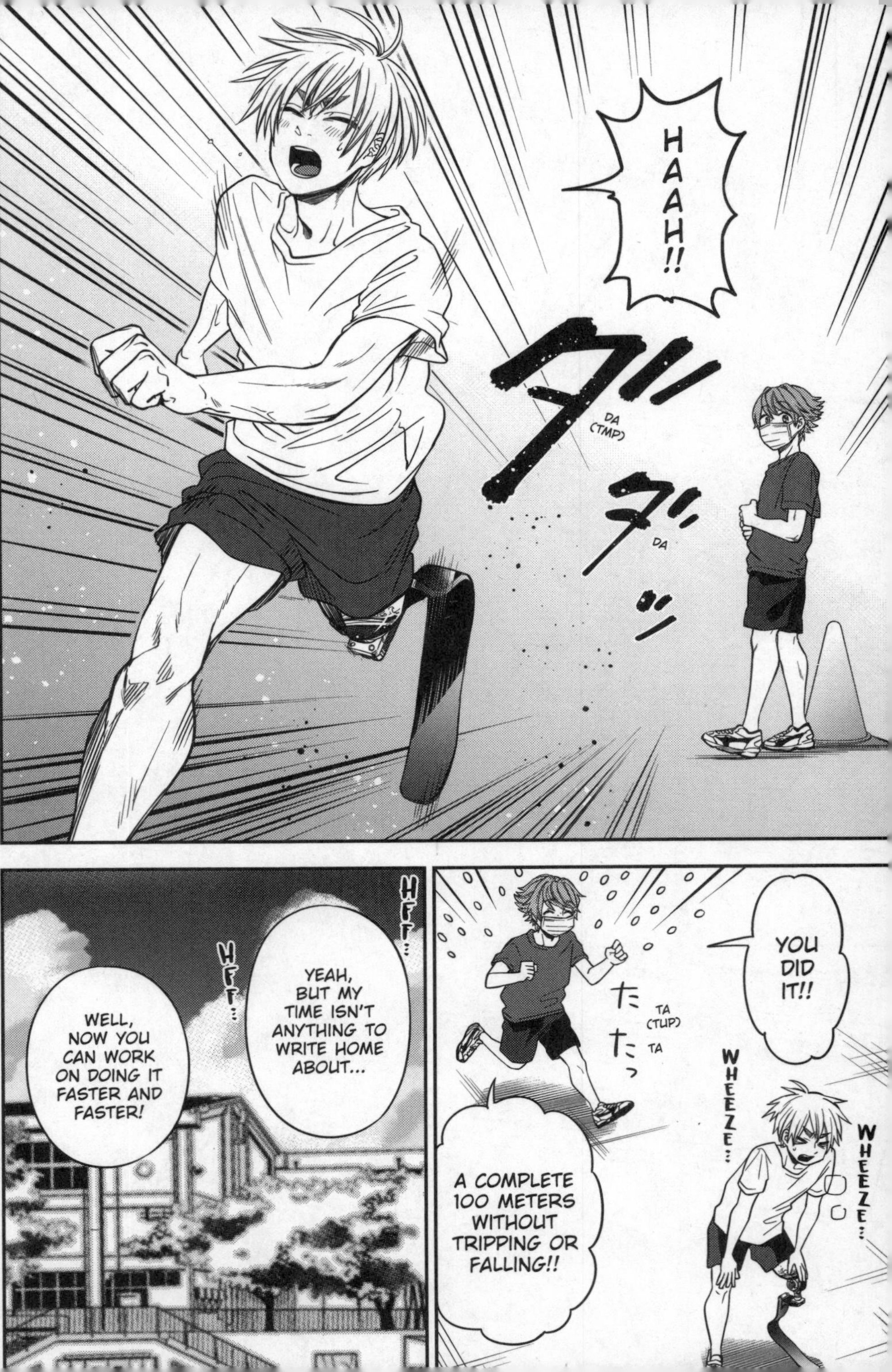
HAAAH!!
ダッ
DA (TMP)
ダッ
DA
YOU DID IT!!
たたっ
TA (TUP) TA
WHEEZE...
WHEEZE...
A COMPLETE 100 METERS WITHOUT TRIPPING OR FALLING!!
HFF...
HFF...
YEAH, BUT MY TIME ISN'T ANYTHING TO WRITE HOME ABOUT...
WELL, NOW YOU CAN WORK ON DOING IT FASTER AND FASTER!

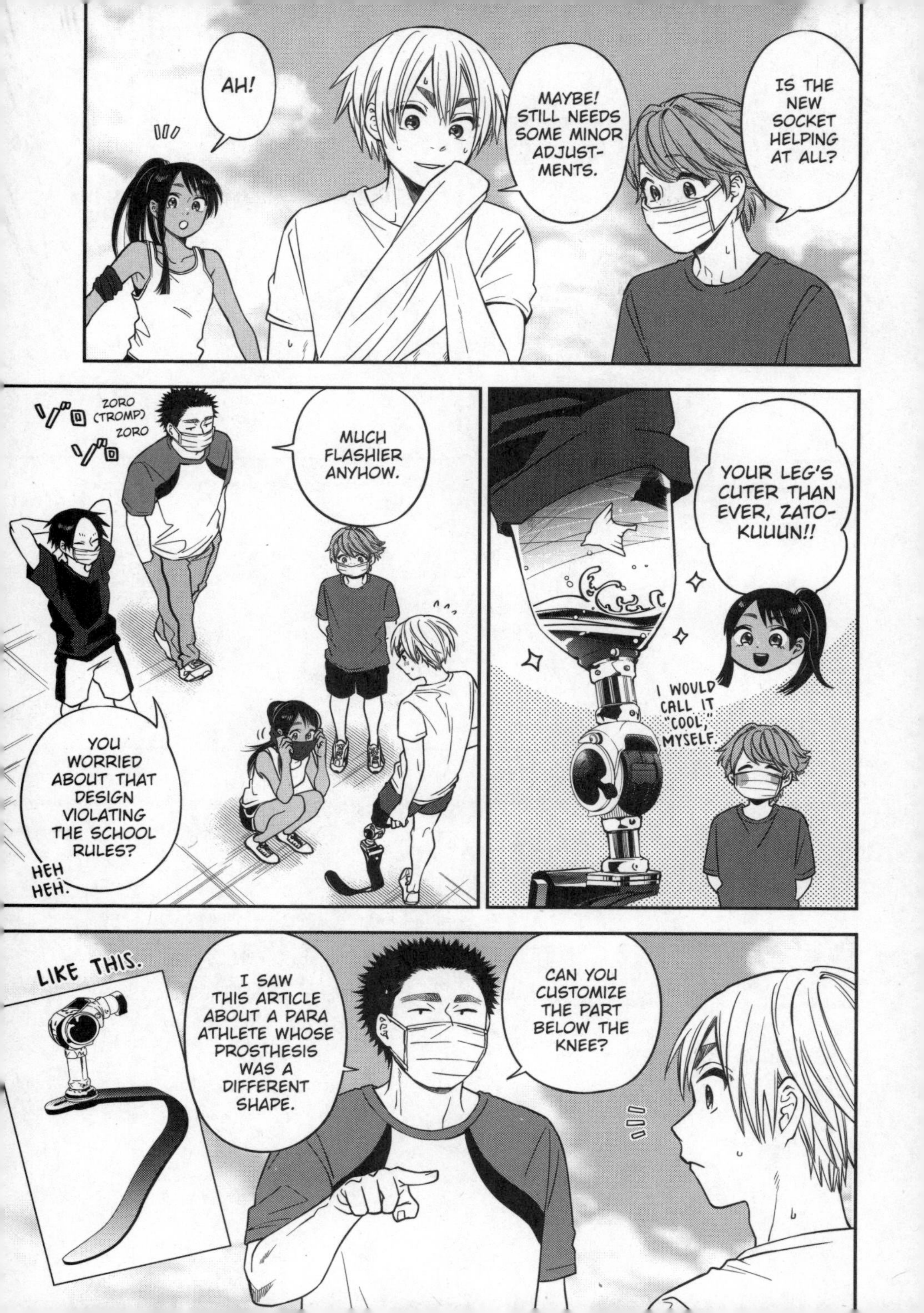
IS THE NEW SOCKET HELPING AT ALL?
MAYBE! STILL NEEDS SOME MINOR ADJUST-MENTS.
AH!
YOUR LEG'S CUTER THAN EVER, ZATO-KUUUN!!
I WOULD CALL IT "COOL," MYSELF.
ZORO (TROMP) ZORO
MUCH FLASHIER ANYHOW.
YOU WORRIED ABOUT THAT DESIGN VIOLATING THE SCHOOL RULES?
HEH HEH.
CAN YOU CUSTOMIZE THE PART BELOW THE KNEE?
I SAW THIS ARTICLE ABOUT A PARA ATHLETE WHOSE PROSTHESIS WAS A DIFFERENT SHAPE.
LIKE THIS.

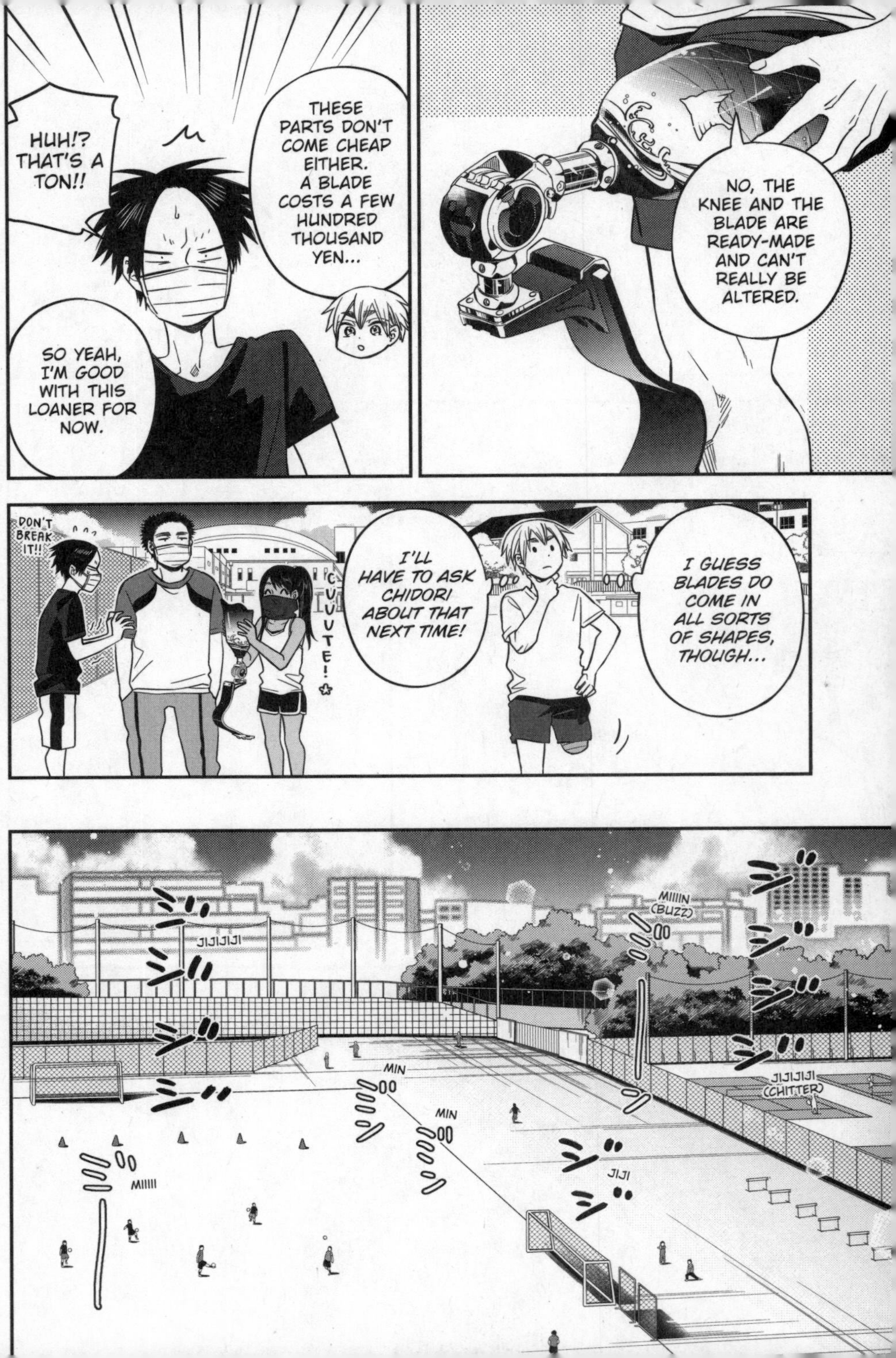
NO, THE KNEE AND THE BLADE ARE READY-MADE AND CAN'T REALLY BE ALTERED.
THESE PARTS DON'T COME CHEAP EITHER. A BLADE COSTS A FEW HUNDRED THOUSAND YEN...
HUH!? THAT'S A TON!!
SO YEAH, I'M GOOD WITH THIS LOANER FOR NOW.
I GUESS BLADES DO COME IN ALL SORTS OF SHAPES, THOUGH...
I'LL HAVE TO ASK CHIDORI ABOUT THAT NEXT TIME!
CUUUTE!☆
DON'T BREAK IT!!
MIIIN (BUZZ)
JIJIJIJI (CHITTER)
JIJI
MIN
MIN
JIJIJIJI
MIIII

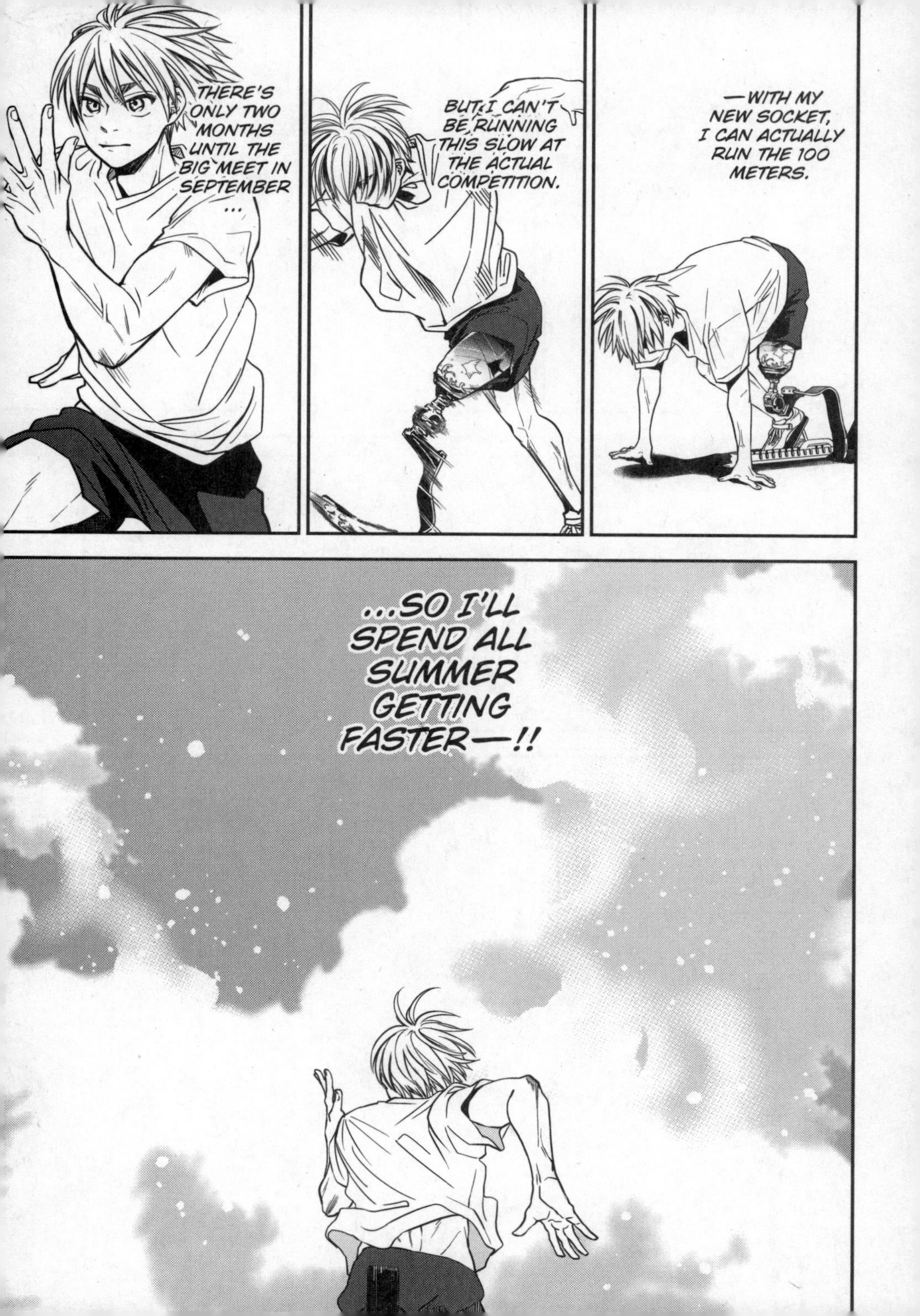
—WITH MY NEW SOCKET, I CAN ACTUALLY RUN THE 100 METERS.
BUT I CAN'T BE RUNNING THIS SLOW AT THE ACTUAL COMPETITION.
THERE'S ONLY TWO MONTHS UNTIL THE BIG MEET IN SEPTEMBER ...
...SO I'LL SPEND ALL SUMMER GETTING FASTER—!!

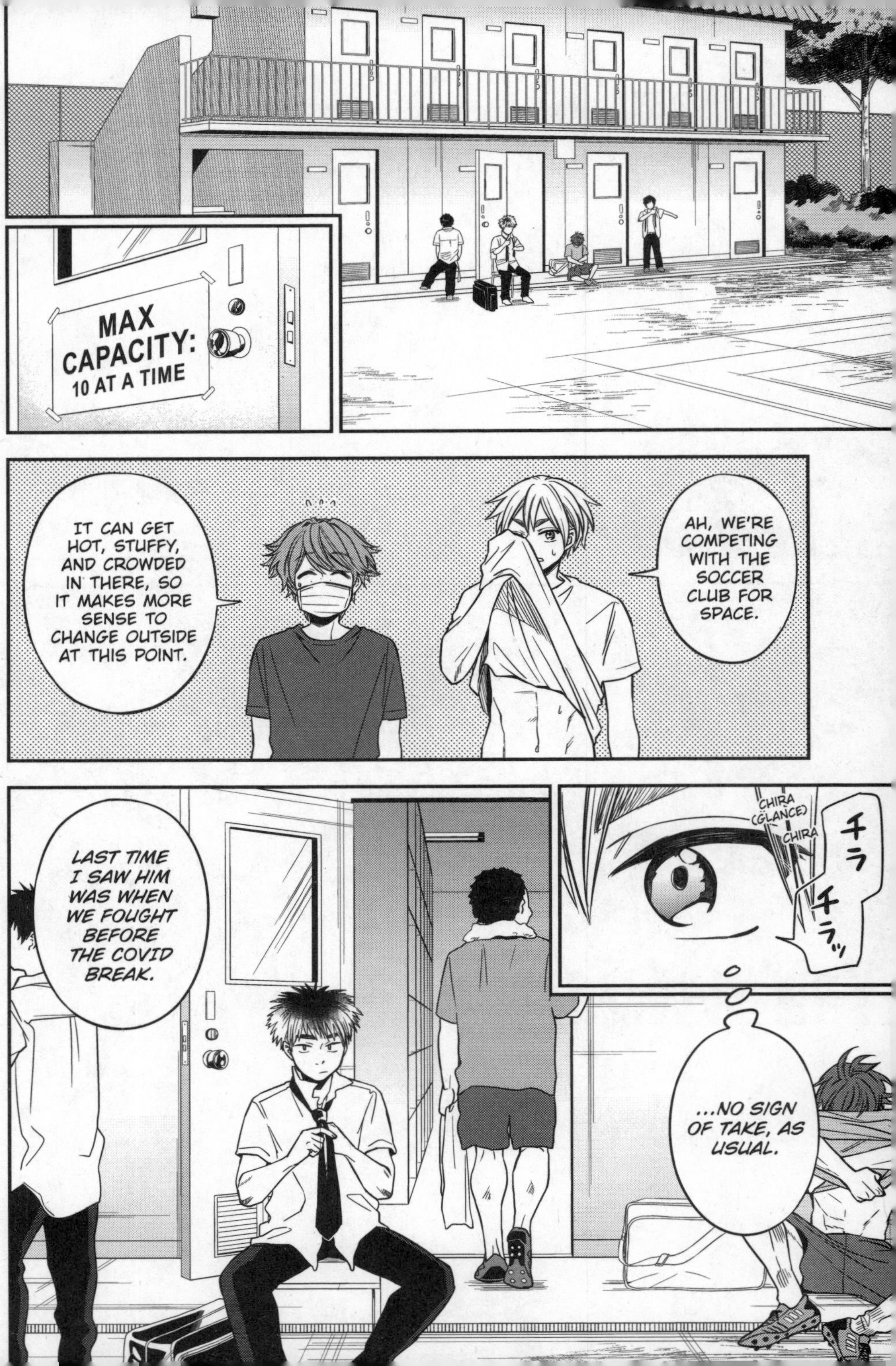
MAX CAPACITY: 10 AT A TIME
AH, WE'RE COMPETING WITH THE SOCCER CLUB FOR SPACE.
IT CAN GET HOT, STUFFY, AND CROWDED IN THERE, SO IT MAKES MORE SENSE TO CHANGE OUTSIDE AT THIS POINT.
CHIRA (GLANCE) CHIRA
チラ
チラッ
...NO SIGN OF TAKE, AS USUAL.
LAST TIME I SAW HIM WAS WHEN WE FOUGHT BEFORE THE COVID BREAK.

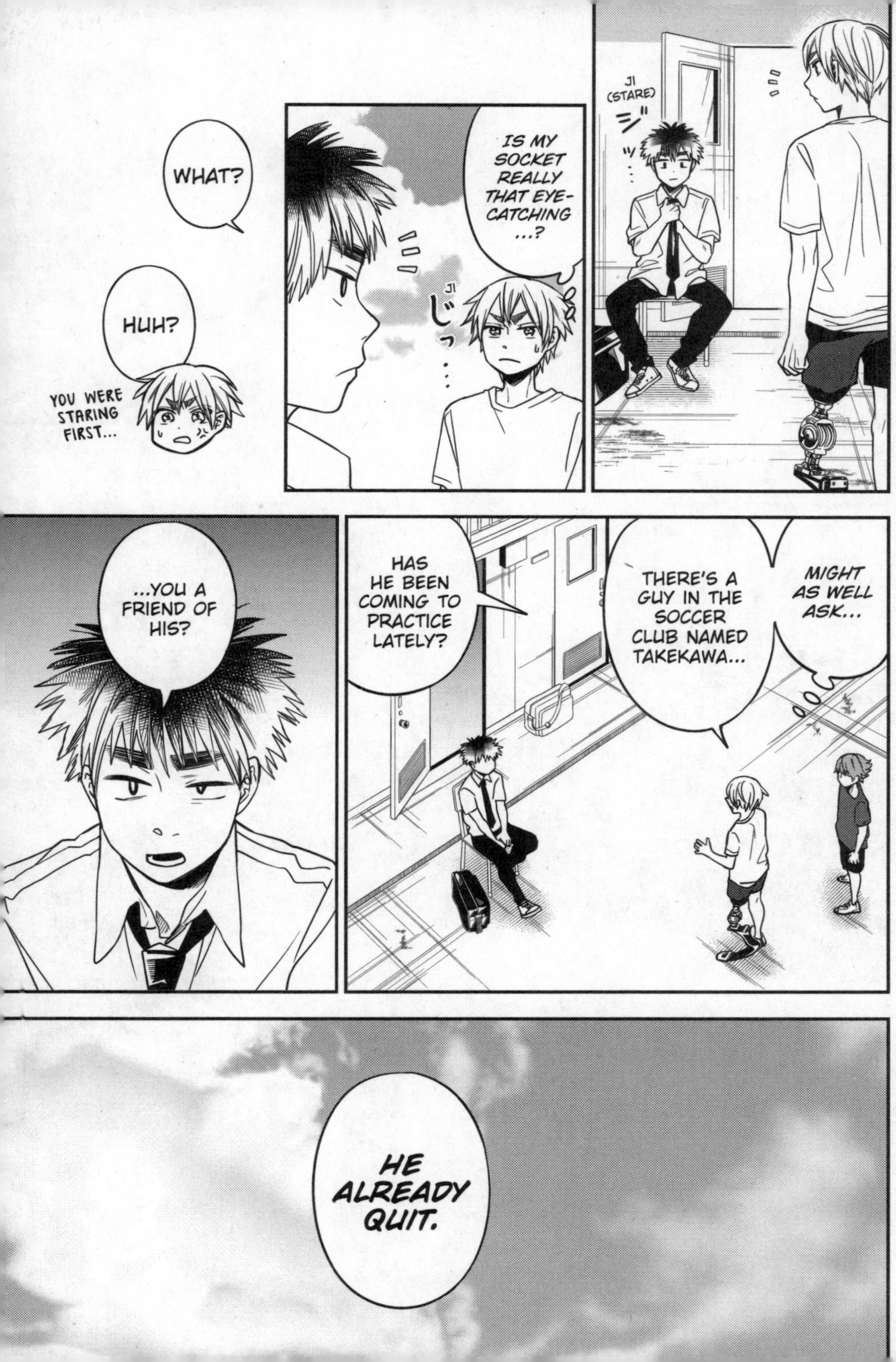
JI (STARE)
IS MY SOCKET REALLY THAT EYE-CATCHING ...?
JI
WHAT?
HUH?
YOU WERE STARING FIRST...
MIGHT AS WELL ASK...
THERE'S A GUY IN THE SOCCER CLUB NAMED TAKEKAWA...
HAS HE BEEN COMING TO PRACTICE LATELY?
...YOU A FRIEND OF HIS?
HE ALREADY QUIT.

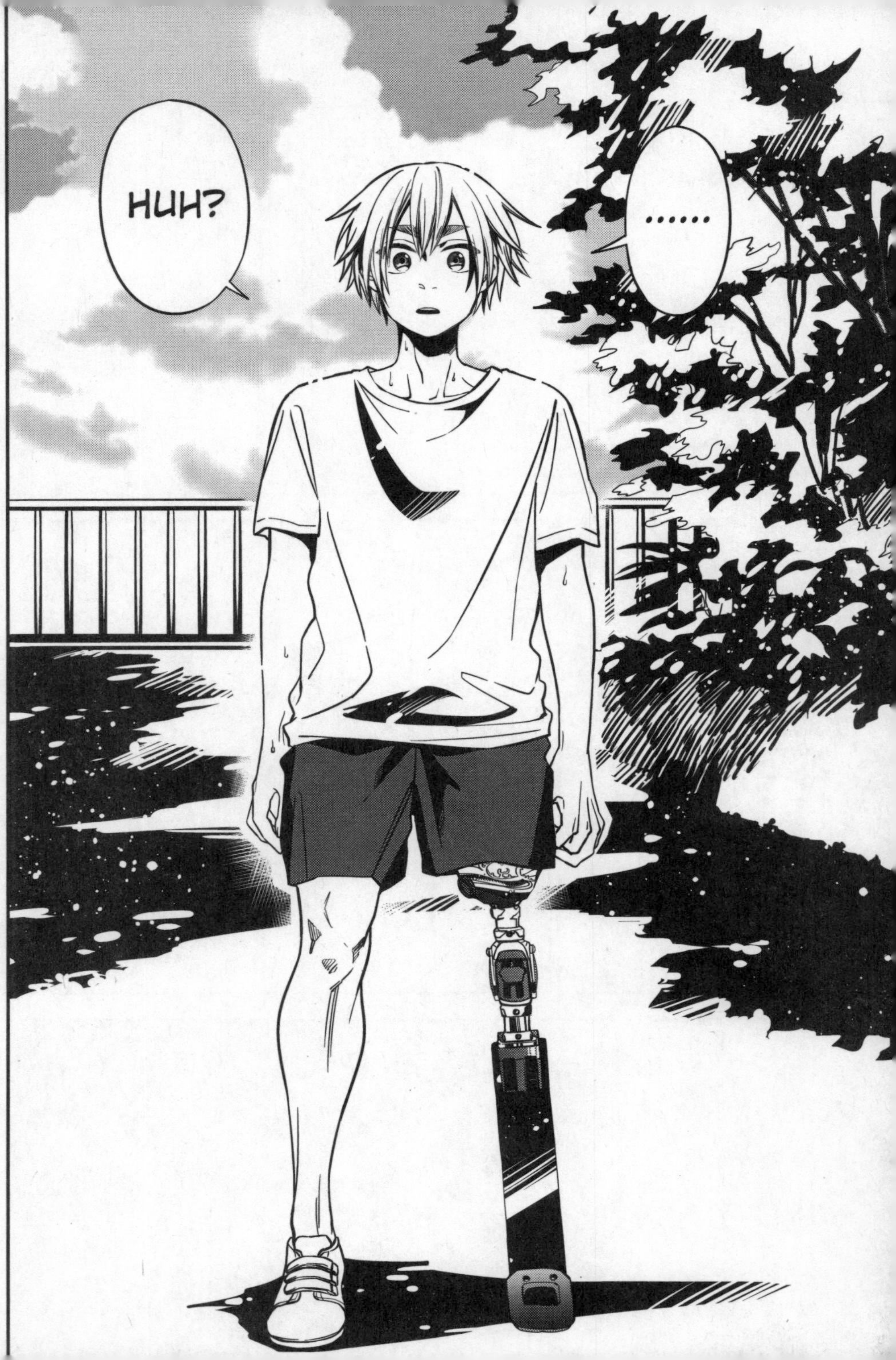
......
HUH?

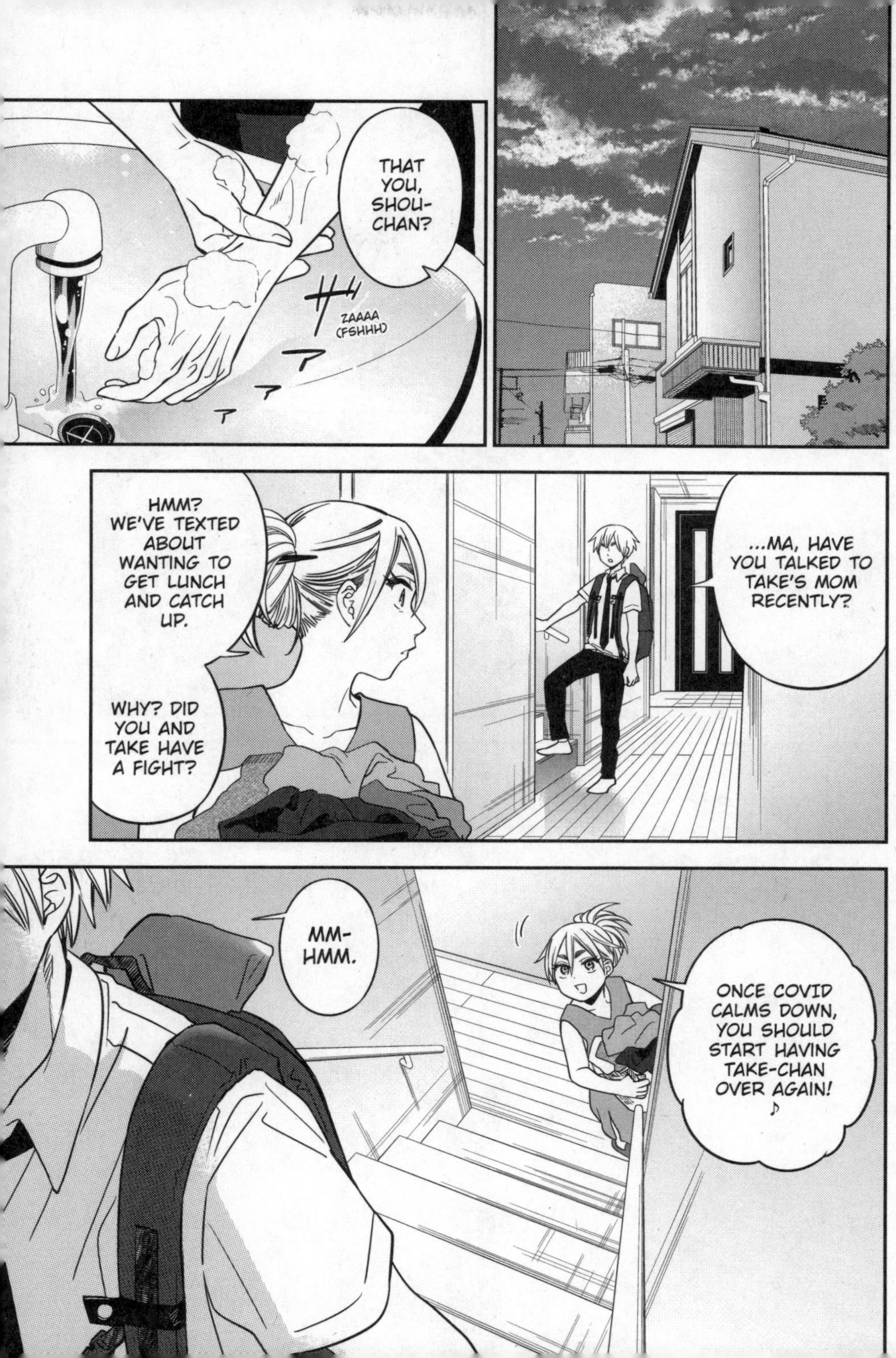
THAT YOU, SHOU-CHAN?
ZAAAA (FSHHH)
...MA, HAVE YOU TALKED TO TAKE'S MOM RECENTLY?
HMM? WE'VE TEXTED ABOUT WANTING TO GET LUNCH AND CATCH UP.
WHY? DID YOU AND TAKE HAVE A FIGHT?
ONCE COVID CALMS DOWN, YOU SHOULD START HAVING TAKE-CHAN OVER AGAIN! ♪
MM-HMM.

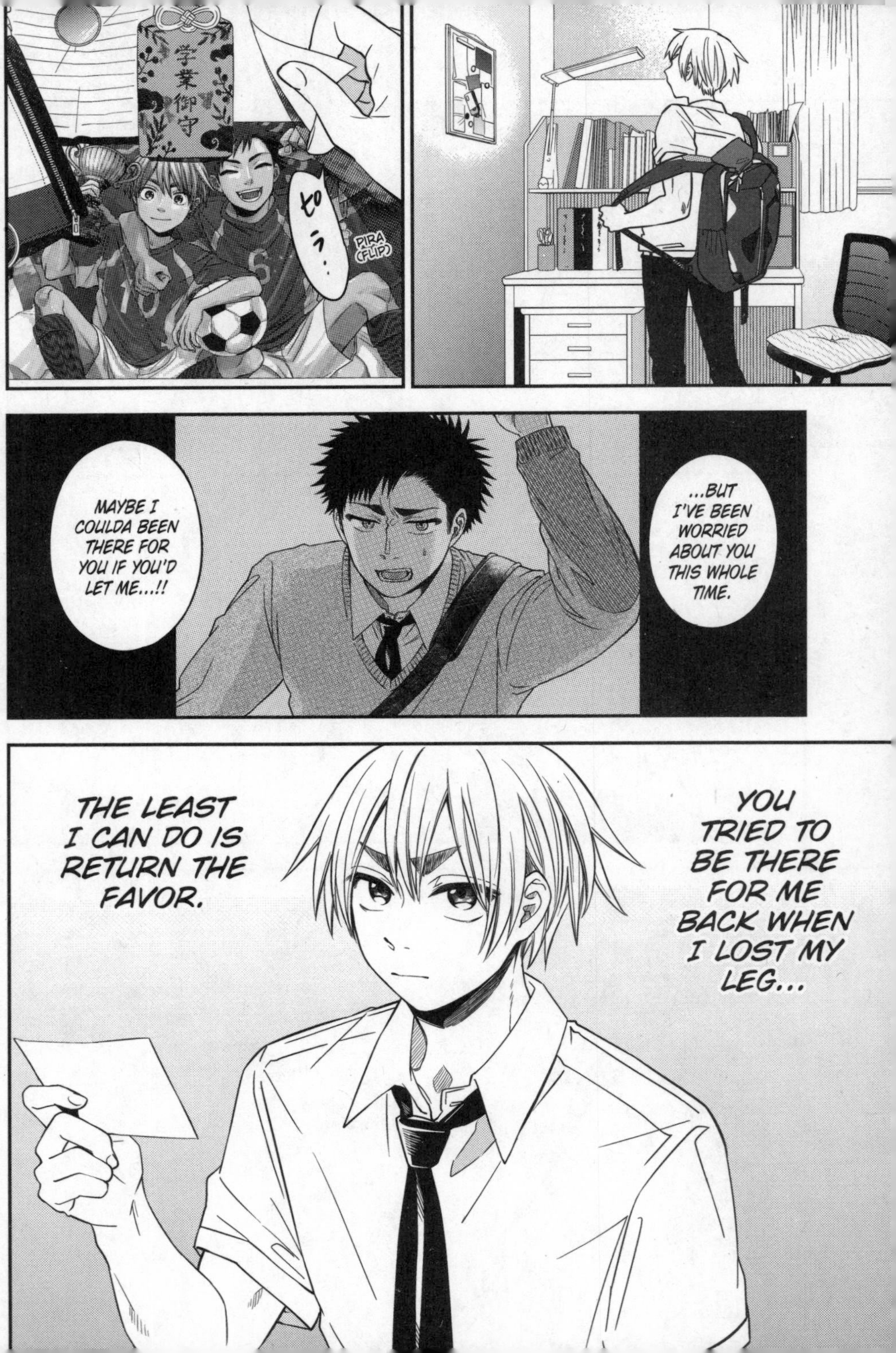
学業御守
ぴら‥
PIRA (FLIP)
...BUT I'VE BEEN WORRIED ABOUT YOU THIS WHOLE TIME.
MAYBE I COULDA BEEN THERE FOR YOU IF YOU'D LET ME...!!
YOU TRIED TO BE THERE FOR ME BACK WHEN I LOST MY LEG...
THE LEAST I CAN DO IS RETURN THE FAVOR.

Chapter 32: The Same Path

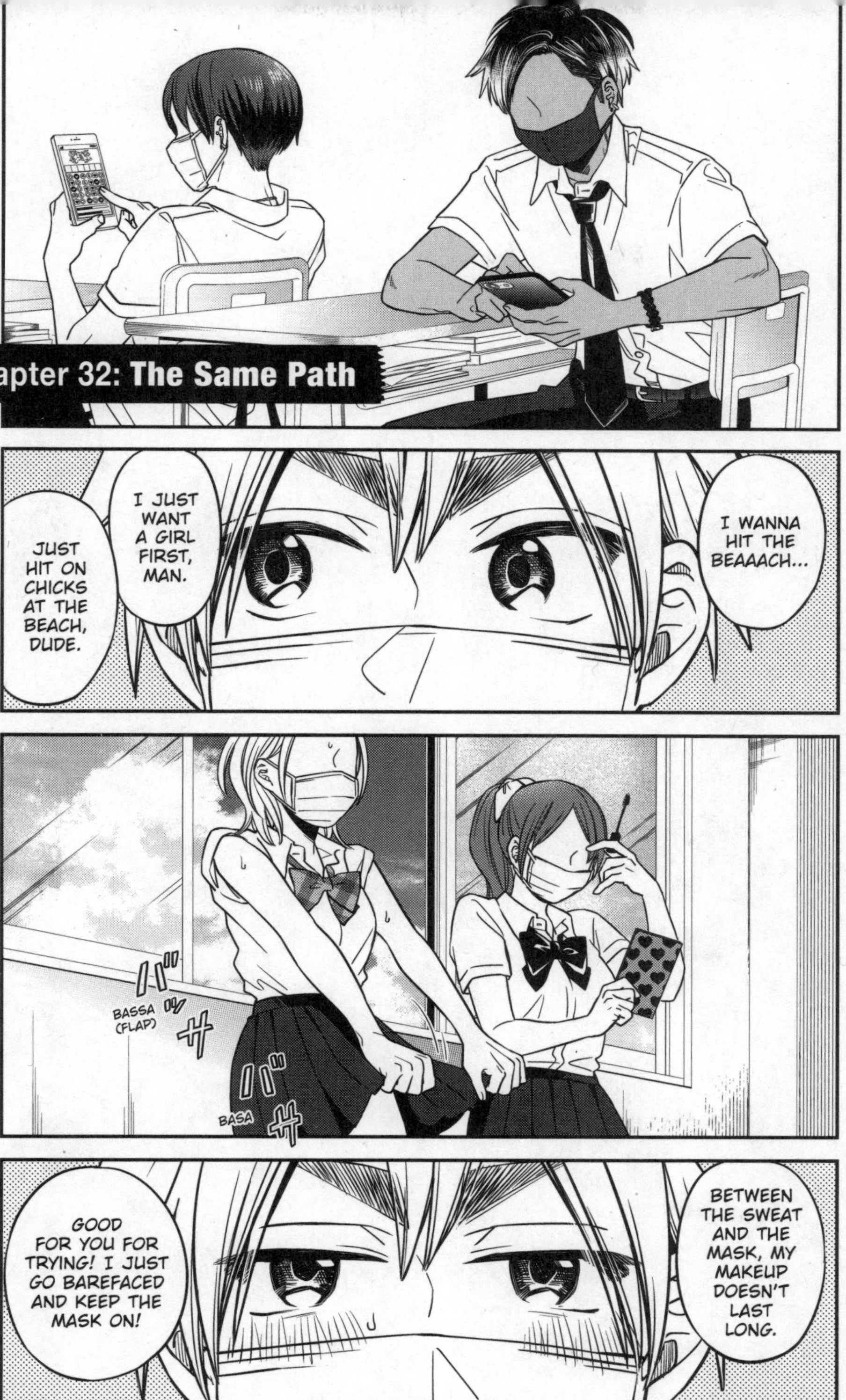
I WANNA HIT THE BEAAACH...
I JUST WANT A GIRL FIRST, MAN.
JUST HIT ON CHICKS AT THE BEACH, DUDE.
BASSA (FLAP)
BASA
BETWEEN THE SWEAT AND THE MASK, MY MAKEUP DOESN'T LAST LONG.
GOOD FOR YOU FOR TRYING! I JUST GO BAREFACED AND KEEP THE MASK ON!

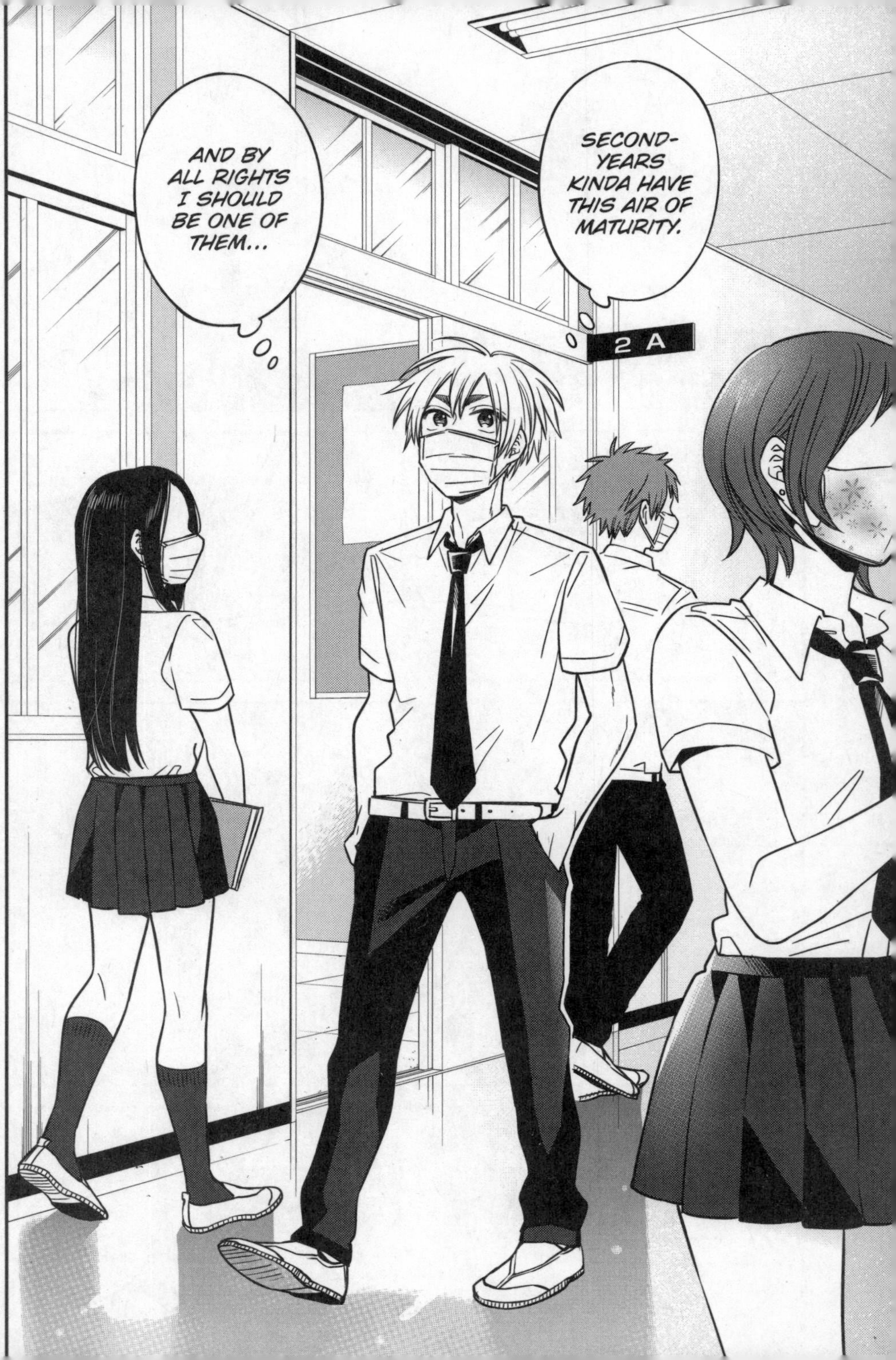
SECOND-YEARS KINDA HAVE THIS AIR OF MATURITY.
AND BY ALL RIGHTS I SHOULD BE ONE OF THEM...
2 A

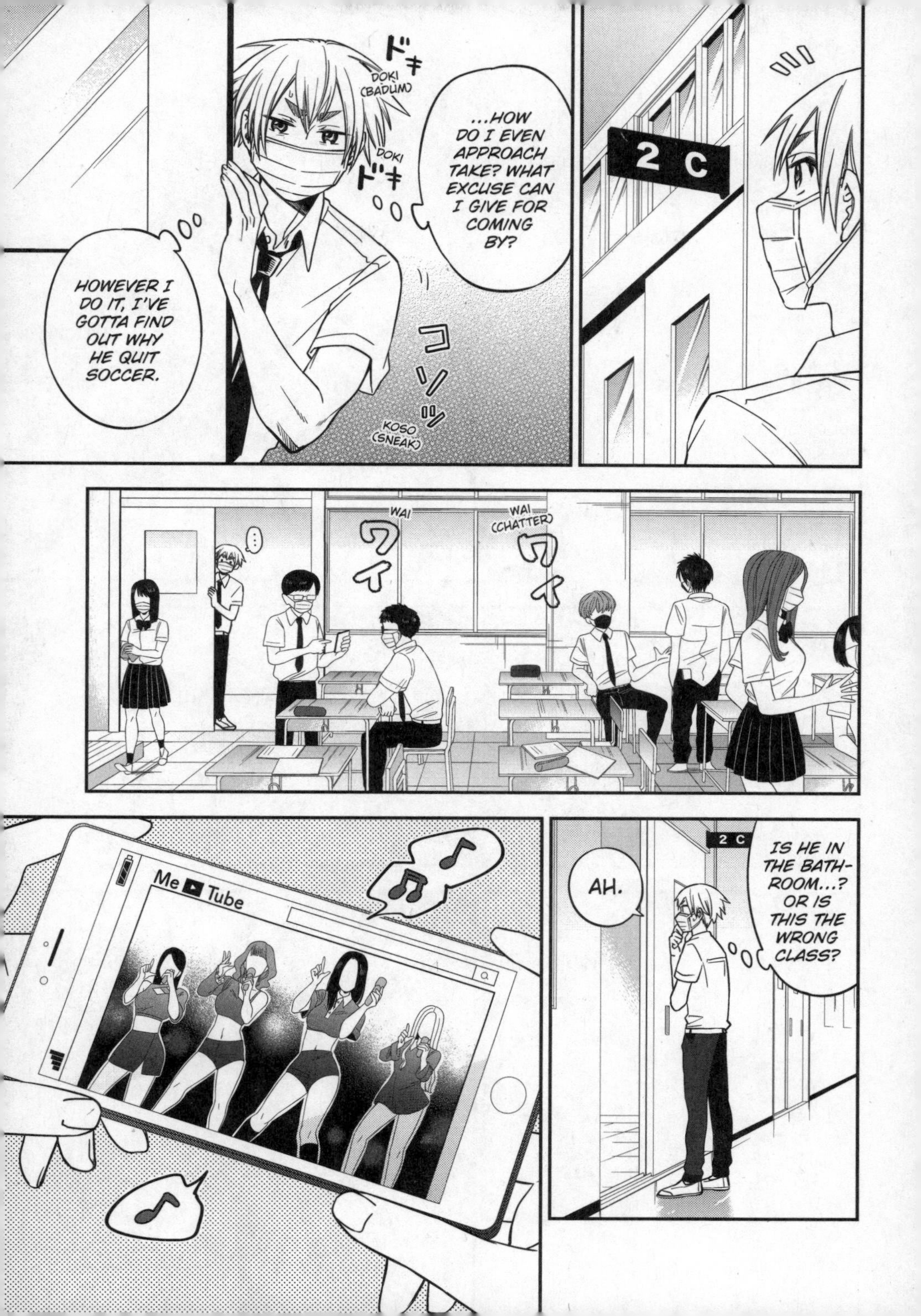
2 C
...HOW DO I EVEN APPROACH TAKE? WHAT EXCUSE CAN I GIVE FOR COMING BY?
DOKI (BADUM)
DOKI
HOWEVER I DO IT, I'VE GOTTA FIND OUT WHY HE QUIT SOCCER.
KOSO (SNEAK)
WAI (CHATTER)
WAI
...
2 C
IS HE IN THE BATH-ROOM...? OR IS THIS THE WRONG CLASS?
AH.
Me Tube

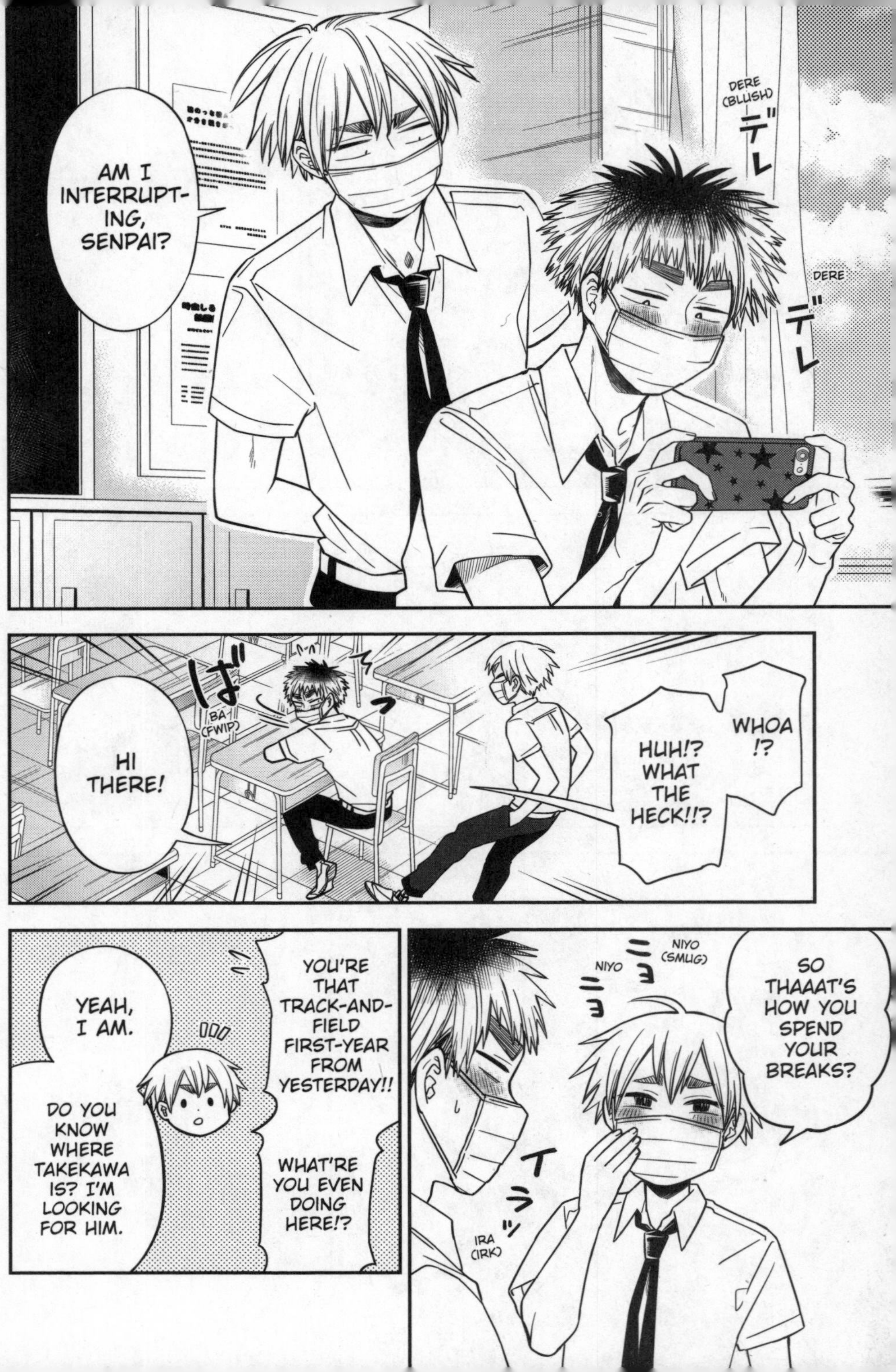
DERE (BLUSH)
デレ
DERE
デレ
AM I INTERRUPTING, SENPAI?
WHOA!?
HUH!? WHAT THE HECK!!?
ば
BA (FWIP)
HI THERE!
SO THAAAT'S HOW YOU SPEND YOUR BREAKS?
NIYO (SMUG)
ニヨ
NIYO
ニヨ
IRA (IRK)
イラッ
YOU'RE THAT TRACK-AND-FIELD FIRST-YEAR FROM YESTERDAY!!
WHAT'RE YOU EVEN DOING HERE!?
YEAH, I AM.
DO YOU KNOW WHERE TAKEKAWA IS? I'M LOOKING FOR HIM.

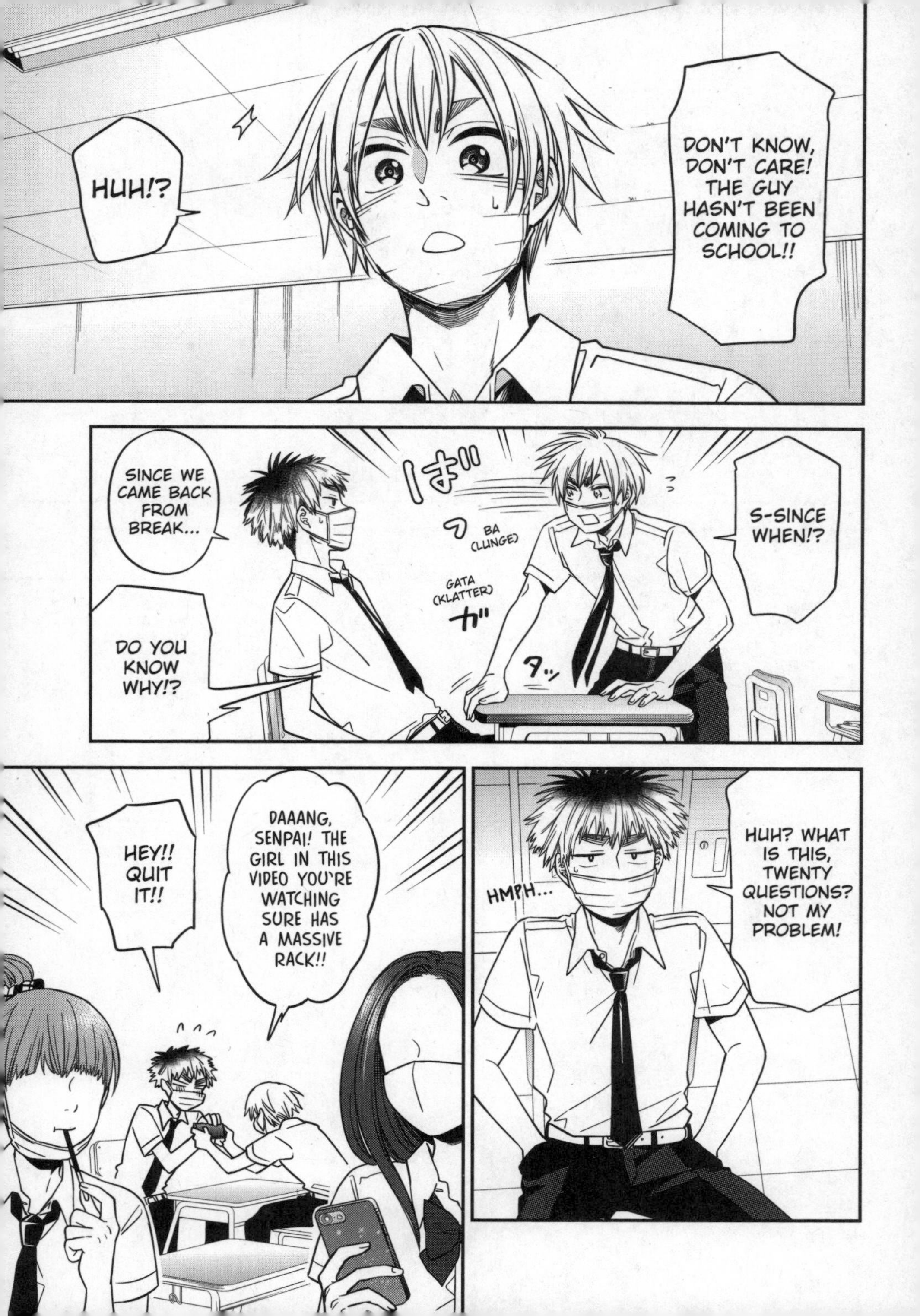

DON'T KNOW, DON'T CARE! THE GUY HASN'T BEEN COMING TO SCHOOL!!
HUH!?
S-SINCE WHEN!?
ばっ
BA (LUNGE)
ガタッ
GATA (KLATTER)
SINCE WE CAME BACK FROM BREAK...
DO YOU KNOW WHY!?
HUH? WHAT IS THIS, TWENTY QUESTIONS? NOT MY PROBLEM!
HMPH...
DAAANG, SENPAI! THE GIRL IN THIS VIDEO YOU'RE WATCHING SURE HAS A MASSIVE RACK!!
HEY!! QUIT IT!!

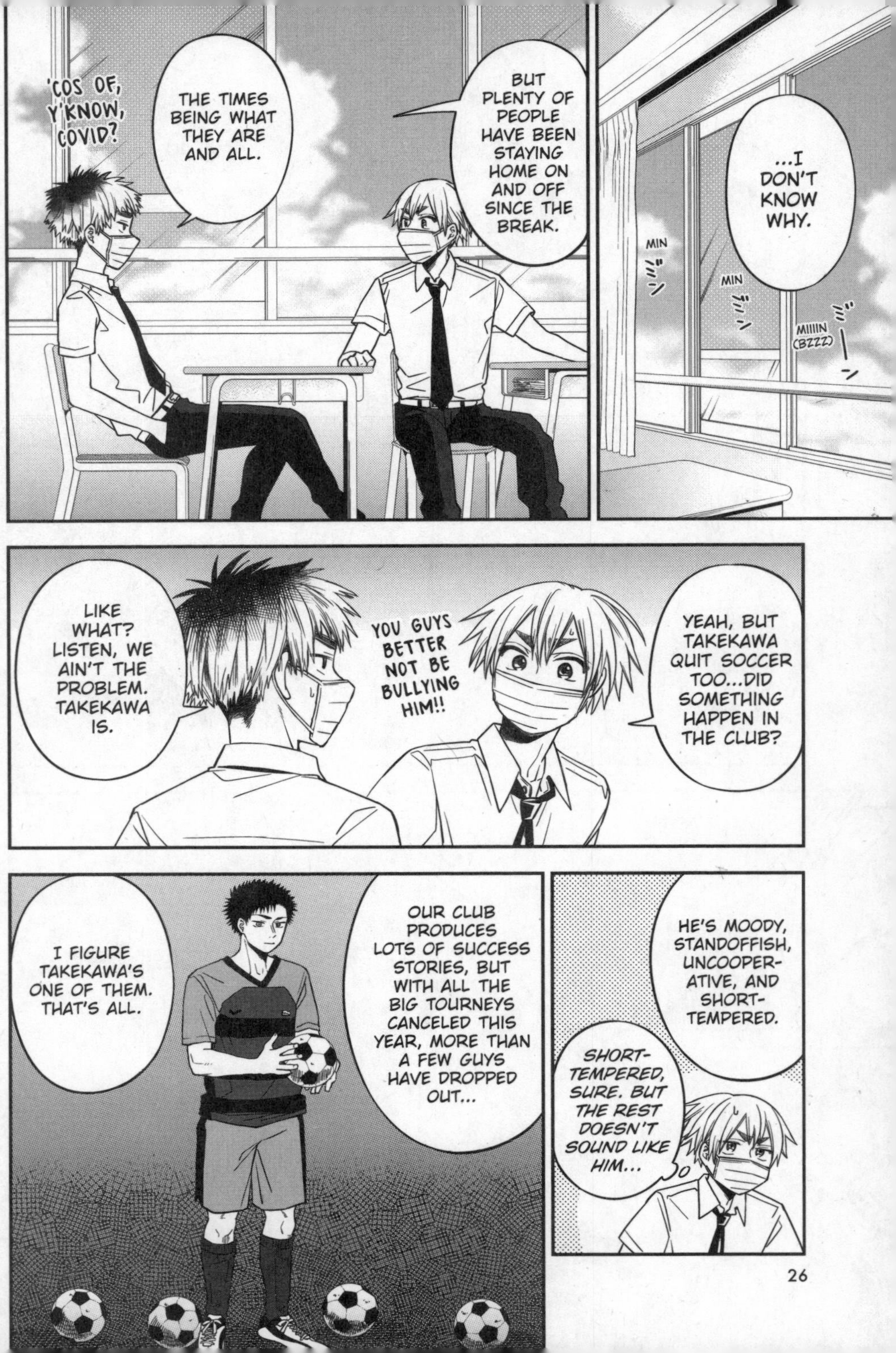
...I DON'T KNOW WHY.
MIN
MIN
MIIIN (BZZZ)
BUT PLENTY OF PEOPLE HAVE BEEN STAYING HOME ON AND OFF SINCE THE BREAK.
THE TIMES BEING WHAT THEY ARE AND ALL.
'COS OF, Y'KNOW, COVID?
YEAH, BUT TAKEKAWA QUIT SOCCER TOO...DID SOMETHING HAPPEN IN THE CLUB?
YOU GUYS BETTER NOT BE BULLYING HIM!!
LIKE WHAT? LISTEN, WE AIN'T THE PROBLEM. TAKEKAWA IS.
HE'S MOODY, STANDOFFISH, UNCOOPER-ATIVE, AND SHORT-TEMPERED.
SHORT-TEMPERED, SURE. BUT THE REST DOESN'T SOUND LIKE HIM...
OUR CLUB PRODUCES LOTS OF SUCCESS STORIES, BUT WITH ALL THE BIG TOURNEYS CANCELED THIS YEAR, MORE THAN A FEW GUYS HAVE DROPPED OUT...
I FIGURE TAKEKAWA'S ONE OF THEM. THAT'S ALL.

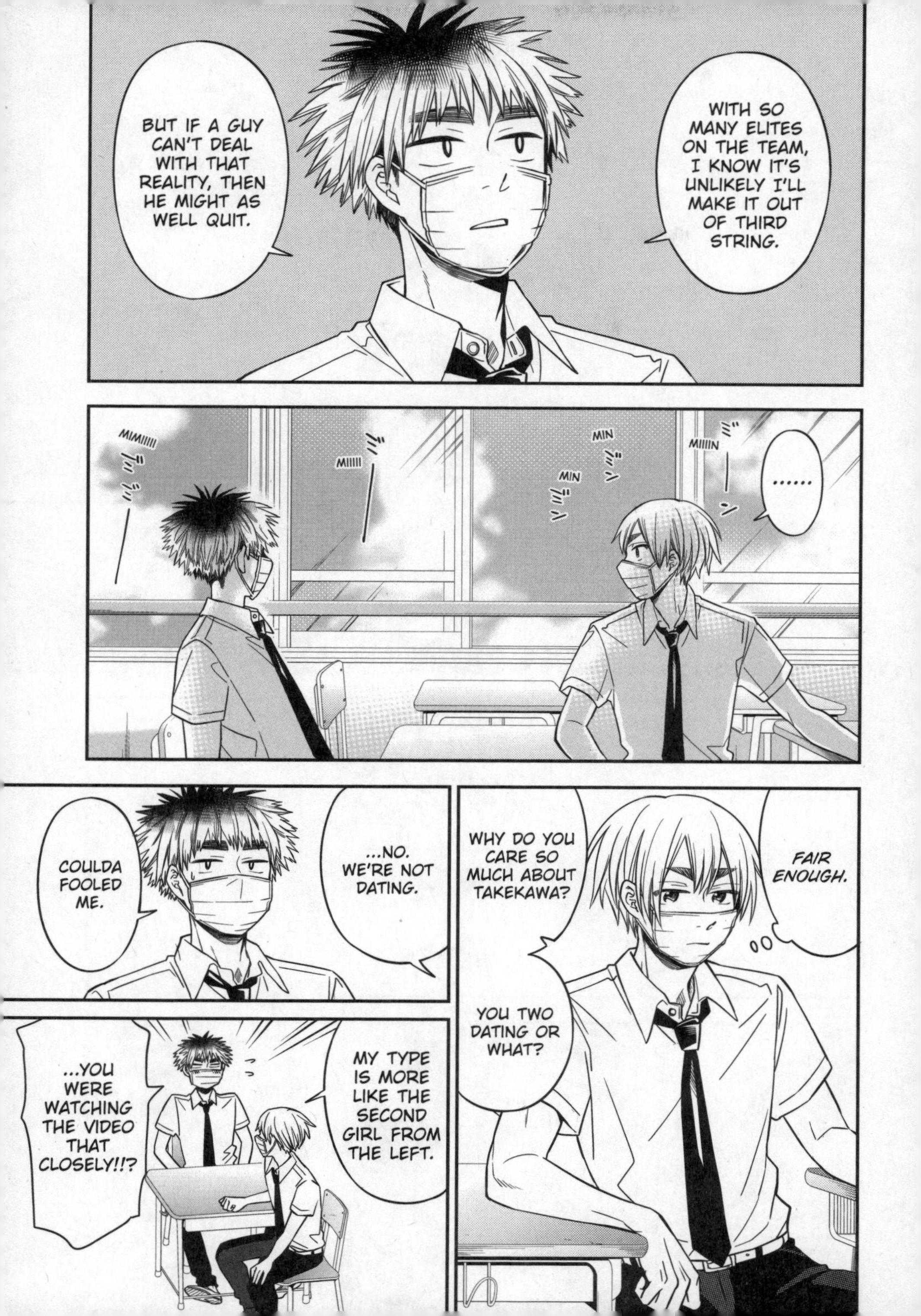

WITH SO MANY ELITES ON THE TEAM, I KNOW IT'S UNLIKELY I'LL MAKE IT OUT OF THIRD STRING.
BUT IF A GUY CAN'T DEAL WITH THAT REALITY, THEN HE MIGHT AS WELL QUIT.
......
MIIIIN
MIN
MIN
MIIIII
MIMIIIIII
FAIR ENOUGH.
WHY DO YOU CARE SO MUCH ABOUT TAKEKAWA?
YOU TWO DATING OR WHAT?
...NO. WE'RE NOT DATING.
COULDA FOOLED ME.
MY TYPE IS MORE LIKE THE SECOND GIRL FROM THE LEFT.
...YOU WERE WATCHING THE VIDEO THAT CLOSELY!!?

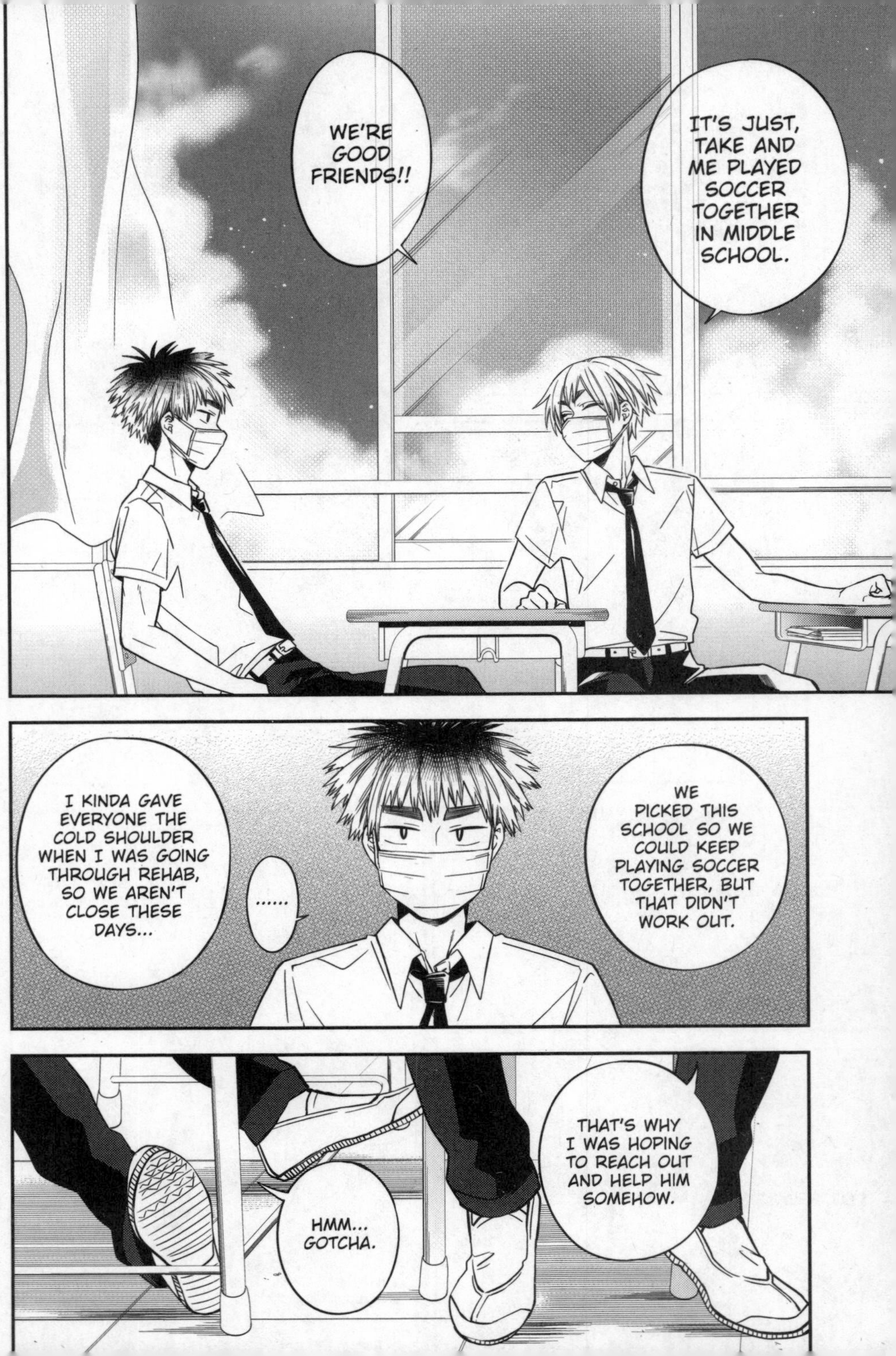
IT'S JUST, TAKE AND ME PLAYED SOCCER TOGETHER IN MIDDLE SCHOOL.
WE'RE GOOD FRIENDS!!
WE PICKED THIS SCHOOL SO WE COULD KEEP PLAYING SOCCER TOGETHER, BUT THAT DIDN'T WORK OUT.
......
I KINDA GAVE EVERYONE THE COLD SHOULDER WHEN I WAS GOING THROUGH REHAB, SO WE AREN'T CLOSE THESE DAYS...
THAT'S WHY I WAS HOPING TO REACH OUT AND HELP HIM SOMEHOW.
HMM... GOTCHA.

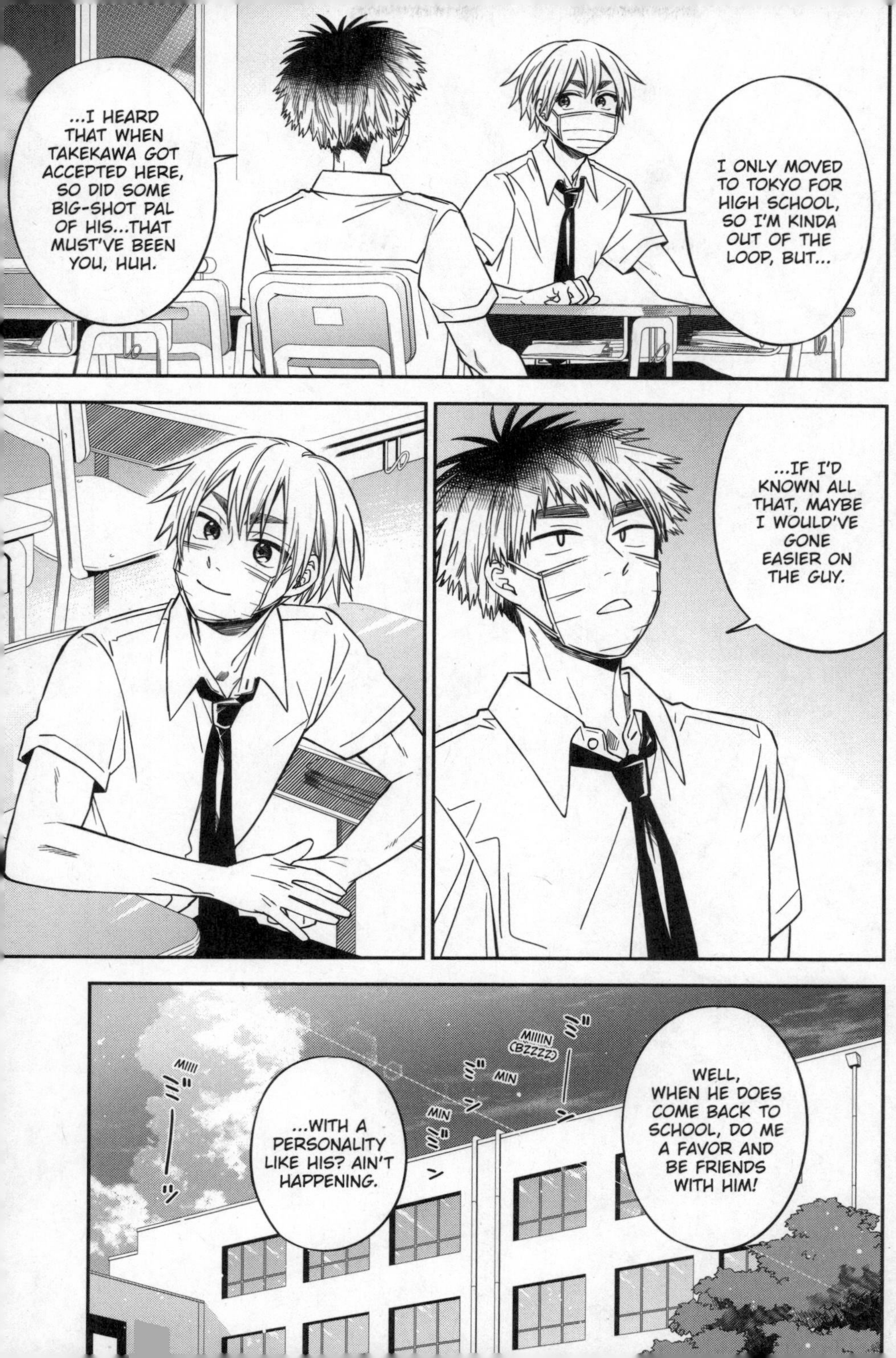
I ONLY MOVED TO TOKYO FOR HIGH SCHOOL, SO I'M KINDA OUT OF THE LOOP, BUT...
...I HEARD THAT WHEN TAKEKAWA GOT ACCEPTED HERE, SO DID SOME BIG-SHOT PAL OF HIS...THAT MUST'VE BEEN YOU, HUH.
...IF I'D KNOWN ALL THAT, MAYBE I WOULD'VE GONE EASIER ON THE GUY.
WELL, WHEN HE DOES COME BACK TO SCHOOL, DO ME A FAVOR AND BE FRIENDS WITH HIM!
MIIIN (BZZZZ)
MIN
MIN
...WITH A PERSONALITY LIKE HIS? AIN'T HAPPENING.
MIIII

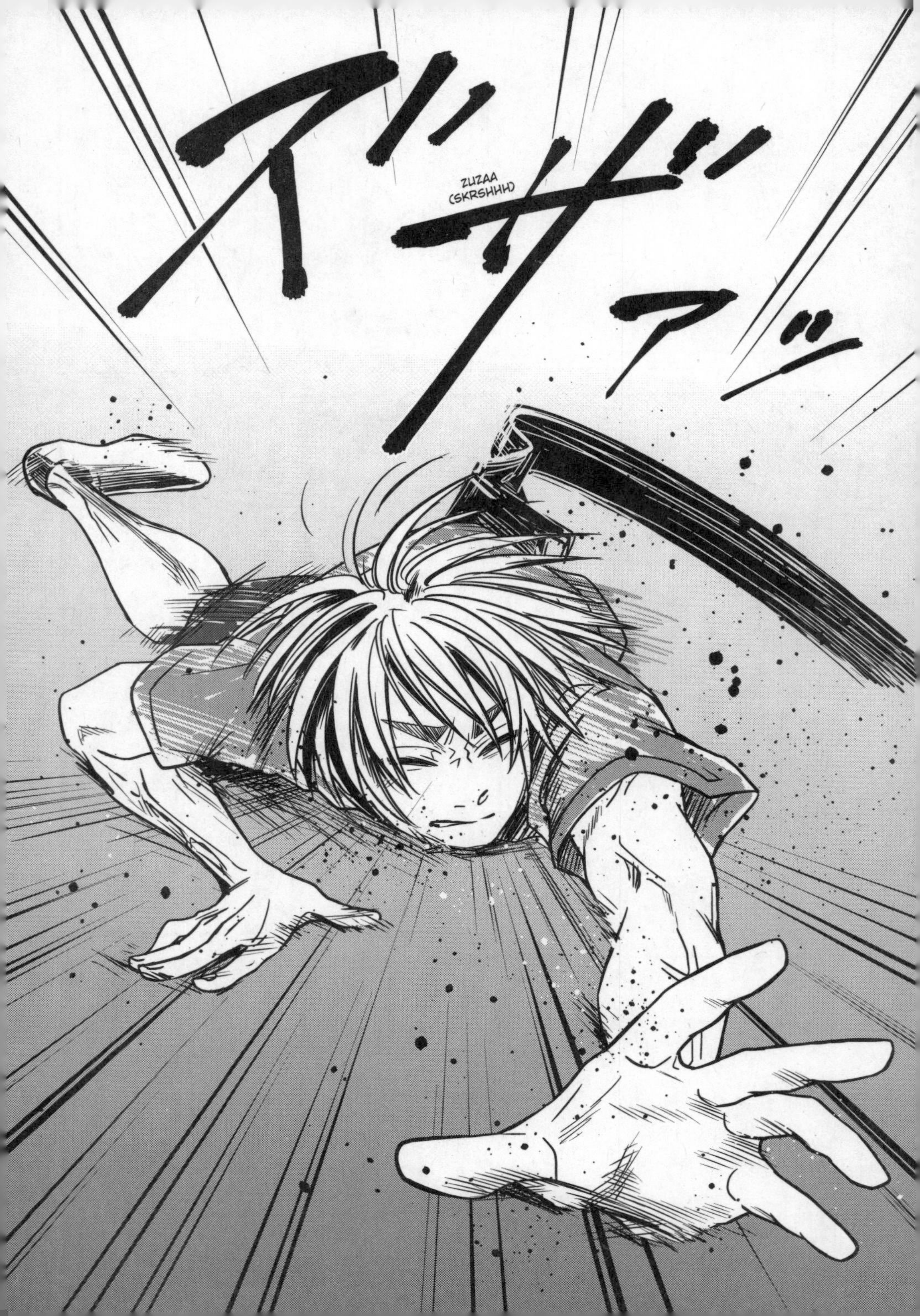
ズザアッ
ZUZAA (SKRSHHH)

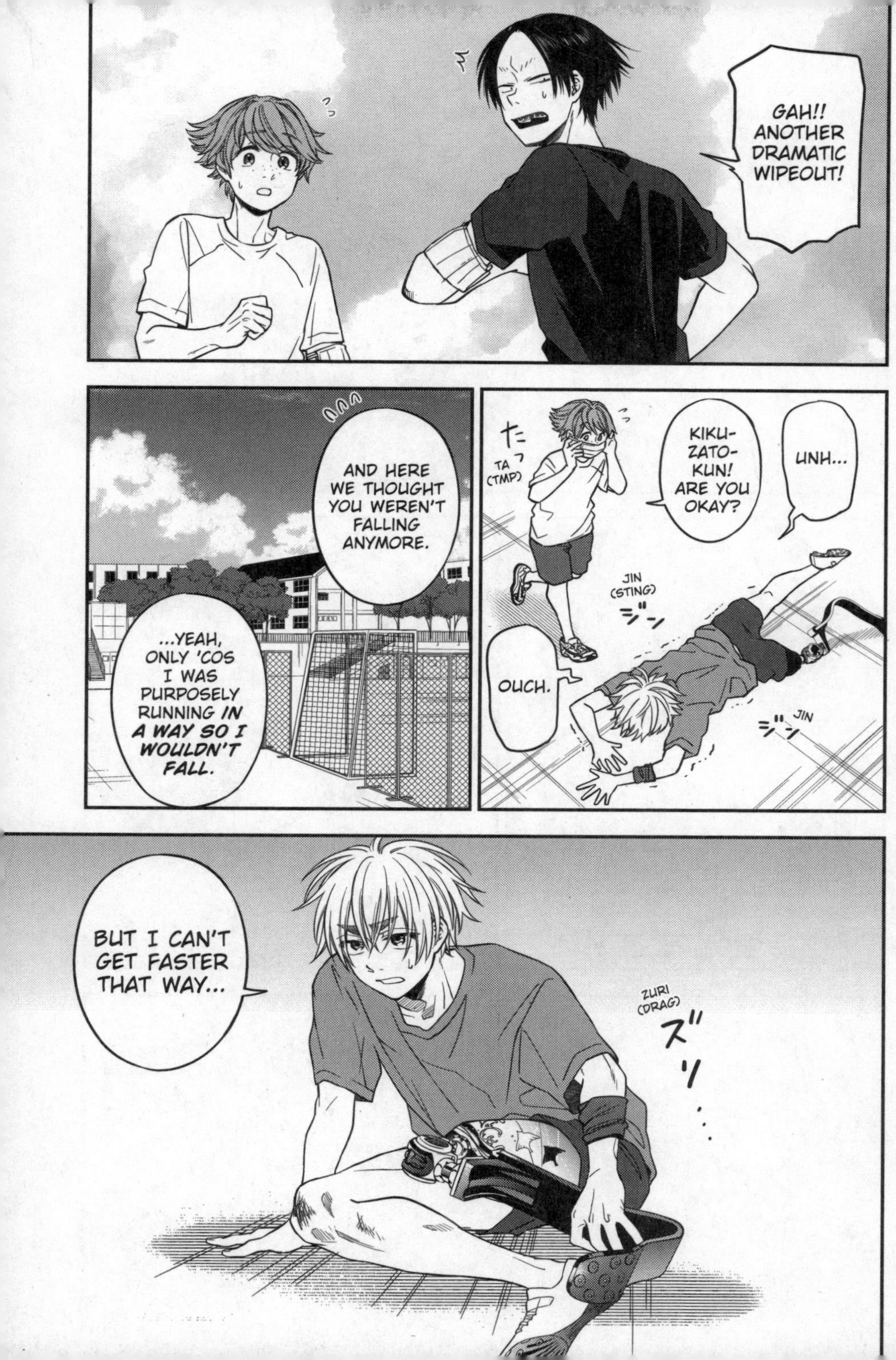
GAH!! ANOTHER DRAMATIC WIPEOUT!
UNH...
KIKUZATO-KUN! ARE YOU OKAY?
TA (TMP)
JIN (STING)
OUCH.
JIN
AND HERE WE THOUGHT YOU WEREN'T FALLING ANYMORE.
...YEAH, ONLY 'COS I WAS PURPOSELY RUNNING *IN A WAY SO I WOULDN'T FALL*.
BUT I CAN'T GET FASTER THAT WAY...
ZURI (DRAG)

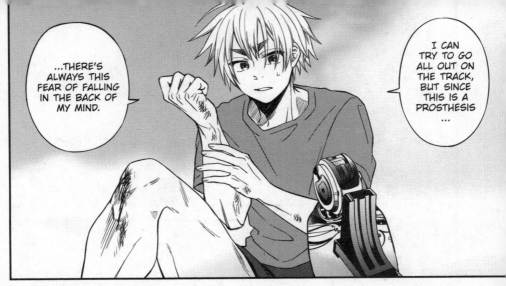

I CAN TRY TO GO ALL OUT ON THE TRACK, BUT SINCE THIS IS A PROSTHESIS ...
...THERE'S ALWAYS THIS FEAR OF FALLING IN THE BACK OF MY MIND.
BUT IF I WANT TO GET FASTER, I HAVE TO PUT EVERYTHING ON THE LINE...
TSUUU (DRIP)
"YOU HAVE NOT YET WITNESSED MY TRUE POWER!" IS IT?
HEH HEH.
HEY! I'M NOT SOME CRINGEY EDGELORD KID!!
PEOPLE WITHOUT PROSTHESES CAN GET A FEEL FOR WHAT IT'S LIKE...
...BY TRYING TO WALK ON STILTS. I READ THAT SOME-WHERE...
DA (DNK)
DA
DA
YEAH, THAT SEEMS CLOSE.
IT'S LIKE A NO-HANDS VERSION OF THAT.

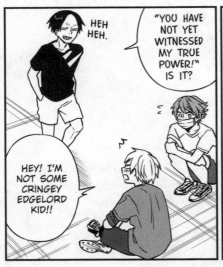

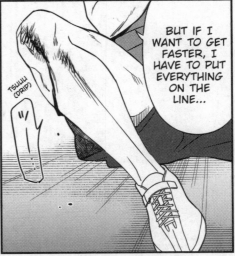

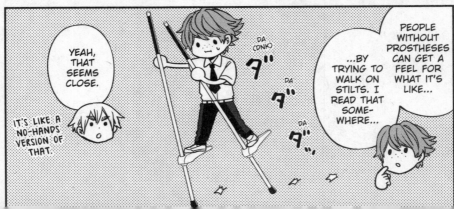

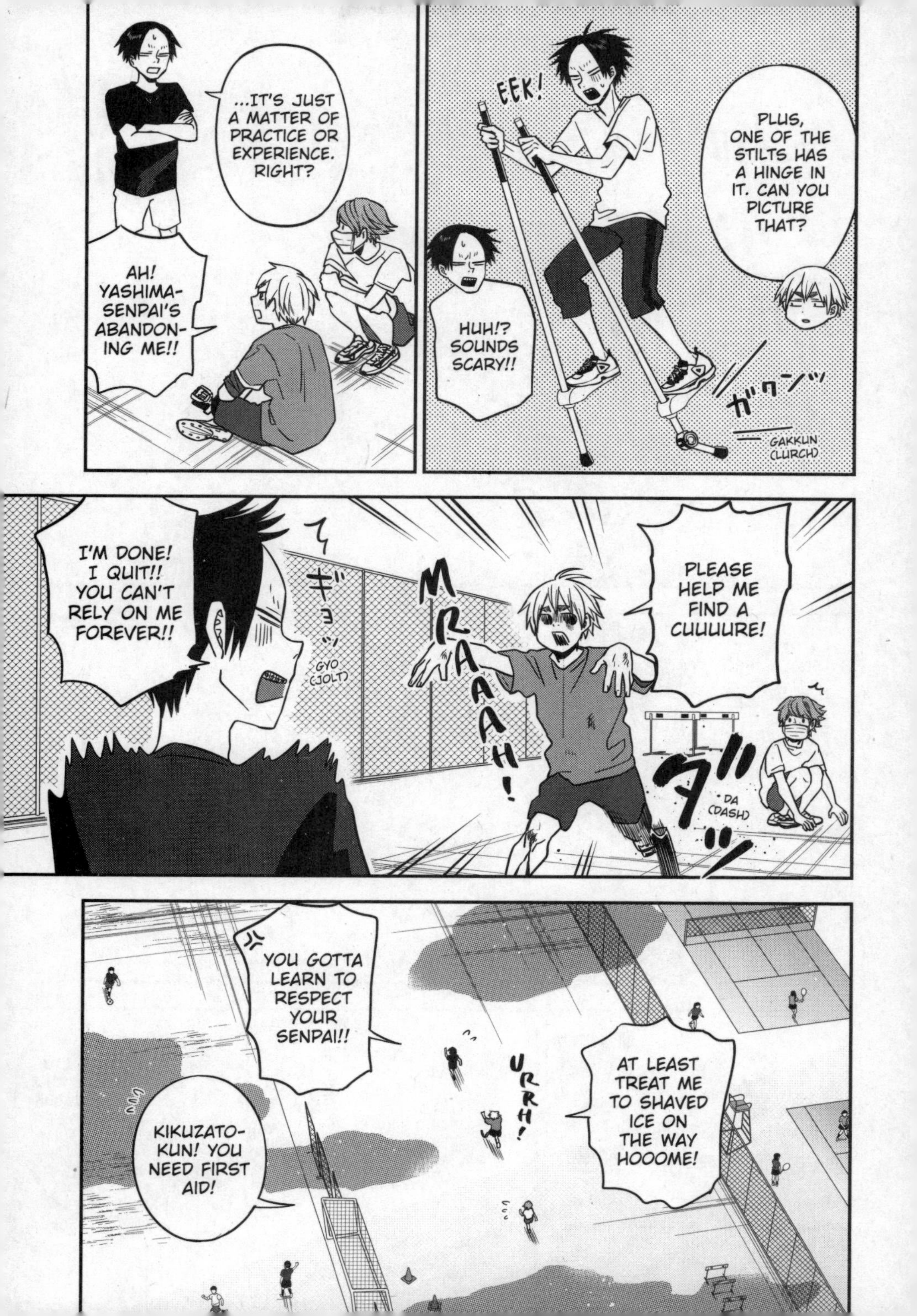
PLUS, ONE OF THE STILTS HAS A HINGE IN IT. CAN YOU PICTURE THAT?
EEK!
HUH!? SOUNDS SCARY!!
ガクンッ
GAKKUN (LURCH)
...IT'S JUST A MATTER OF PRACTICE OR EXPERIENCE. RIGHT?
AH! YASHIMA-SENPAI'S ABANDON-ING ME!!
PLEASE HELP ME FIND A CUUUURE!
ダッ
DA (DASH)
MRAAAAH!
ギョッ
GYO (JOLT)
I'M DONE! I QUIT!! YOU CAN'T RELY ON ME FOREVER!!
AT LEAST TREAT ME TO SHAVED ICE ON THE WAY HOOOME!
URRH!
YOU GOTTA LEARN TO RESPECT YOUR SENPAI!!
KIKUZATO-KUN! YOU NEED FIRST AID!

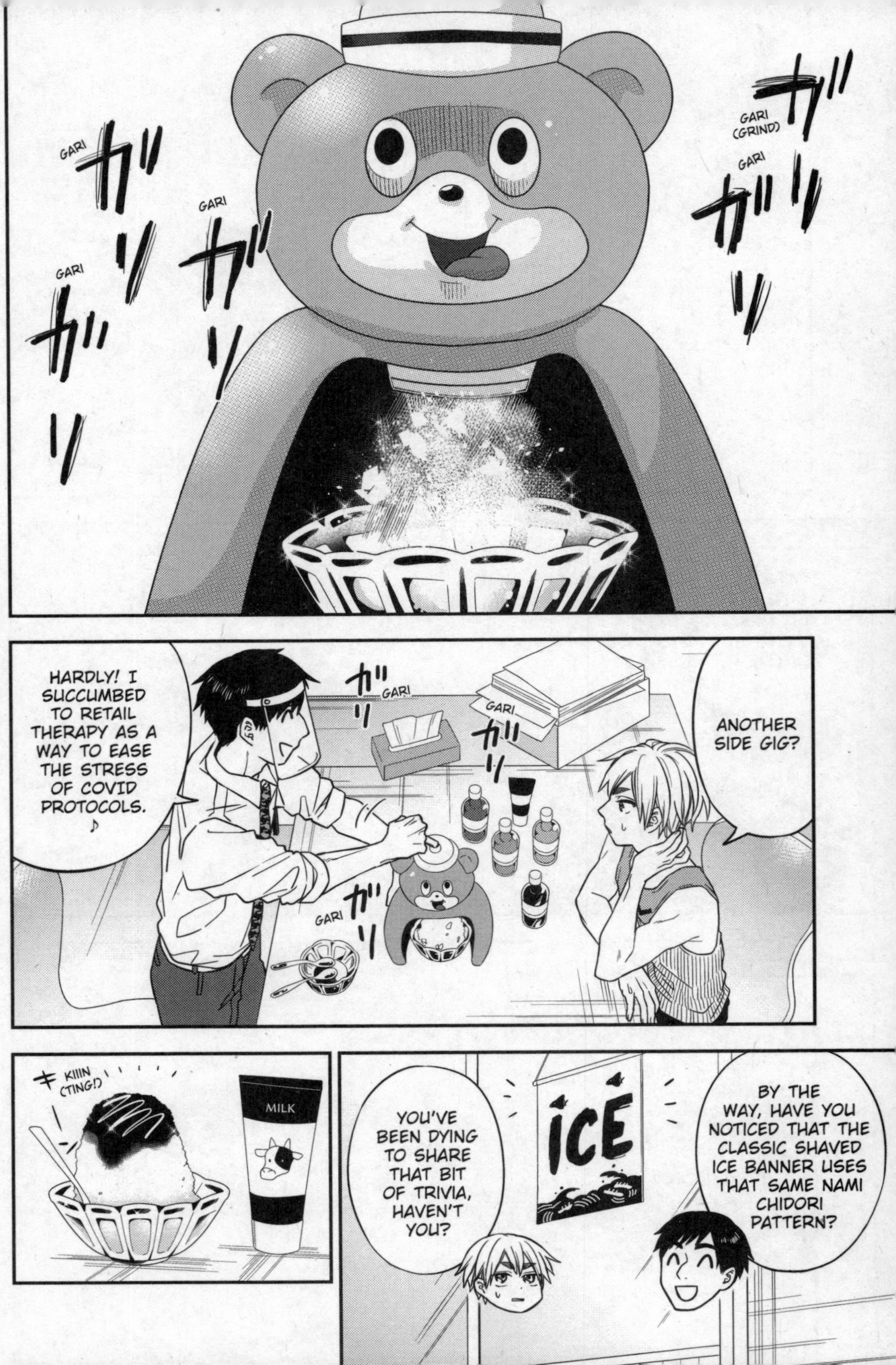

GARI (GRIND)
GARI
GARI
GARI
GARI
ANOTHER SIDE GIG?
GARI
GARI
GARI
HARDLY! I SUCCUMBED TO RETAIL THERAPY AS A WAY TO EASE THE STRESS OF COVID PROTOCOLS. ♪
BY THE WAY, HAVE YOU NOTICED THAT THE CLASSIC SHAVED ICE BANNER USES THAT SAME NAMI CHIDORI PATTERN?
ICE
YOU'VE BEEN DYING TO SHARE THAT BIT OF TRIVIA, HAVEN'T YOU?
KIIIN (TING!)
MILK

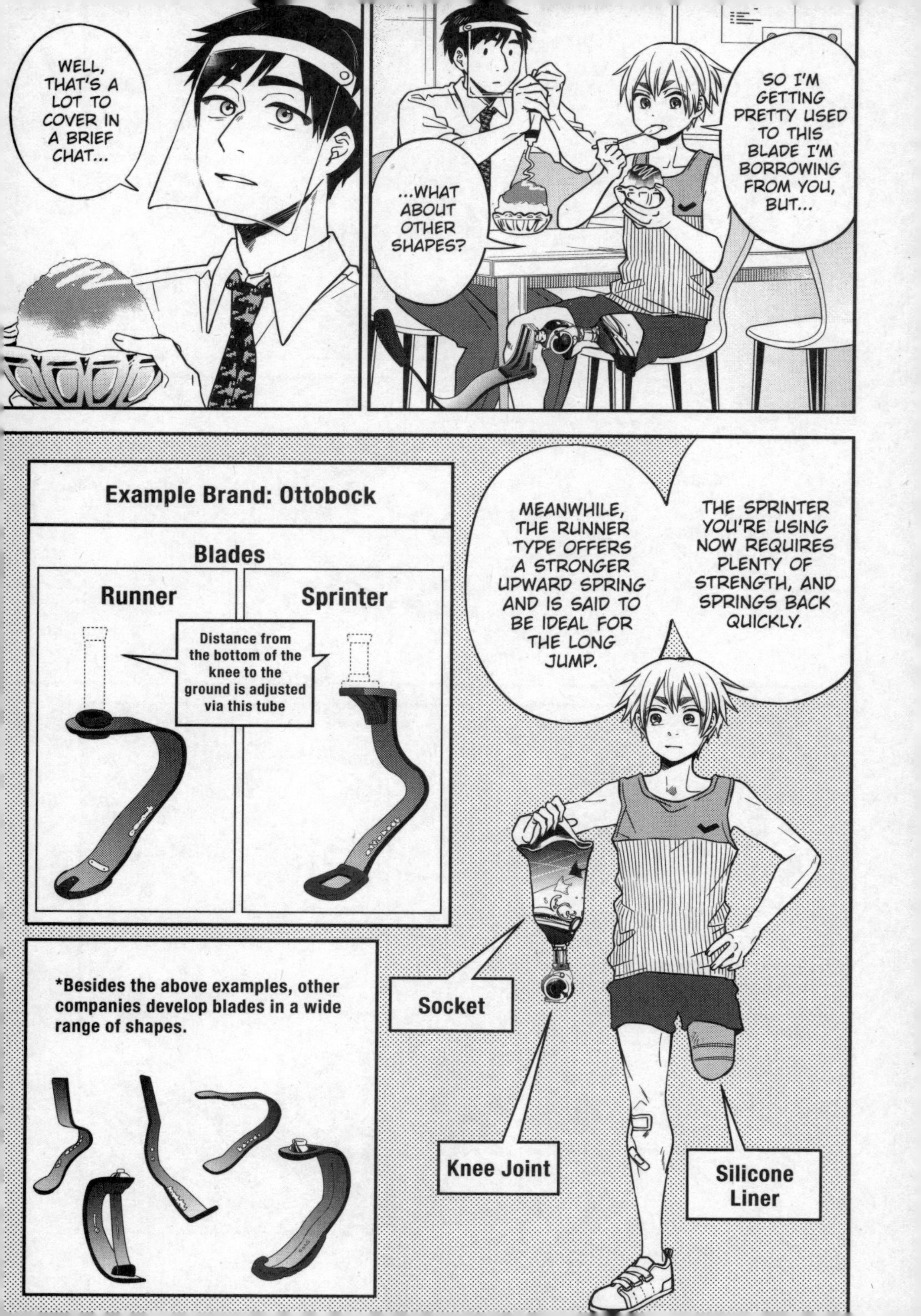
SO I'M GETTING PRETTY USED TO THIS BLADE I'M BORROWING FROM YOU, BUT...
...WHAT ABOUT OTHER SHAPES?
WELL, THAT'S A LOT TO COVER IN A BRIEF CHAT...
THE SPRINTER YOU'RE USING NOW REQUIRES PLENTY OF STRENGTH, AND SPRINGS BACK QUICKLY.
MEANWHILE, THE RUNNER TYPE OFFERS A STRONGER UPWARD SPRING AND IS SAID TO BE IDEAL FOR THE LONG JUMP.
Example Brand: Ottobock
Blades
Runner
Sprinter
Distance from the bottom of the knee to the ground is adjusted via this tube
Socket
Knee Joint
Silicone Liner
*Besides the above examples, other companies develop blades in a wide range of shapes.

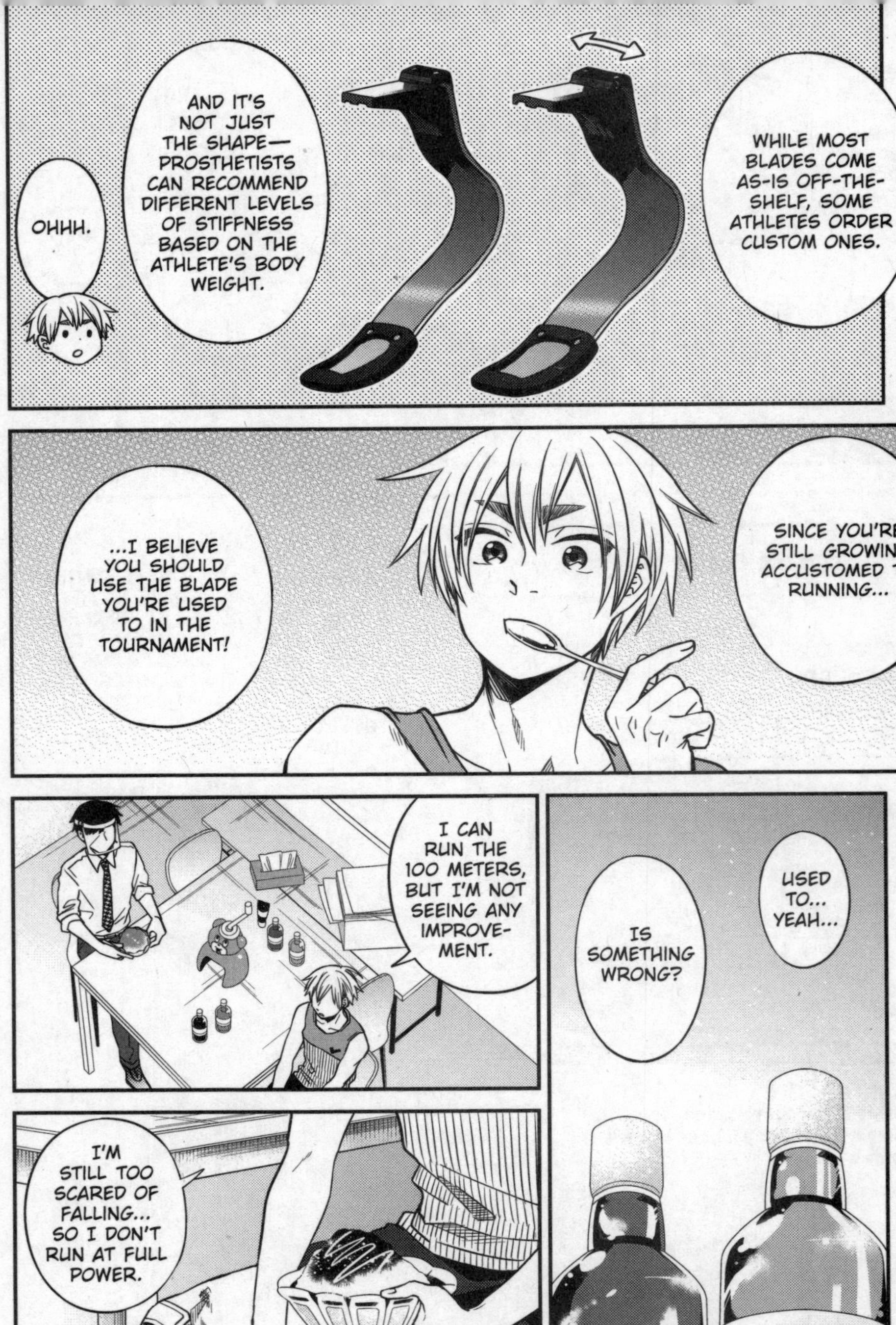
WHILE MOST BLADES COME AS-IS OFF-THE-SHELF, SOME ATHLETES ORDER CUSTOM ONES.
AND IT'S NOT JUST THE SHAPE— PROSTHETISTS CAN RECOMMEND DIFFERENT LEVELS OF STIFFNESS BASED ON THE ATHLETE'S BODY WEIGHT.
OHHH.
SINCE YOU'RE STILL GROWING ACCUSTOMED TO RUNNING...
...I BELIEVE YOU SHOULD USE THE BLADE YOU'RE USED TO IN THE TOURNAMENT!
USED TO... YEAH...
IS SOMETHING WRONG?
Lemon
I CAN RUN THE 100 METERS, BUT I'M NOT SEEING ANY IMPROVE- MENT.
I'M STILL TOO SCARED OF FALLING... SO I DON'T RUN AT FULL POWER.

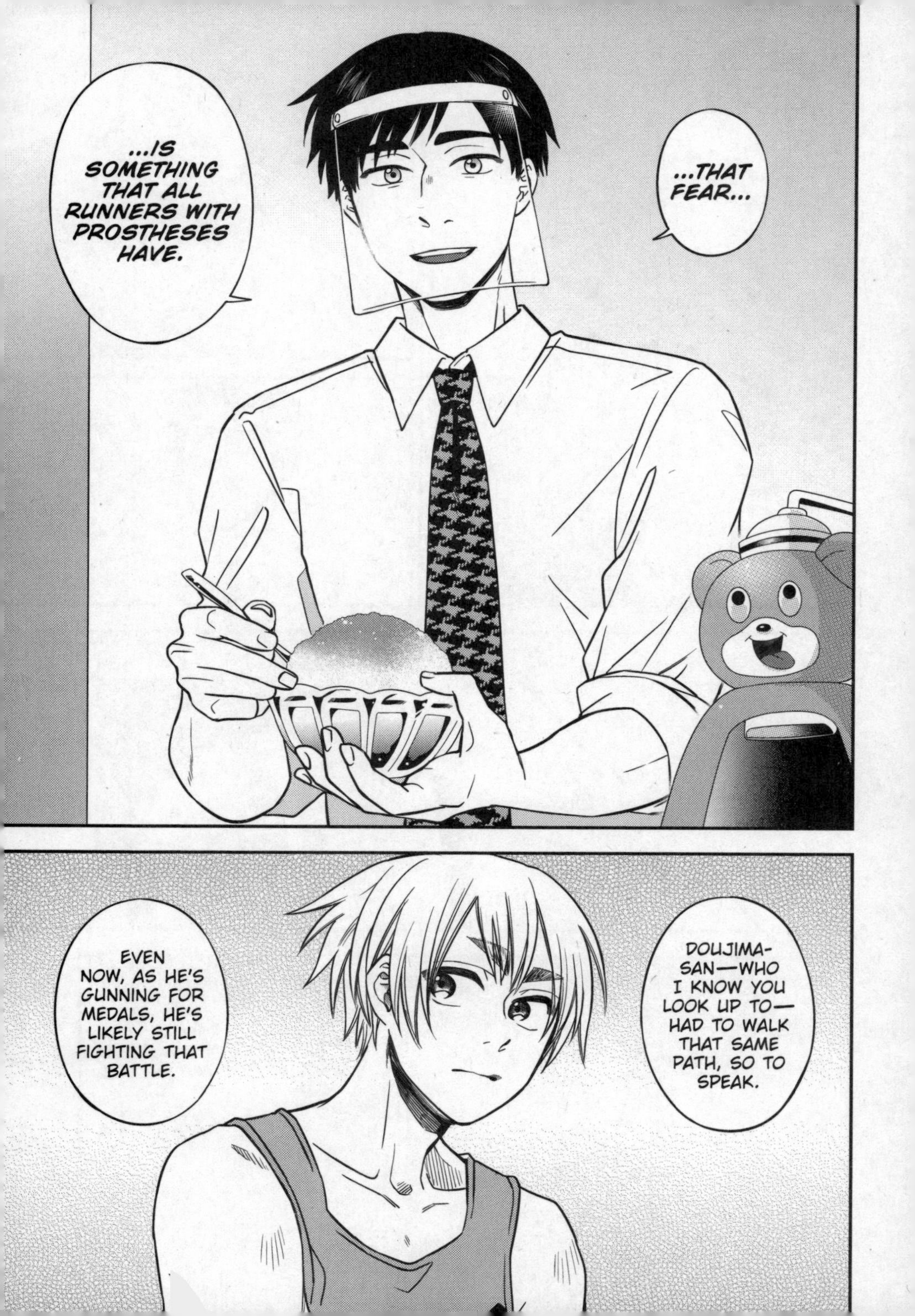
...THAT FEAR...
...IS SOMETHING THAT ALL RUNNERS WITH PROSTHESES HAVE.
DOUJIMA-SAN—WHO I KNOW YOU LOOK UP TO—HAD TO WALK THAT SAME PATH, SO TO SPEAK.
EVEN NOW, AS HE'S GUNNING FOR MEDALS, HE'S LIKELY STILL FIGHTING THAT BATTLE.

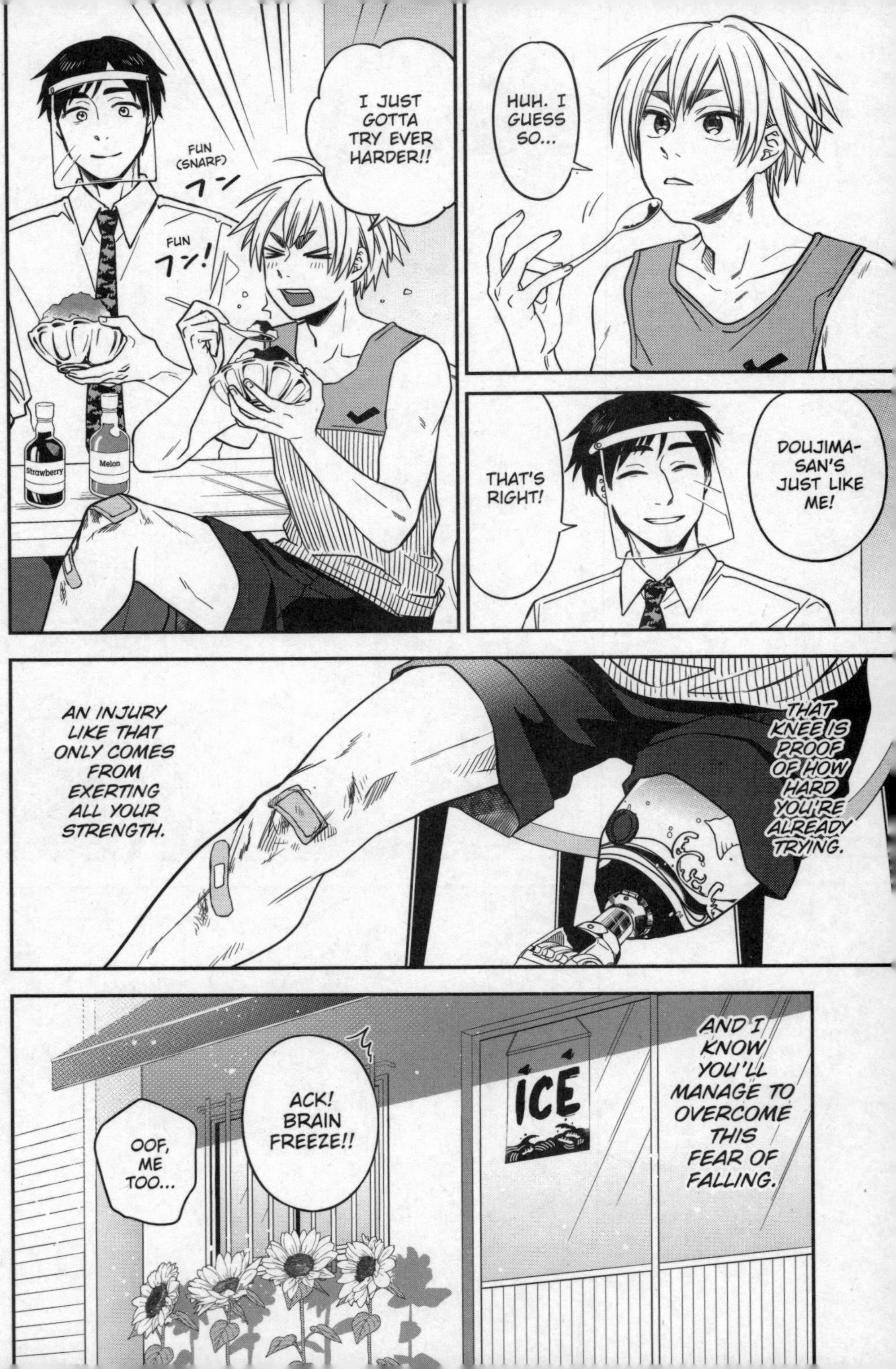
HUH. I GUESS SO...
DOUJIMA-SAN'S JUST LIKE ME!
THAT'S RIGHT!
I JUST GOTTA TRY EVER HARDER!!
FUN (SNARF)
フン
FUN
フン!
Strawberry
Melon
THAT KNEE IS PROOF OF HOW HARD YOU'RE ALREADY TRYING.
AN INJURY LIKE THAT ONLY COMES FROM EXERTING ALL YOUR STRENGTH.
AND I KNOW YOU'LL MANAGE TO OVERCOME THIS FEAR OF FALLING.
ICE
ACK! BRAIN FREEZE!!
OOF, ME TOO...

Chapter 33: Those I'm Bringing

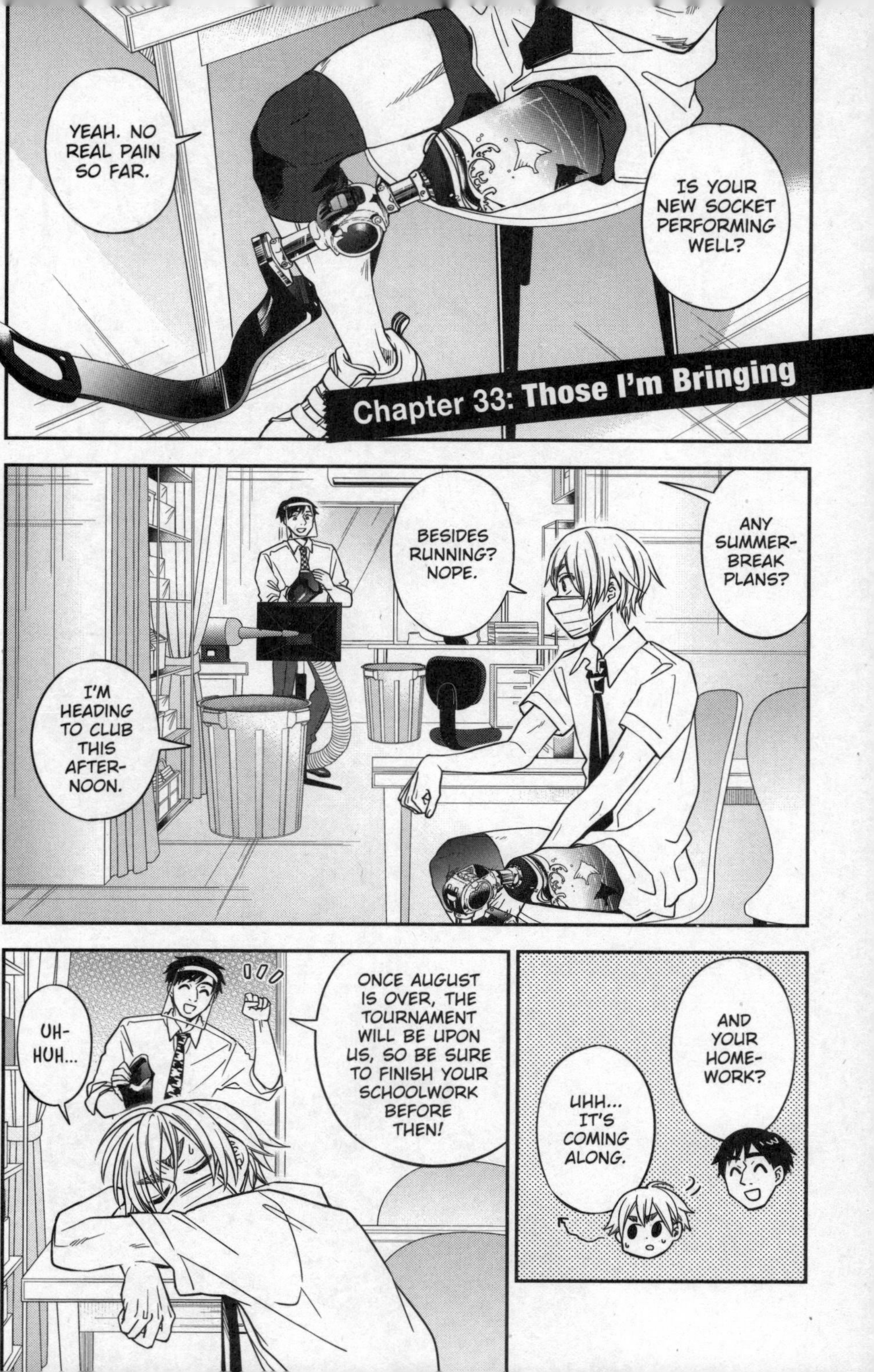
IS YOUR NEW SOCKET PERFORMING WELL?
YEAH. NO REAL PAIN SO FAR.
Chapter 33: Those I'm Bringing
ANY SUMMER-BREAK PLANS?
BESIDES RUNNING? NOPE.
I'M HEADING TO CLUB THIS AFTER-NOON.
AND YOUR HOME-WORK?
UHH... IT'S COMING ALONG.
ONCE AUGUST IS OVER, THE TOURNAMENT WILL BE UPON US, SO BE SURE TO FINISH YOUR SCHOOLWORK BEFORE THEN!
UH-HUH...

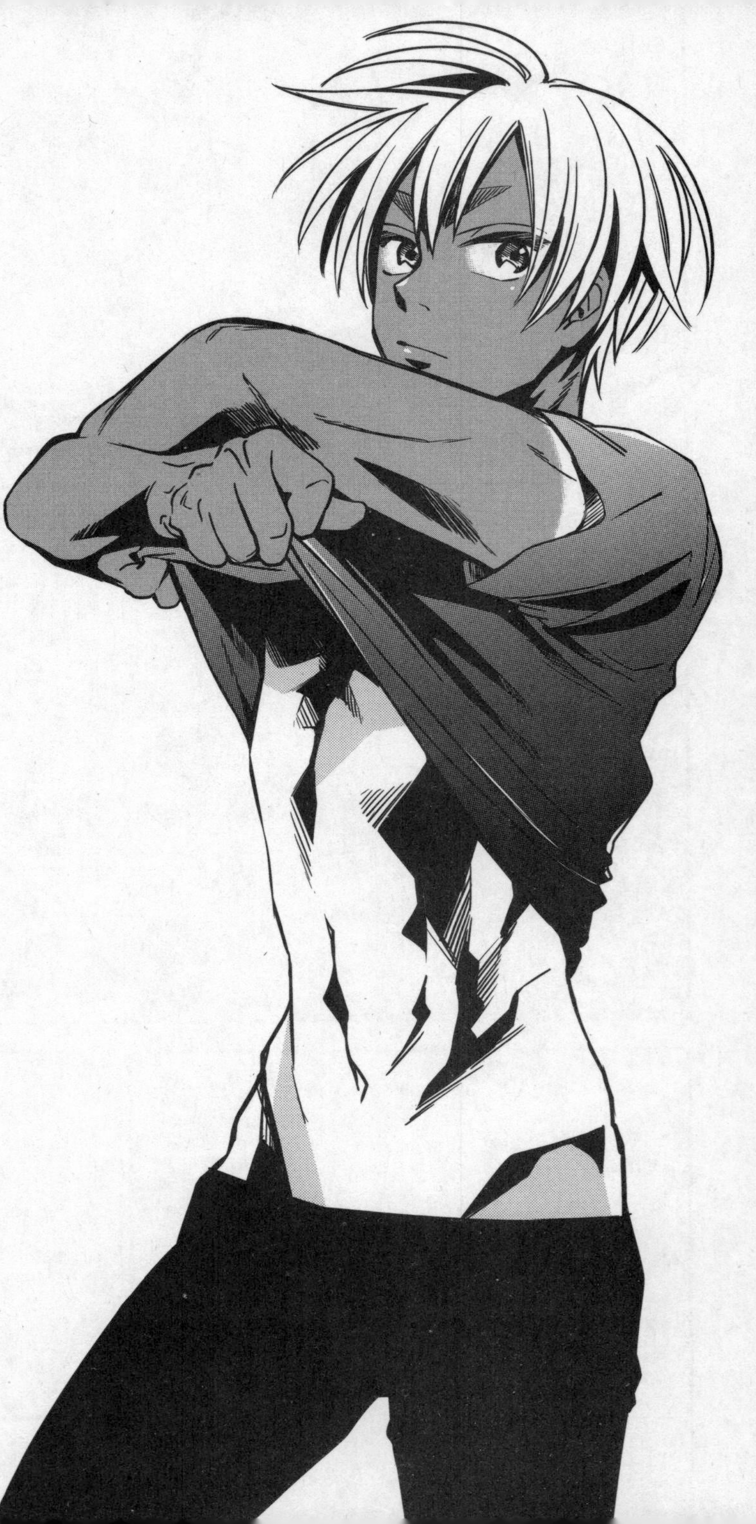

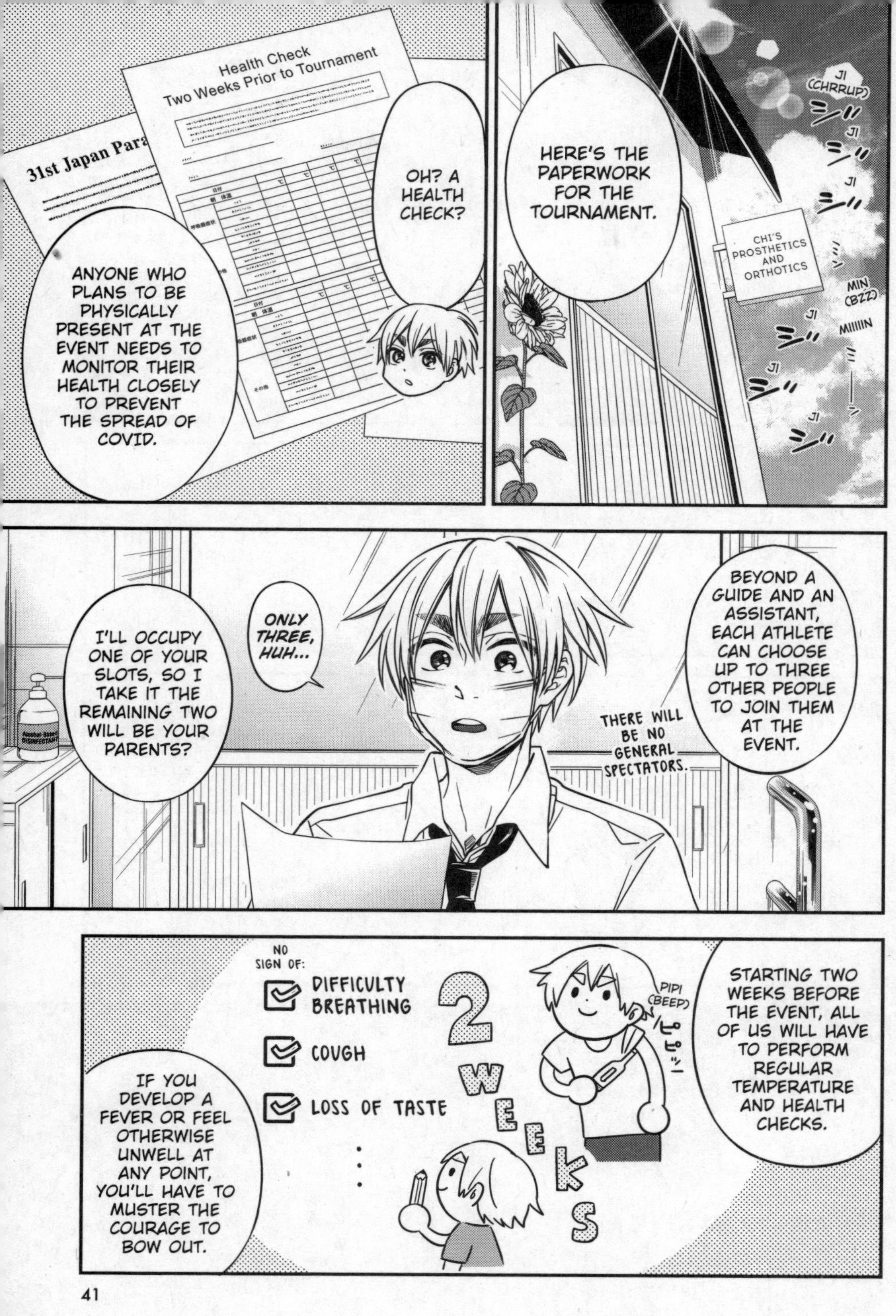
JI (CHRRUP)
ジッ
JI
ジッ
JI
ジッ
CHI'S PROSTHETICS AND ORTHOTICS
MIN (BZZ)
MIIIIIN
ミーーン
JI
ジッ
JI
ジッ
JI
ジッ
HERE'S THE PAPERWORK FOR THE TOURNAMENT.
OH? A HEALTH CHECK?
Health Check Two Weeks Prior to Tournament
31st Japan Para
ANYONE WHO PLANS TO BE PHYSICALLY PRESENT AT THE EVENT NEEDS TO MONITOR THEIR HEALTH CLOSELY TO PREVENT THE SPREAD OF COVID.
BEYOND A GUIDE AND AN ASSISTANT, EACH ATHLETE CAN CHOOSE UP TO THREE OTHER PEOPLE TO JOIN THEM AT THE EVENT.
THERE WILL BE NO GENERAL SPECTATORS.
ONLY THREE, HUH...
I'LL OCCUPY ONE OF YOUR SLOTS, SO I TAKE IT THE REMAINING TWO WILL BE YOUR PARENTS?
STARTING TWO WEEKS BEFORE THE EVENT, ALL OF US WILL HAVE TO PERFORM REGULAR TEMPERATURE AND HEALTH CHECKS.
PIPI (BEEP)
ピピッ
2 WEEKS
NO SIGN OF:
DIFFICULTY BREATHING
COUGH
LOSS OF TASTE
IF YOU DEVELOP A FEVER OR FEEL OTHERWISE UNWELL AT ANY POINT, YOU'LL HAVE TO MUSTER THE COURAGE TO BOW OUT.

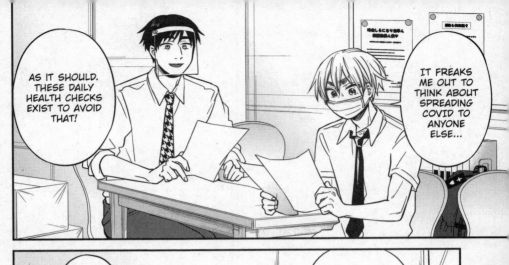

IT FREAKS ME OUT TO THINK ABOUT SPREADING COVID TO ANYONE ELSE...
AS IT SHOULD. THESE DAILY HEALTH CHECKS EXIST TO AVOID THAT!
DO YOU THINK YOU CAN EXPLAIN ALL THIS TO YOUR PARENTS?
Alcohol-Base DISINFECTAN
WHAT AM I, A TODDLER?
'COURSE I CAN!!
THE DAY BEFORE THE EVENT, YOU'LL GO TO RECEIVE YOUR CLASS DESIGNATION.
BE SURE TO HAVE THAT PAPERWORK FILLED OUT AND READY AS WELL!
THE MEDICAL CERTIFICATE, THE X-RAYS, AND...
SO MUCH TO HANDLE... BRAIN'S ABOUT TO BUST...
UGH...
JIIIN (KREEE)
JIIIN
JIIIN

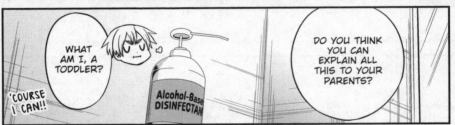

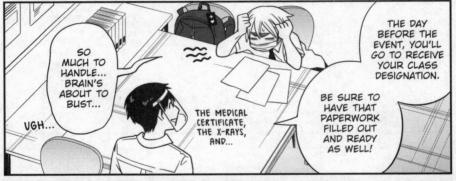

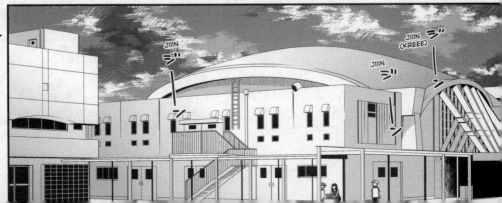

IS THIS THE REMOTE MEET?

JAAF 2020

National High School Remote Track and Field Championship Series

OH.

Points — Girls' 1500m

Grade Level	⌄	Region
Search by Name		School

Rank	Points	Ti...
	1082.0	4:
	045.0	4:2
	0	4:22.67
	1009.0	4:25.57

LOOKS LIKE RANKINGS ON AN ARCADE GAME.

YOU CAN SEARCH BY EVENT, GRADE LEVEL, OR EVEN REGION.

YEAH, WE'RE GONNA SEE THE RANKINGS FOR THE ATHLETES WHO FINISHED AND SUBMITTED THEIR TIMES.

...AND BE MOTIVATED TO COMPETE FOR REAL!

THIS WAY, ATHLETES NATIONWIDE CAN GET THEIR NAMES UP ON THESE CHARTS...

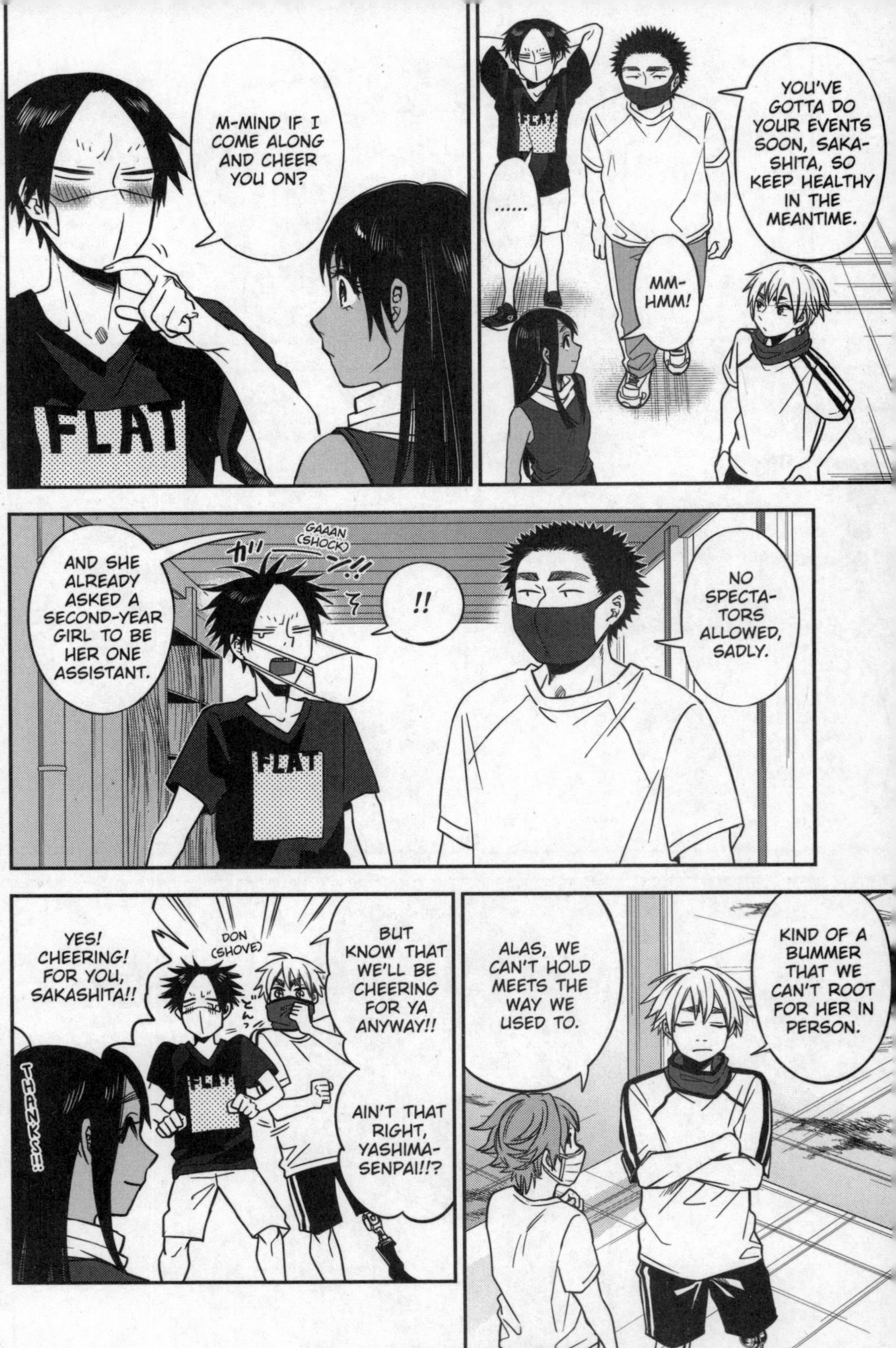
YOU'VE GOTTA DO YOUR EVENTS SOON, SAKASHITA, SO KEEP HEALTHY IN THE MEANTIME.
MM-HMM!
......
M-MIND IF I COME ALONG AND CHEER YOU ON?
NO SPECTATORS ALLOWED, SADLY.
!!
GAAAN (SHOCK)
AND SHE ALREADY ASKED A SECOND-YEAR GIRL TO BE HER ONE ASSISTANT.
KIND OF A BUMMER THAT WE CAN'T ROOT FOR HER IN PERSON.
ALAS, WE CAN'T HOLD MEETS THE WAY WE USED TO.
BUT KNOW THAT WE'LL BE CHEERING FOR YA ANYWAY!!
AIN'T THAT RIGHT, YASHIMA-SENPAI!!?
DON (SHOVE)
YES! CHEERING! FOR YOU, SAKASHITA!!
THANKS!!

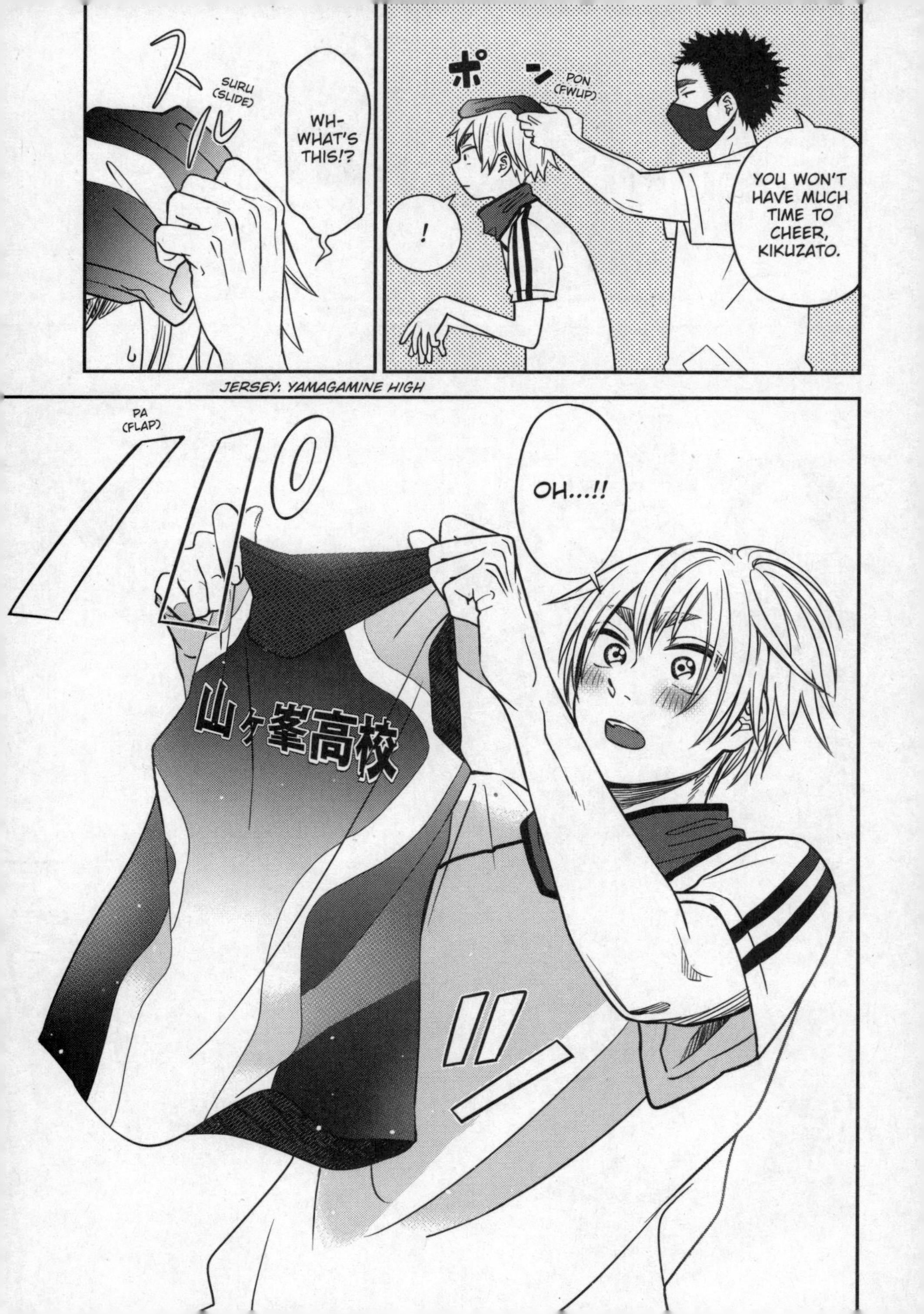
ポン
PON (FWUP)
YOU WON'T HAVE MUCH TIME TO CHEER, KIKUZATO.
!
スル
SURU (SLIDE)
WH- WHAT'S THIS!?
JERSEY: YAMAGAMINE HIGH
OH...!!
パ
PA (FLAP)
山ヶ峰高校

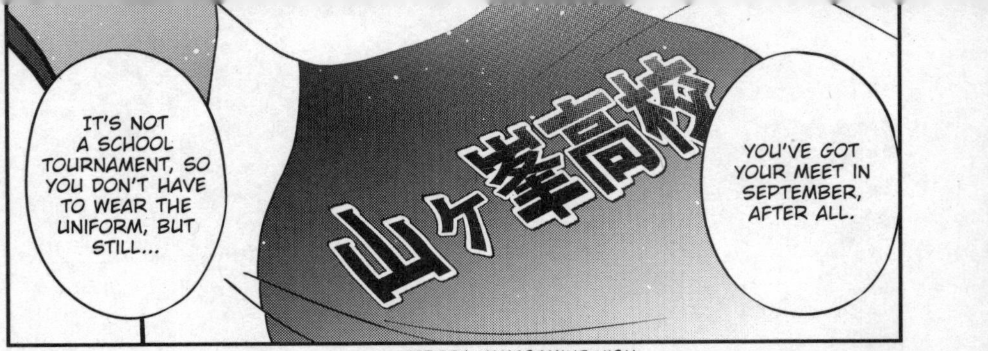
YOU'VE GOT YOUR MEET IN SEPTEMBER, AFTER ALL.
山ヶ峯高校
IT'S NOT A SCHOOL TOURNAMENT, SO YOU DON'T HAVE TO WEAR THE UNIFORM, BUT STILL...

JERSEY: YAMAGAMINE HIGH

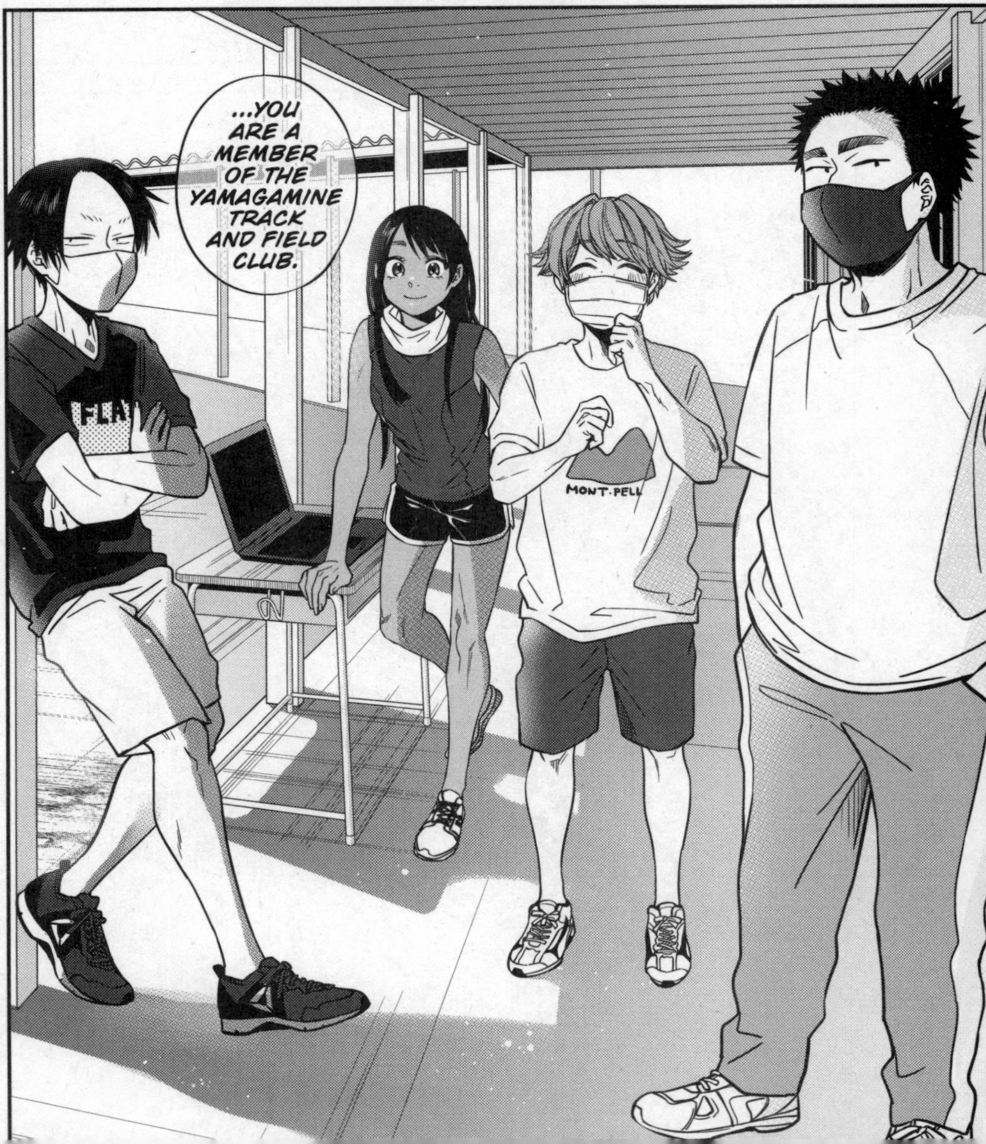
...YOU ARE A MEMBER OF THE YAMAGAMINE TRACK AND FIELD CLUB.
MONT.PELL

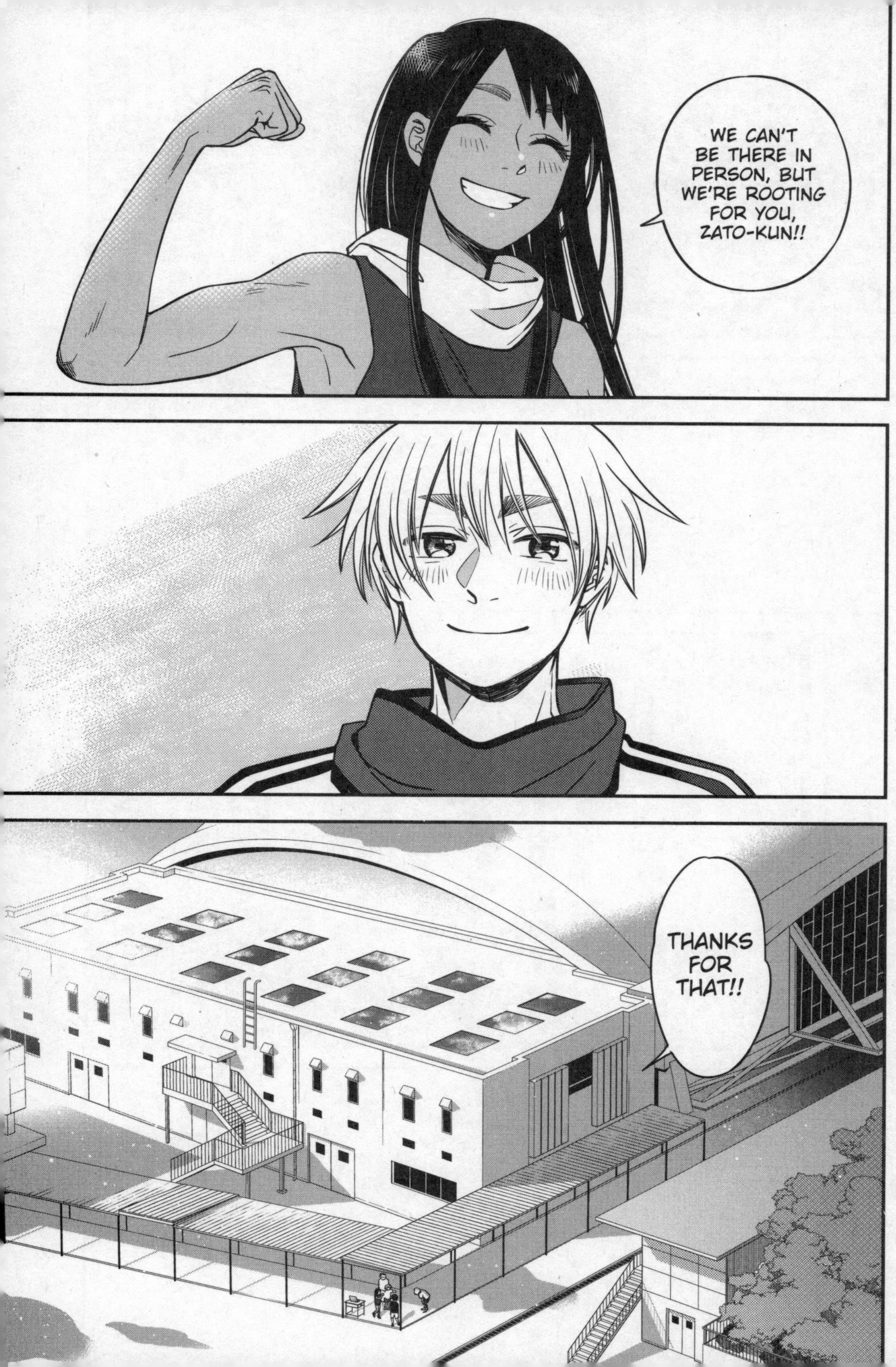
WE CAN'T BE THERE IN PERSON, BUT WE'RE ROOTING FOR YOU, ZATO-KUN!!
THANKS FOR THAT!!

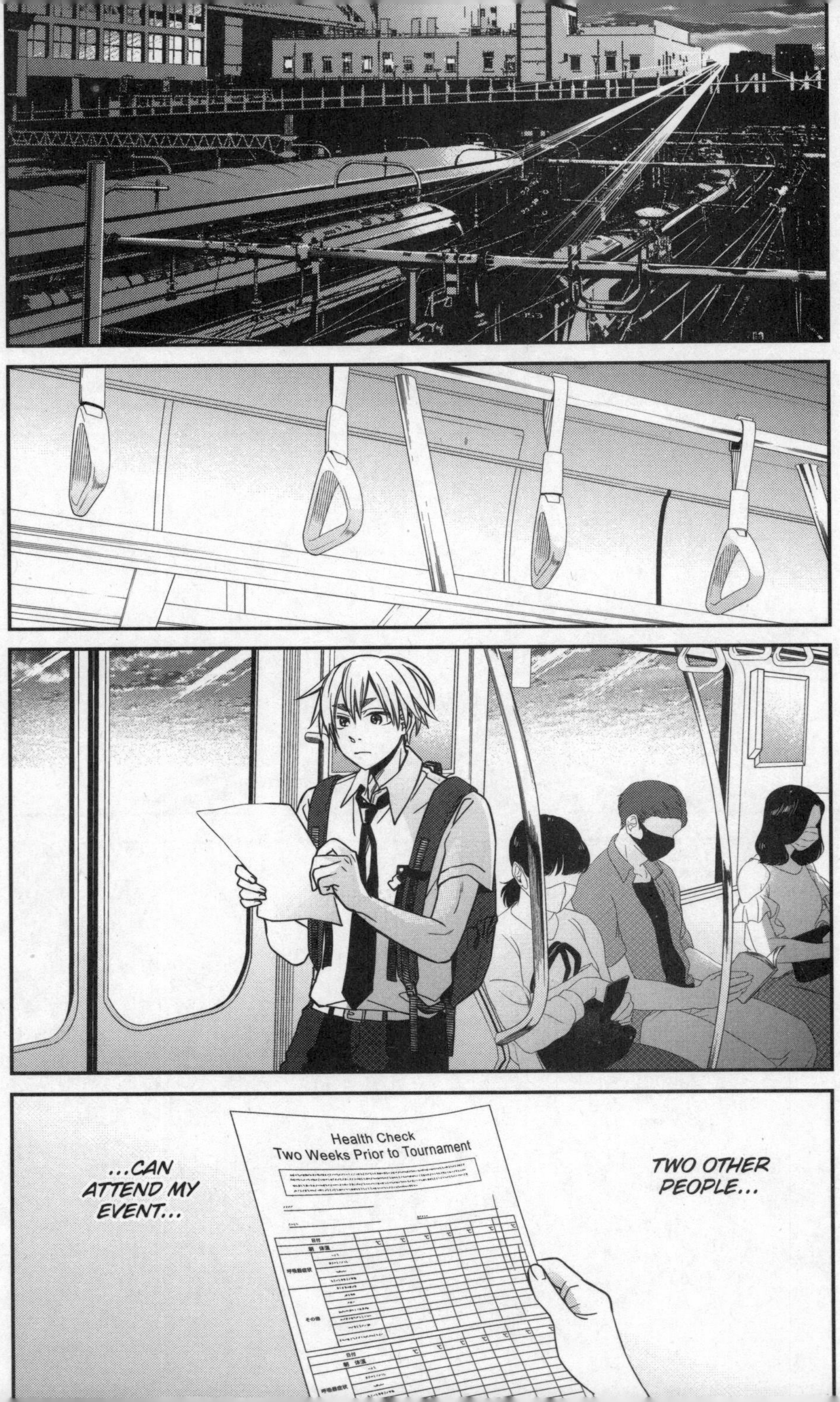
TWO OTHER PEOPLE...
Health Check
Two Weeks Prior to Tournament
...CAN ATTEND MY EVENT...

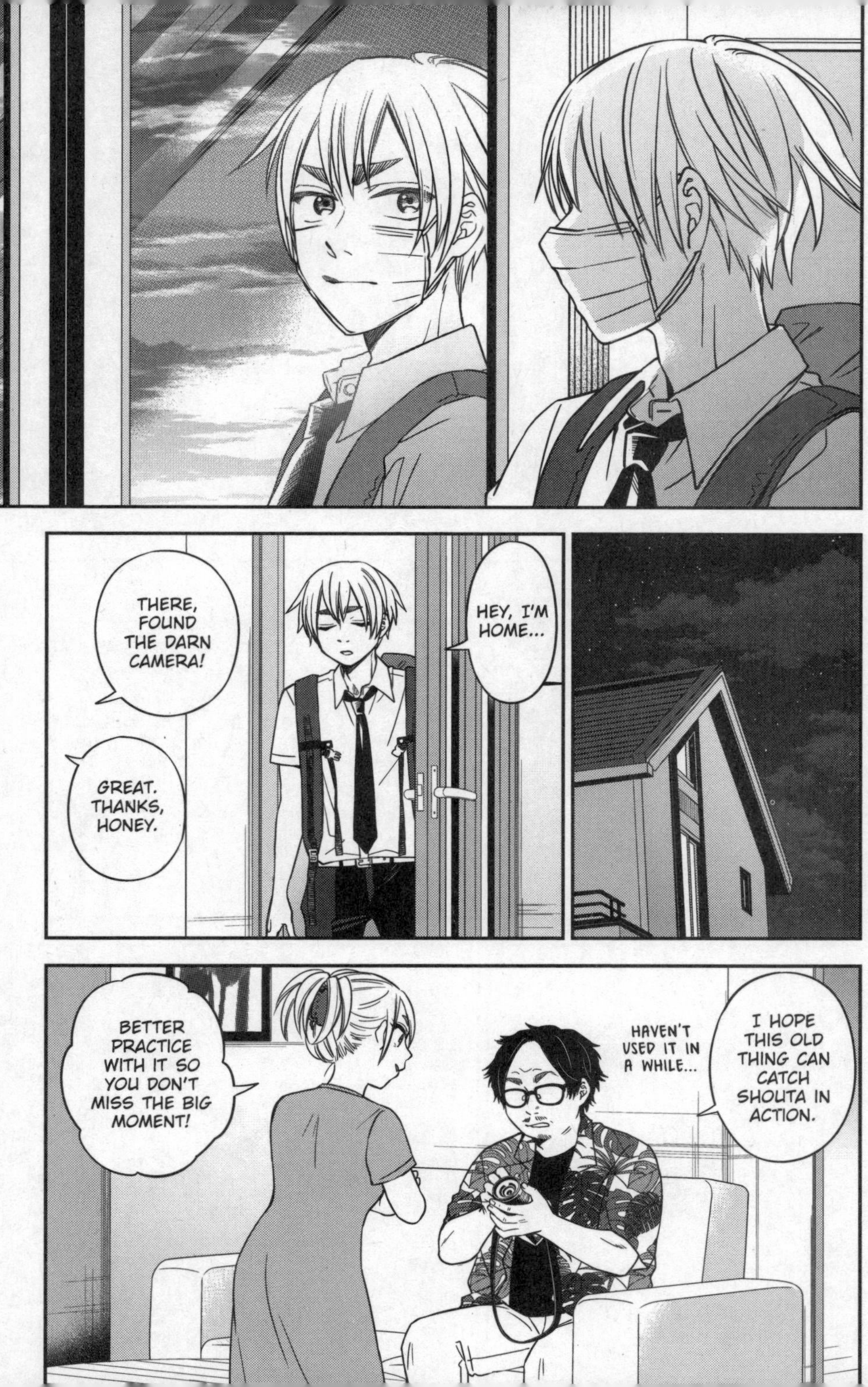
HEY, I'M HOME...
THERE, FOUND THE DARN CAMERA!
GREAT. THANKS, HONEY.
I HOPE THIS OLD THING CAN CATCH SHOUTA IN ACTION.
HAVEN'T USED IT IN A WHILE...
BETTER PRACTICE WITH IT SO YOU DON'T MISS THE BIG MOMENT!

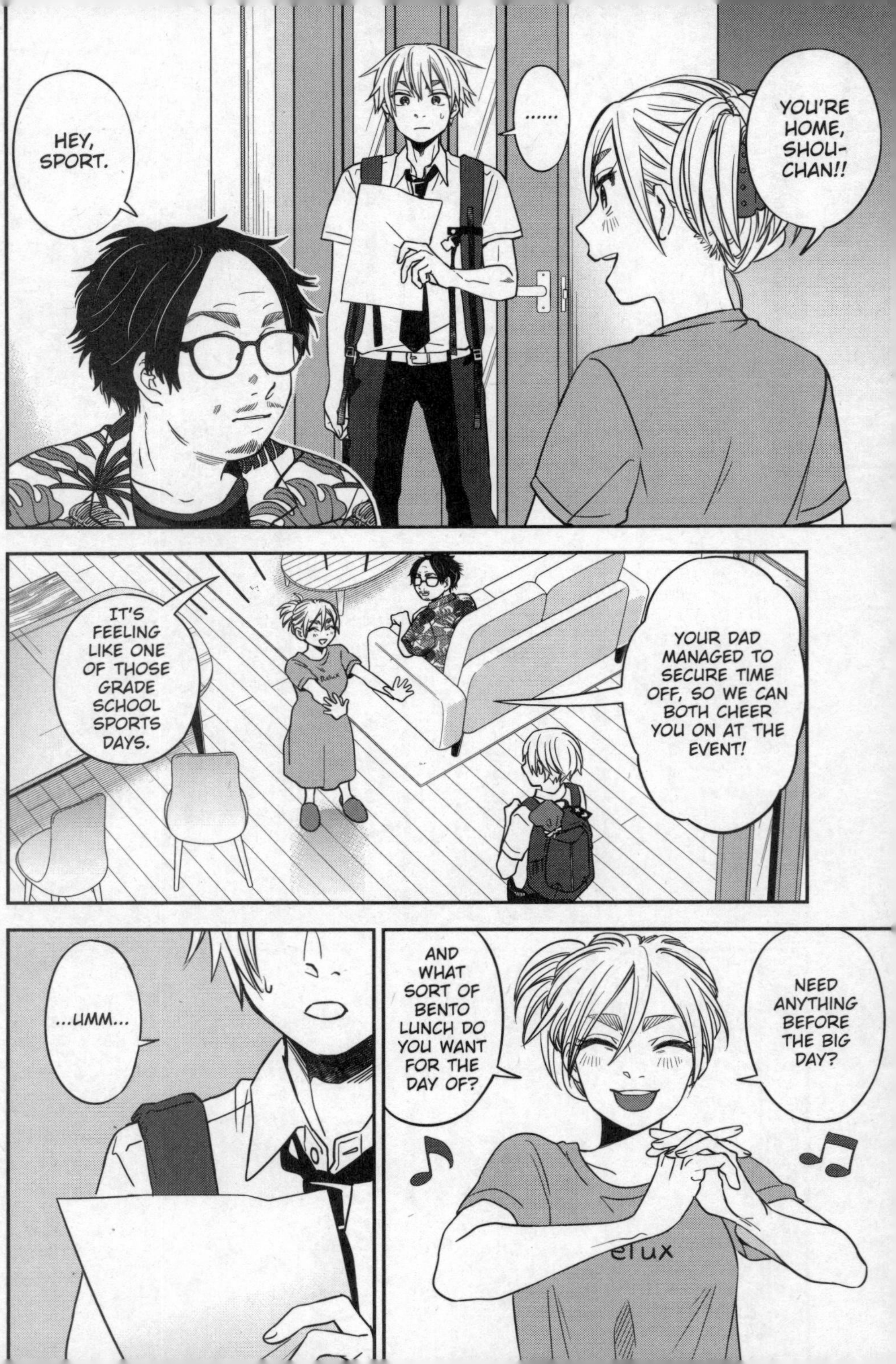
YOU'RE HOME, SHOU-CHAN!!
......
HEY, SPORT.
YOUR DAD MANAGED TO SECURE TIME OFF, SO WE CAN BOTH CHEER YOU ON AT THE EVENT!
IT'S FEELING LIKE ONE OF THOSE GRADE SCHOOL SPORTS DAYS.
NEED ANYTHING BEFORE THE BIG DAY?
AND WHAT SORT OF BENTO LUNCH DO YOU WANT FOR THE DAY OF?
...UMM...

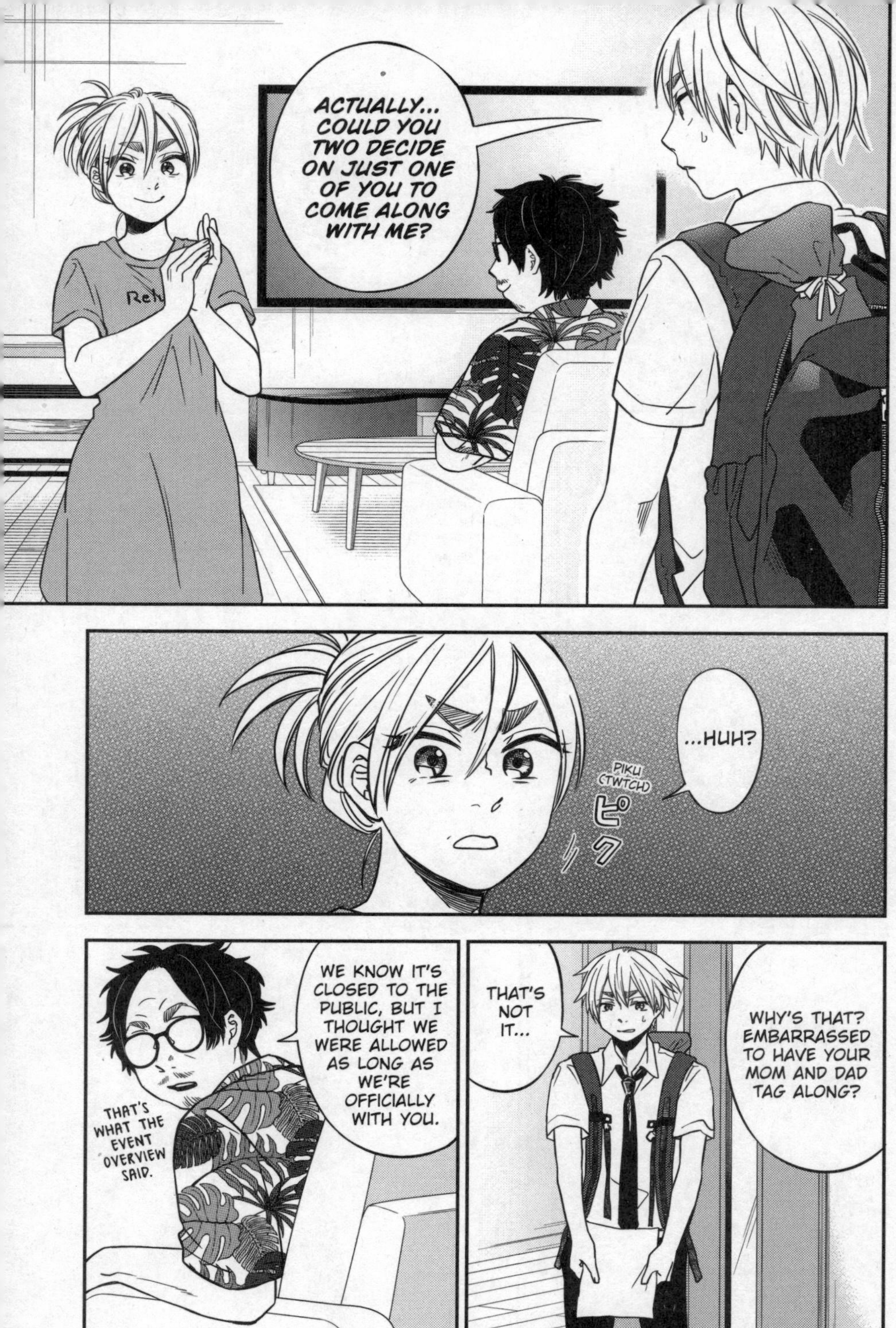
ACTUALLY... COULD YOU TWO DECIDE ON JUST ONE OF YOU TO COME ALONG WITH ME?
...HUH?
PIKU (TWTCH)
ピク
WHY'S THAT? EMBARRASSED TO HAVE YOUR MOM AND DAD TAG ALONG?
THAT'S NOT IT...
WE KNOW IT'S CLOSED TO THE PUBLIC, BUT I THOUGHT WE WERE ALLOWED AS LONG AS WE'RE OFFICIALLY WITH YOU.
THAT'S WHAT THE EVENT OVERVIEW SAID.

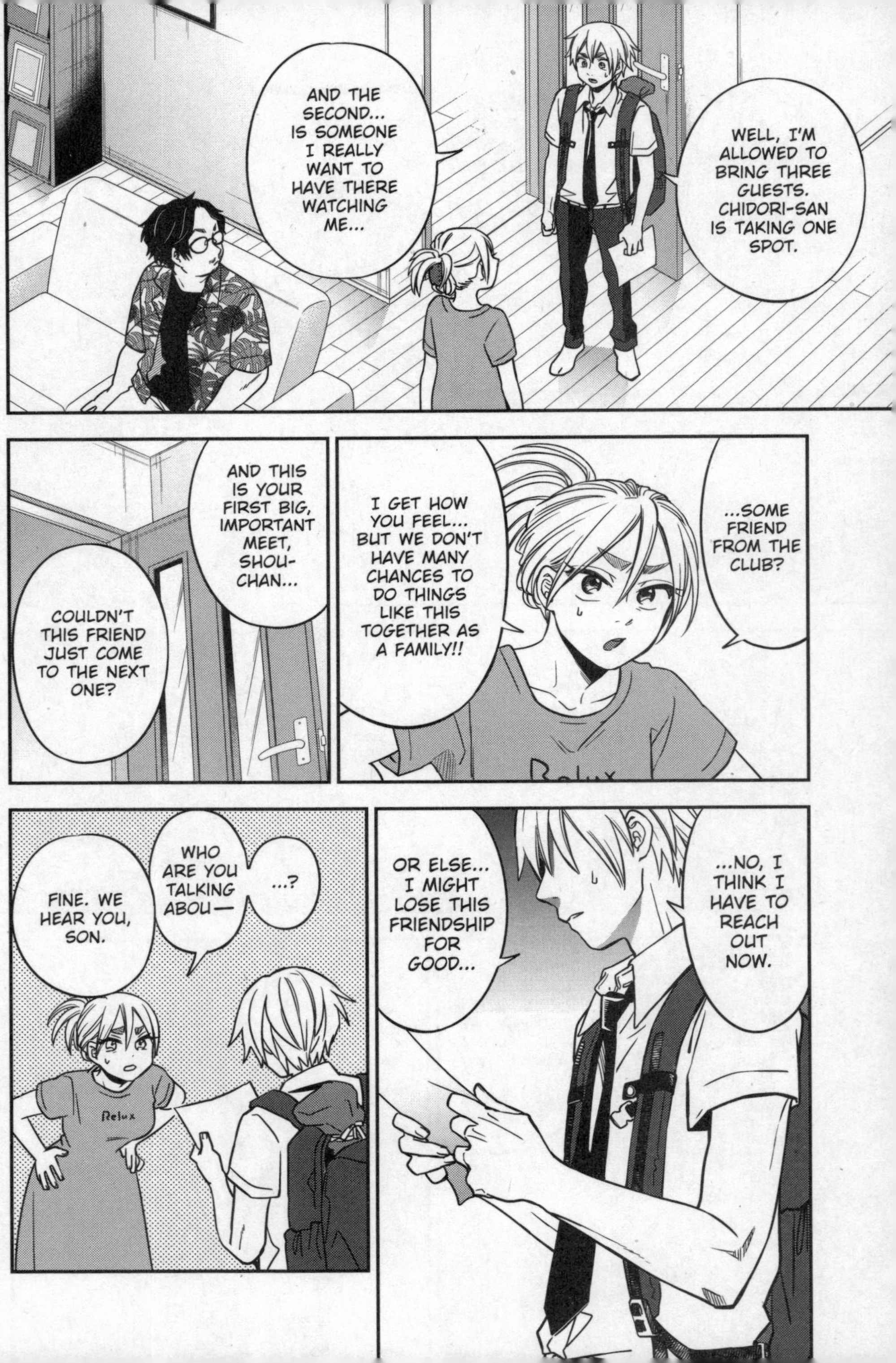
WELL, I'M ALLOWED TO BRING THREE GUESTS. CHIDORI-SAN IS TAKING ONE SPOT.
AND THE SECOND... IS SOMEONE I REALLY WANT TO HAVE THERE WATCHING ME...
...SOME FRIEND FROM THE CLUB?
I GET HOW YOU FEEL... BUT WE DON'T HAVE MANY CHANCES TO DO THINGS LIKE THIS TOGETHER AS A FAMILY!!
AND THIS IS YOUR FIRST BIG, IMPORTANT MEET, SHOU-CHAN...
COULDN'T THIS FRIEND JUST COME TO THE NEXT ONE?
...NO, I THINK I HAVE TO REACH OUT NOW.
OR ELSE... I MIGHT LOSE THIS FRIENDSHIP FOR GOOD...
...?
WHO ARE YOU TALKING ABOU—
FINE. WE HEAR YOU, SON.

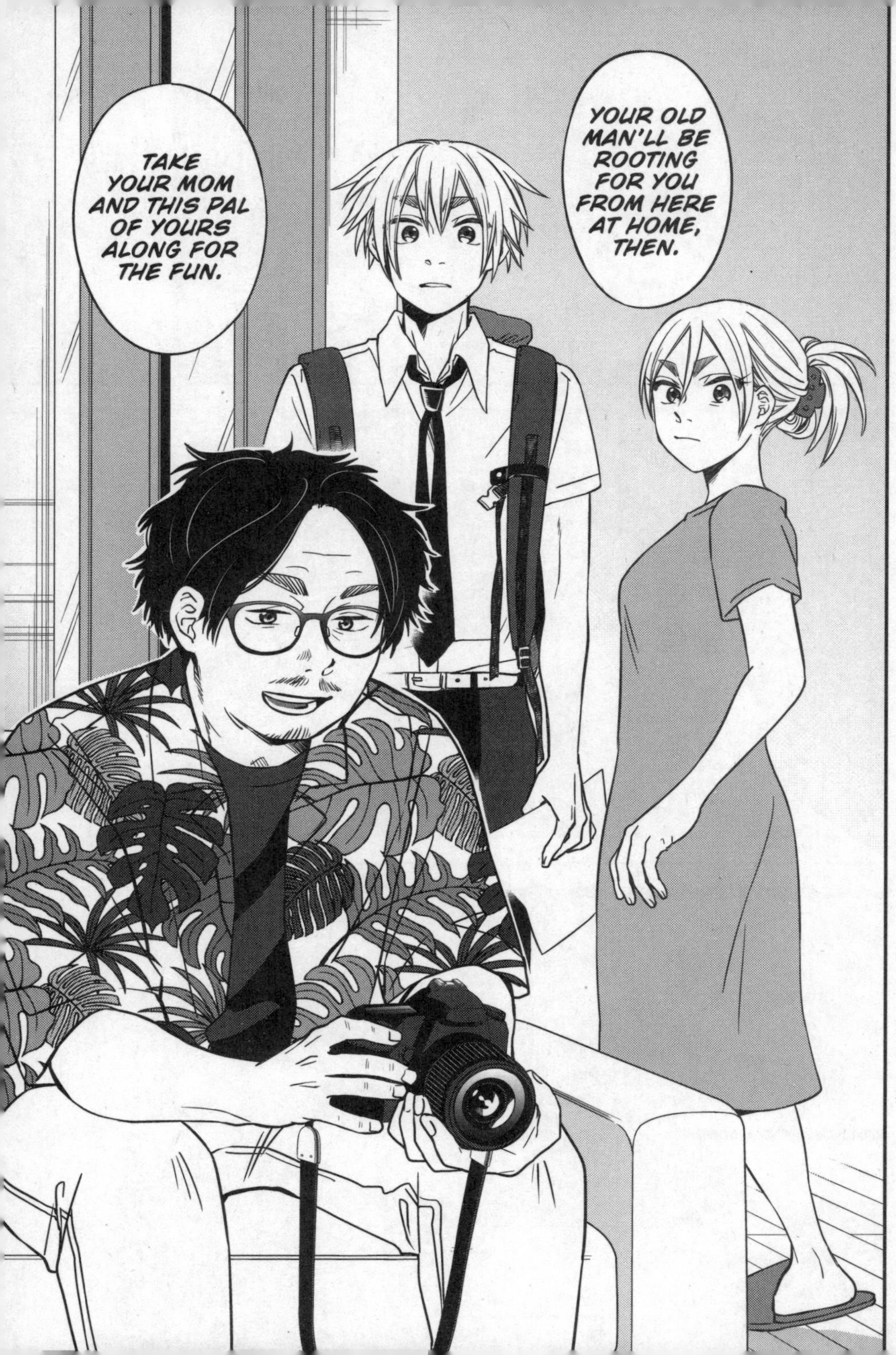
YOUR OLD MAN'LL BE ROOTING FOR YOU FROM HERE AT HOME, THEN.
TAKE YOUR MOM AND THIS PAL OF YOURS ALONG FOR THE FUN.

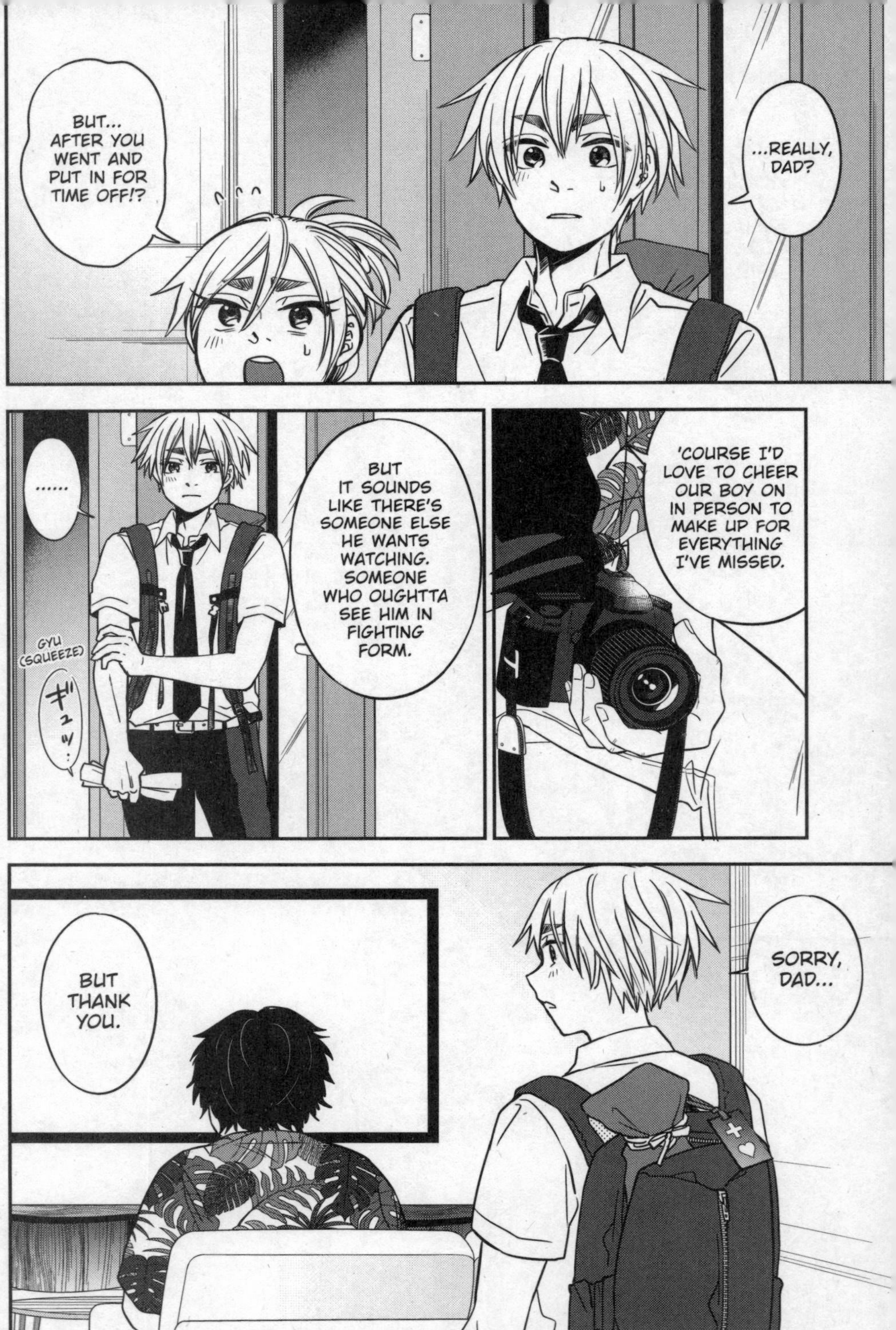
...REALLY, DAD?
BUT... AFTER YOU WENT AND PUT IN FOR TIME OFF!?
'COURSE I'D LOVE TO CHEER OUR BOY ON IN PERSON TO MAKE UP FOR EVERYTHING I'VE MISSED.
BUT IT SOUNDS LIKE THERE'S SOMEONE ELSE HE WANTS WATCHING. SOMEONE WHO OUGHTTA SEE HIM IN FIGHTING FORM.
......
GYU (SQUEEZE)
ギュッ…
SORRY, DAD...
BUT THANK YOU.

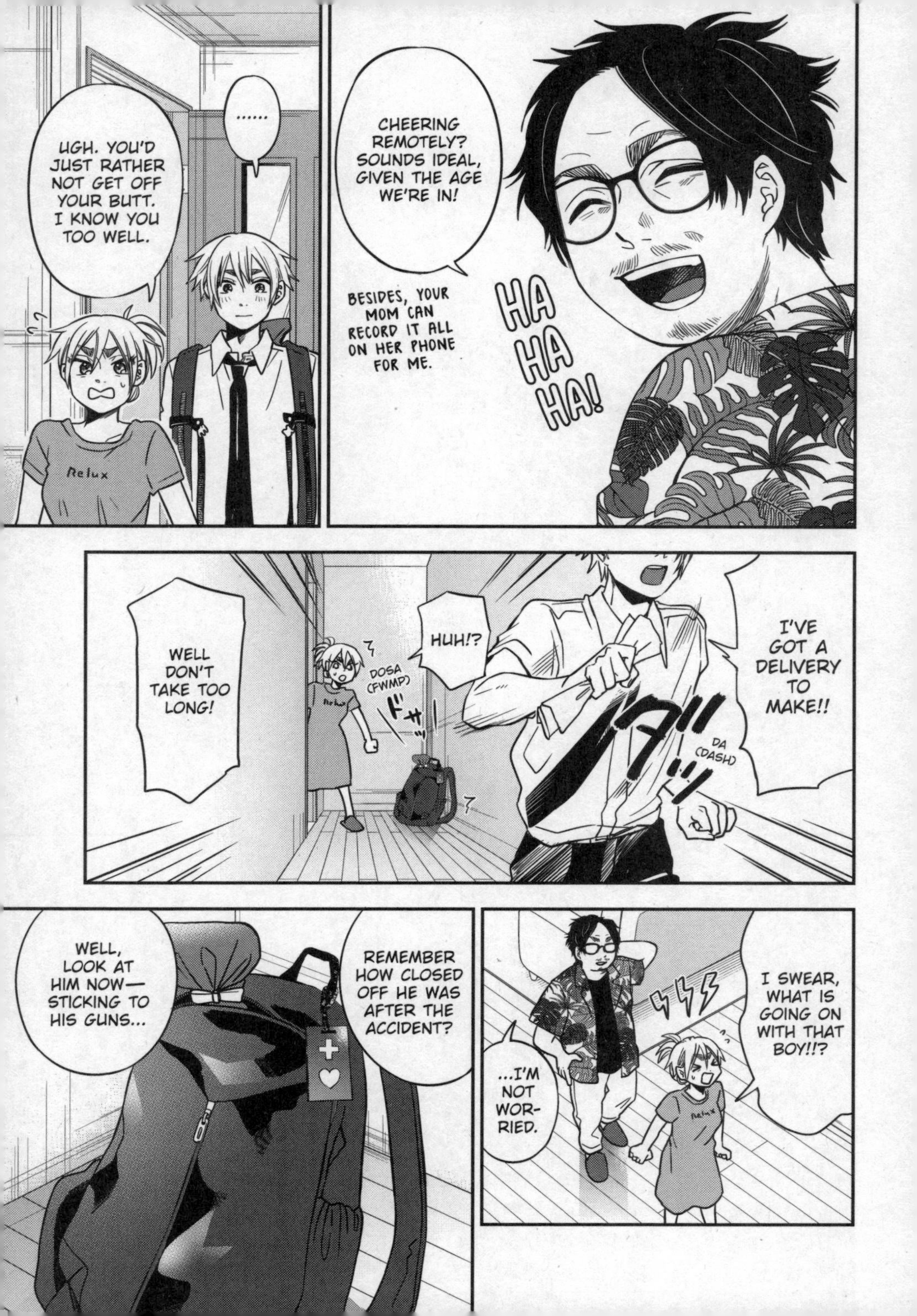
CHEERING REMOTELY? SOUNDS IDEAL, GIVEN THE AGE WE'RE IN!
HA HA HA!
BESIDES, YOUR MOM CAN RECORD IT ALL ON HER PHONE FOR ME.
......
UGH. YOU'D JUST RATHER NOT GET OFF YOUR BUTT. I KNOW YOU TOO WELL.
Relux
I'VE GOT A DELIVERY TO MAKE!!
DA (DASH)
HUH!?
DOSA (FWMP)
WELL DON'T TAKE TOO LONG!
I SWEAR, WHAT IS GOING ON WITH THAT BOY!!?
...I'M NOT WORRIED.
REMEMBER HOW CLOSED OFF HE WAS AFTER THE ACCIDENT?
WELL, LOOK AT HIM NOW—STICKING TO HIS GUNS...

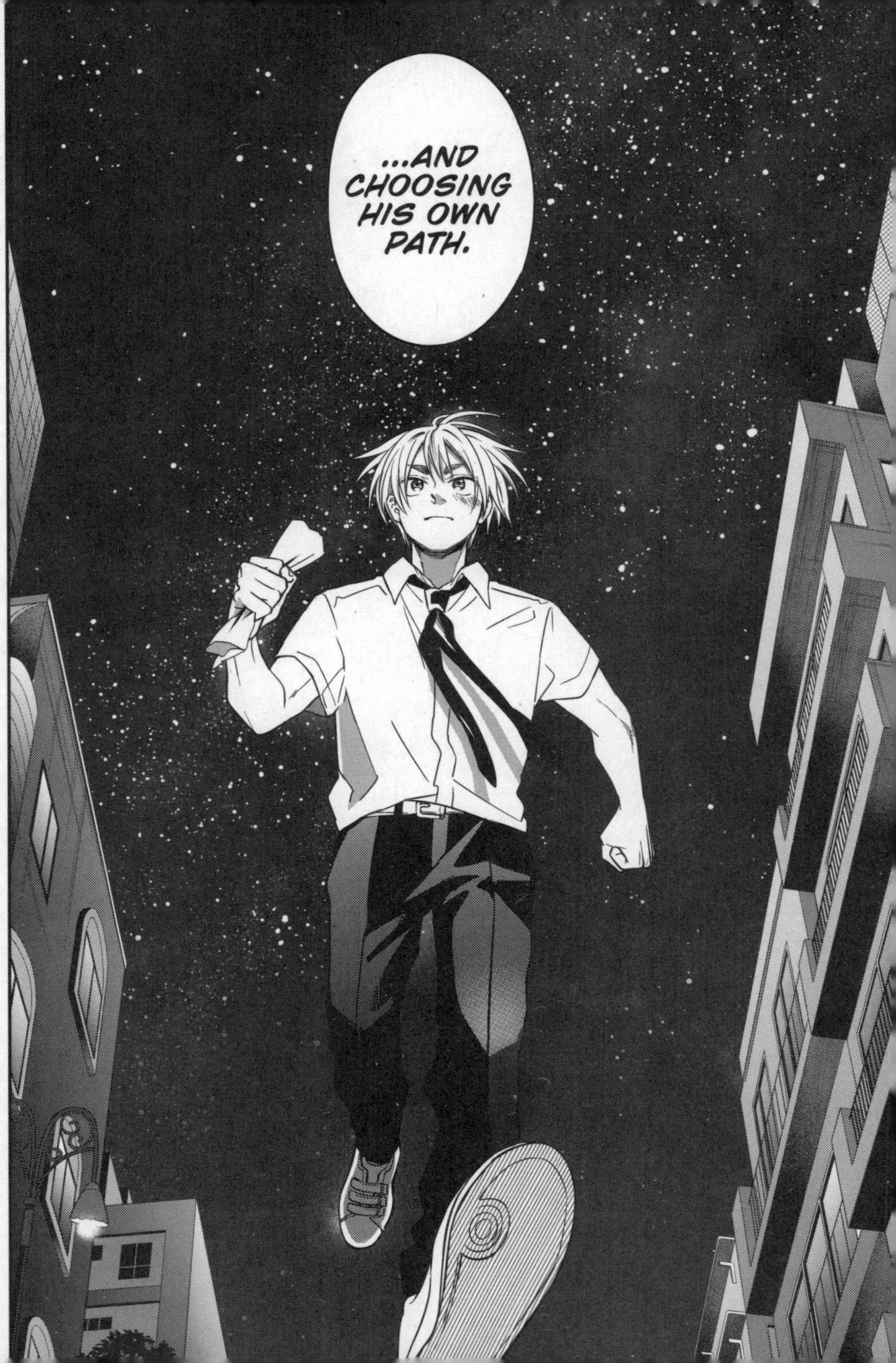
...AND CHOOSING HIS OWN PATH.

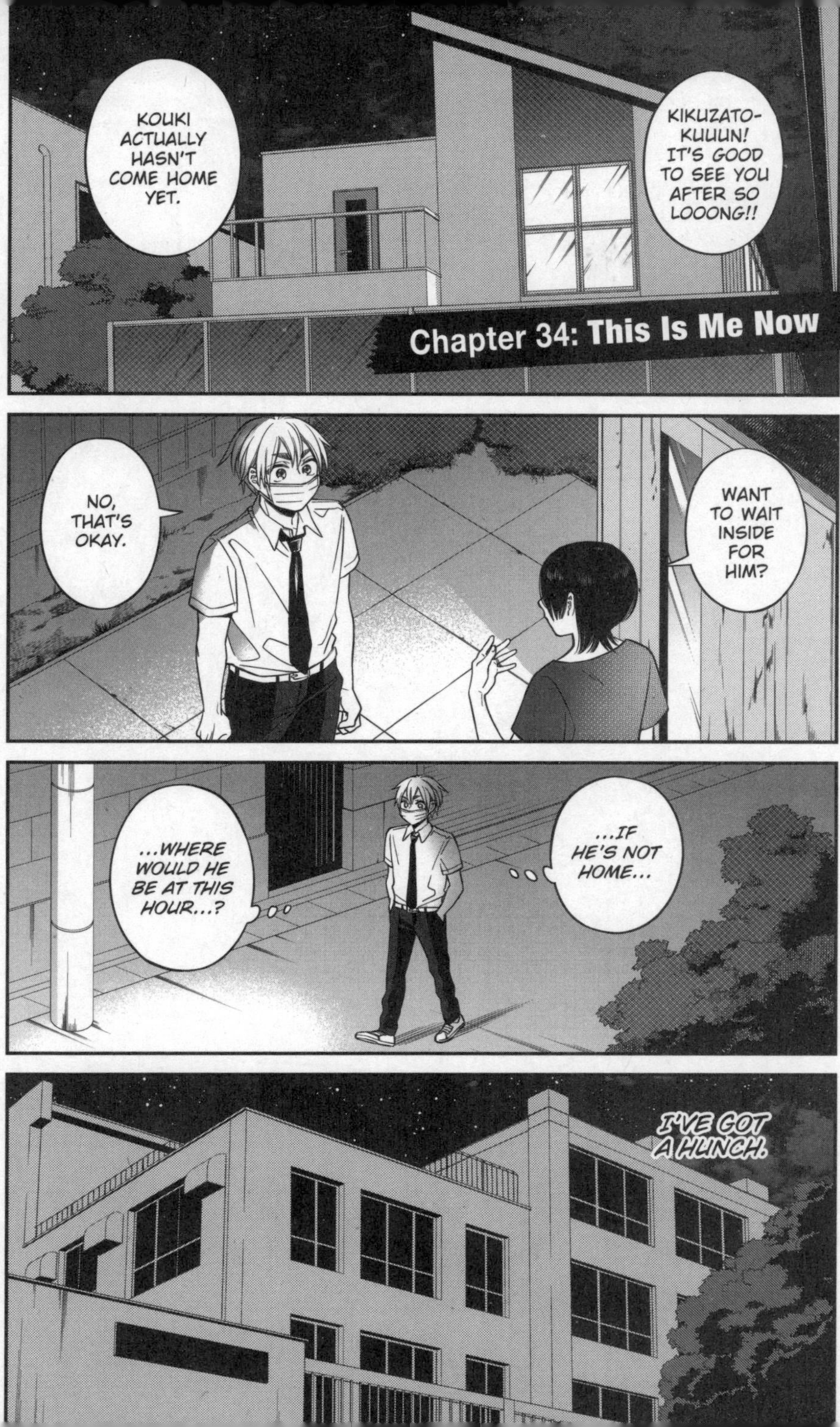
KIKUZATO-KUUUN! IT'S GOOD TO SEE YOU AFTER SO LOOONG!!
KOUKI ACTUALLY HASN'T COME HOME YET.
Chapter 34: This Is Me Now
WANT TO WAIT INSIDE FOR HIM?
NO, THAT'S OKAY.
...IF HE'S NOT HOME...
...WHERE WOULD HE BE AT THIS HOUR...?
I'VE GOT A HUNCH.

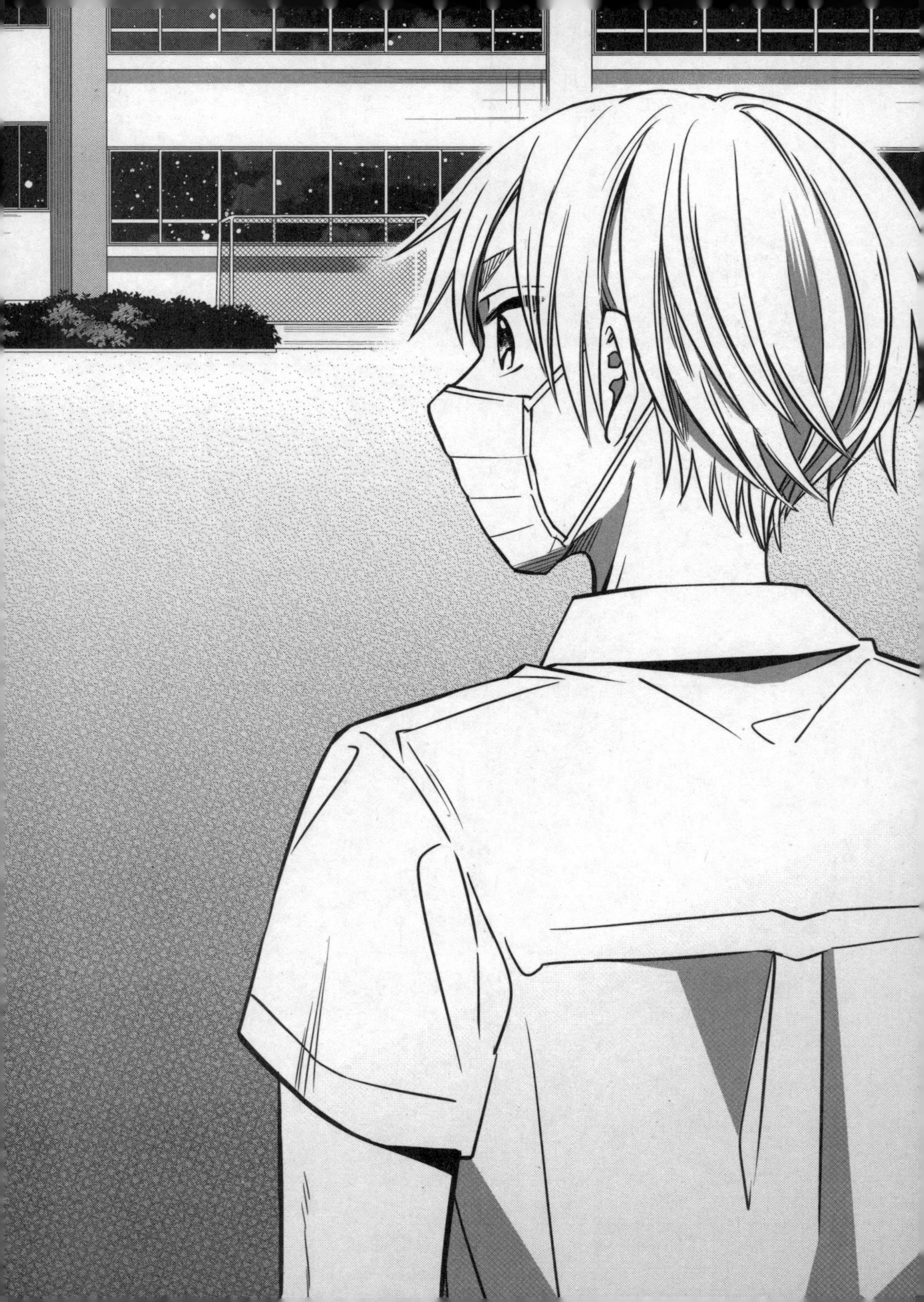

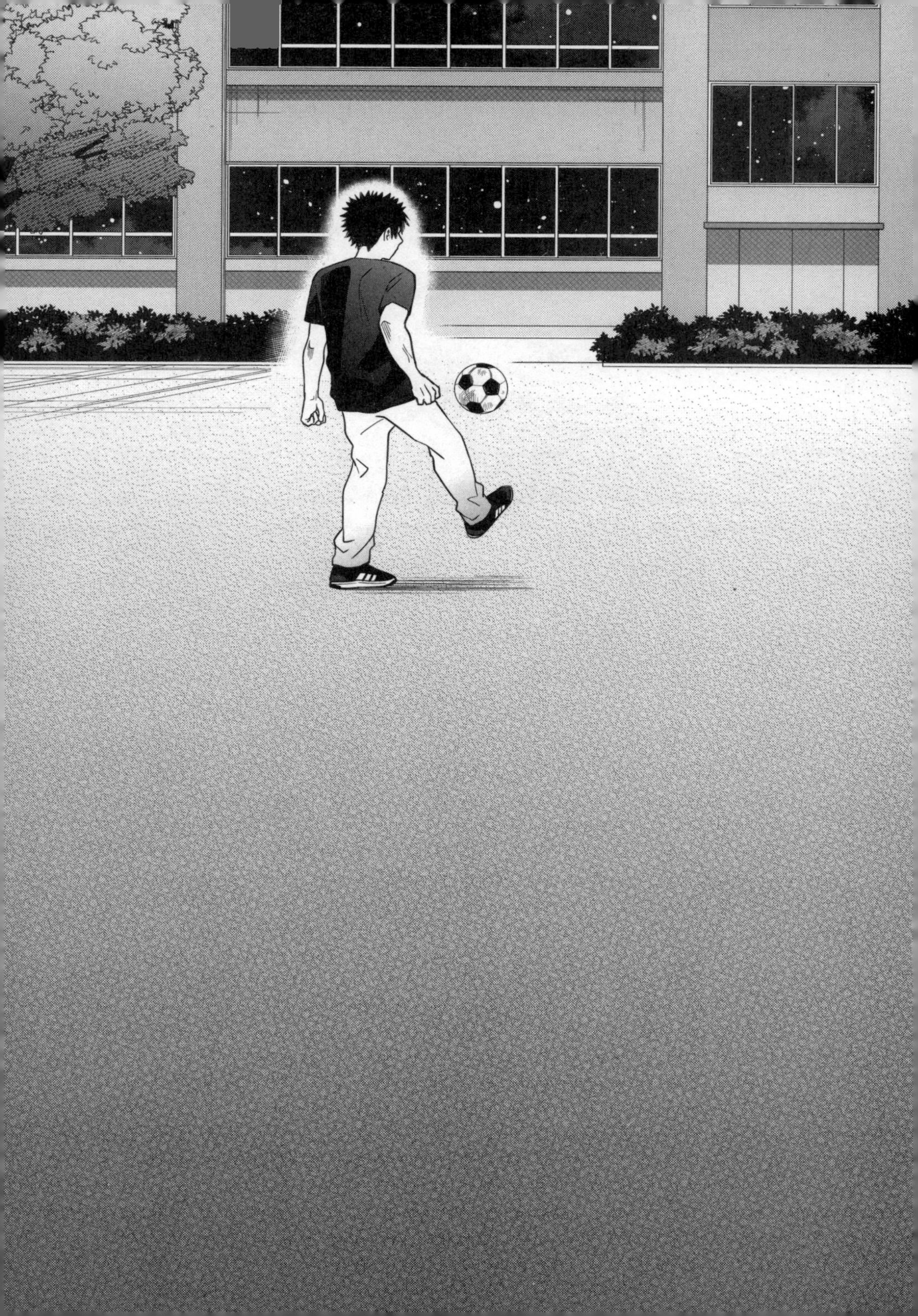

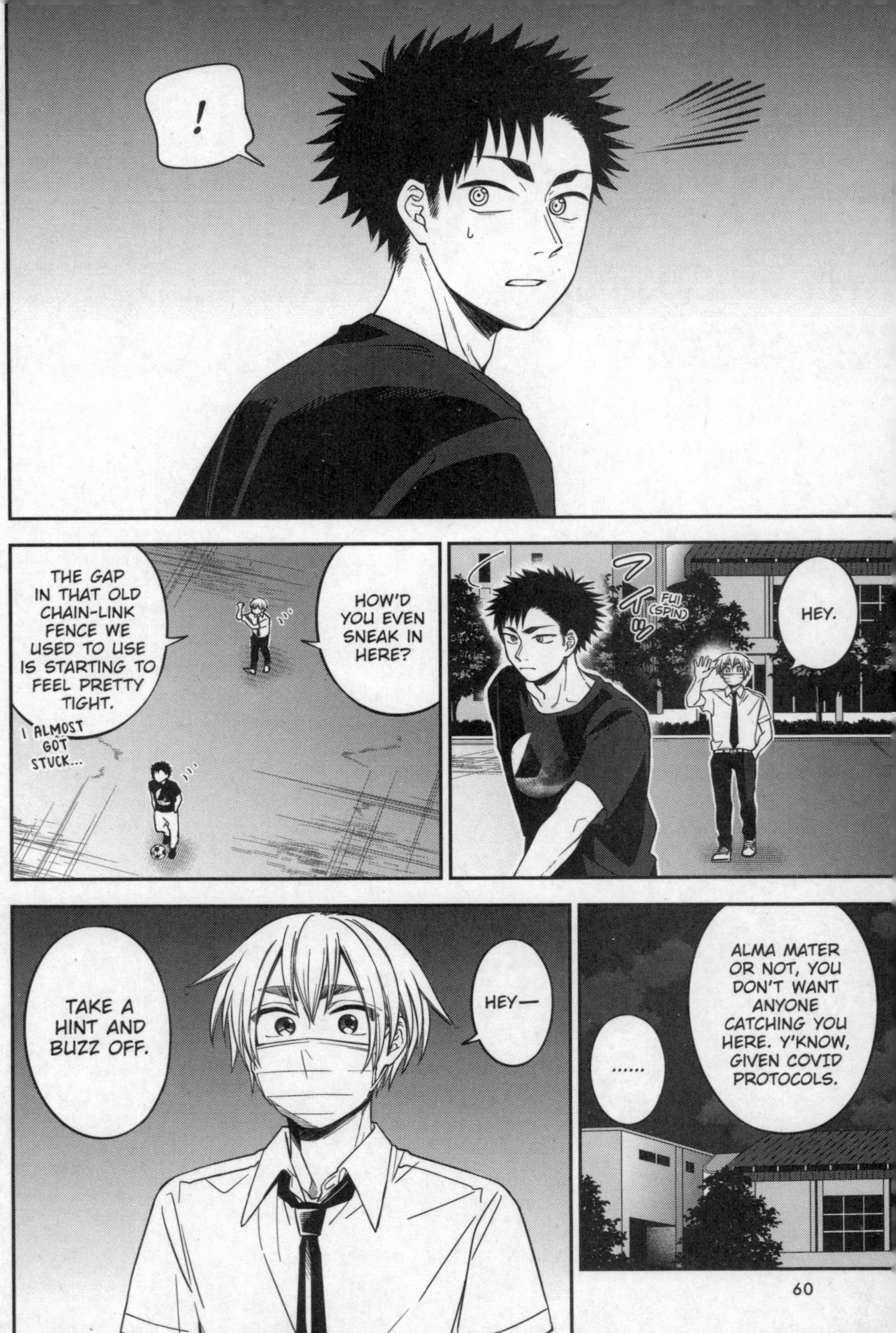
!
HEY.
FUI (SPIN)
HOW'D YOU EVEN SNEAK IN HERE?
THE GAP IN THAT OLD CHAIN-LINK FENCE WE USED TO USE IS STARTING TO FEEL PRETTY TIGHT.
I ALMOST GOT STUCK...
ALMA MATER OR NOT, YOU DON'T WANT ANYONE CATCHING YOU HERE. Y'KNOW, GIVEN COVID PROTOCOLS.
......
HEY—
TAKE A HINT AND BUZZ OFF.

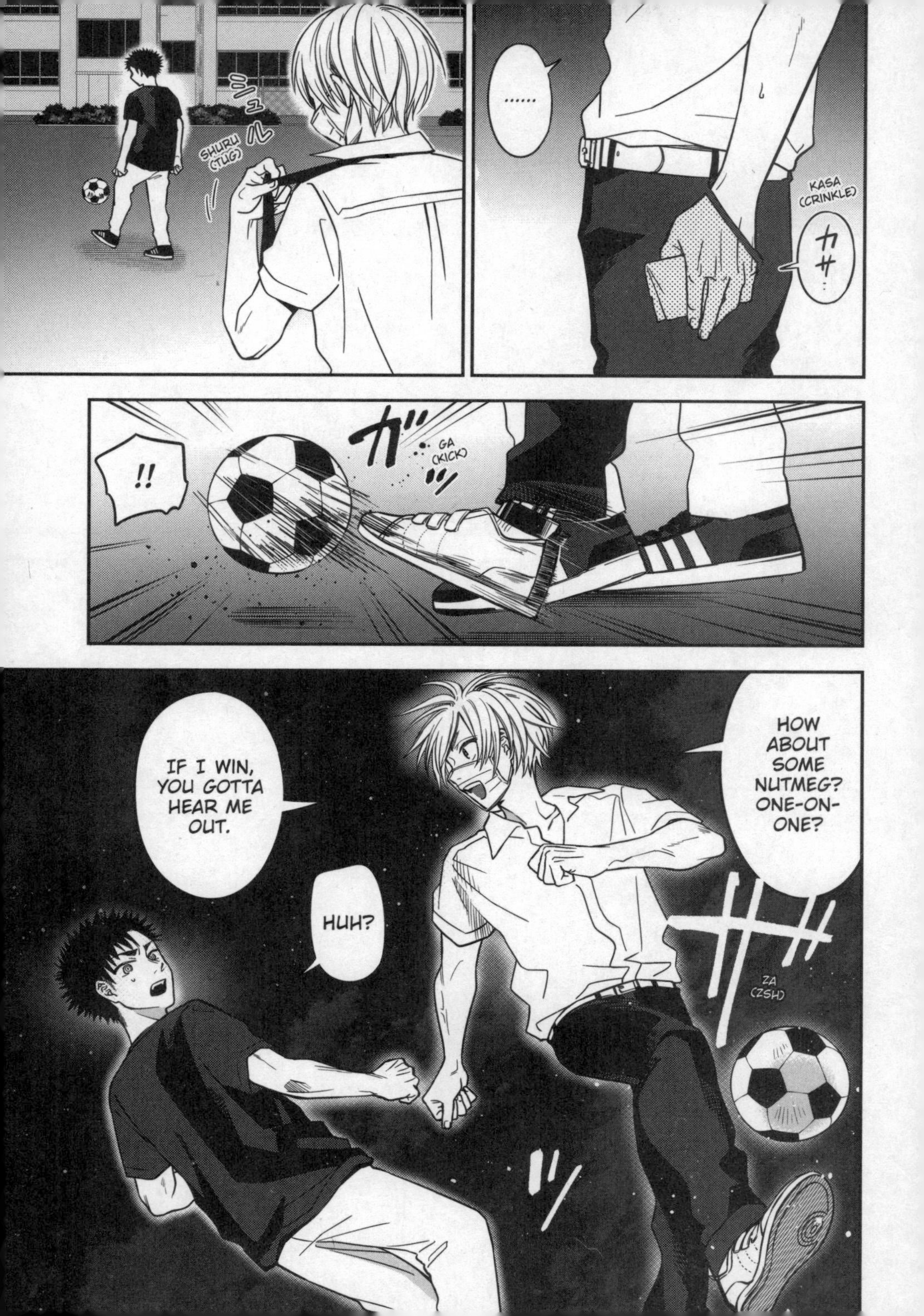
......
KASA (CRINKLE)
カサ…
シュル
SHURU (TUG)
ガッ
GA (KICK)
!!
HOW ABOUT SOME NUTMEG? ONE-ON-ONE?
IF I WIN, YOU GOTTA HEAR ME OUT.
HUH?
ZA (ZSH)

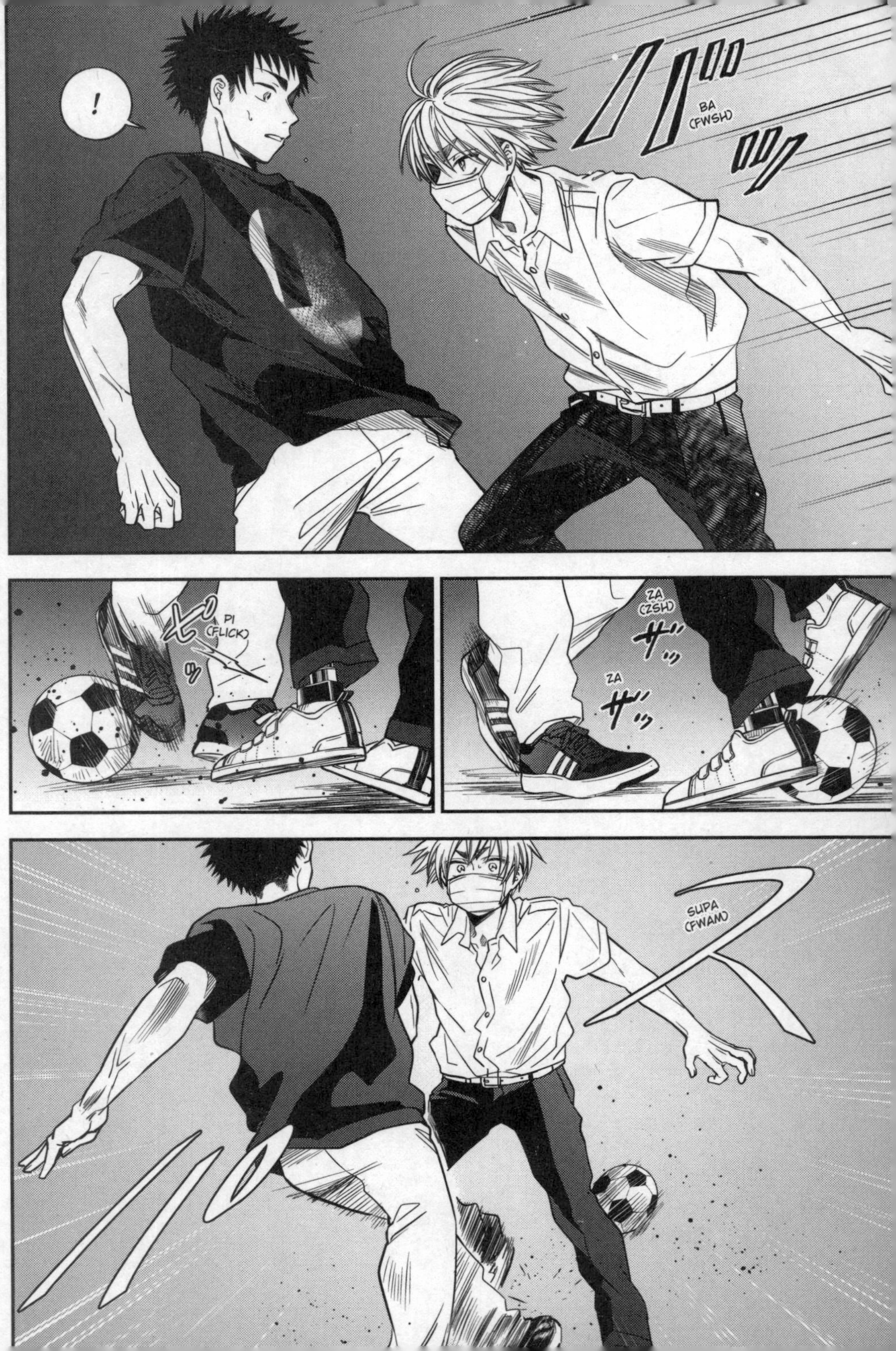
BA (FWSH)
!
ZA (ZSH)
ZA
PI (FLICK)
SUPA (FWAM)

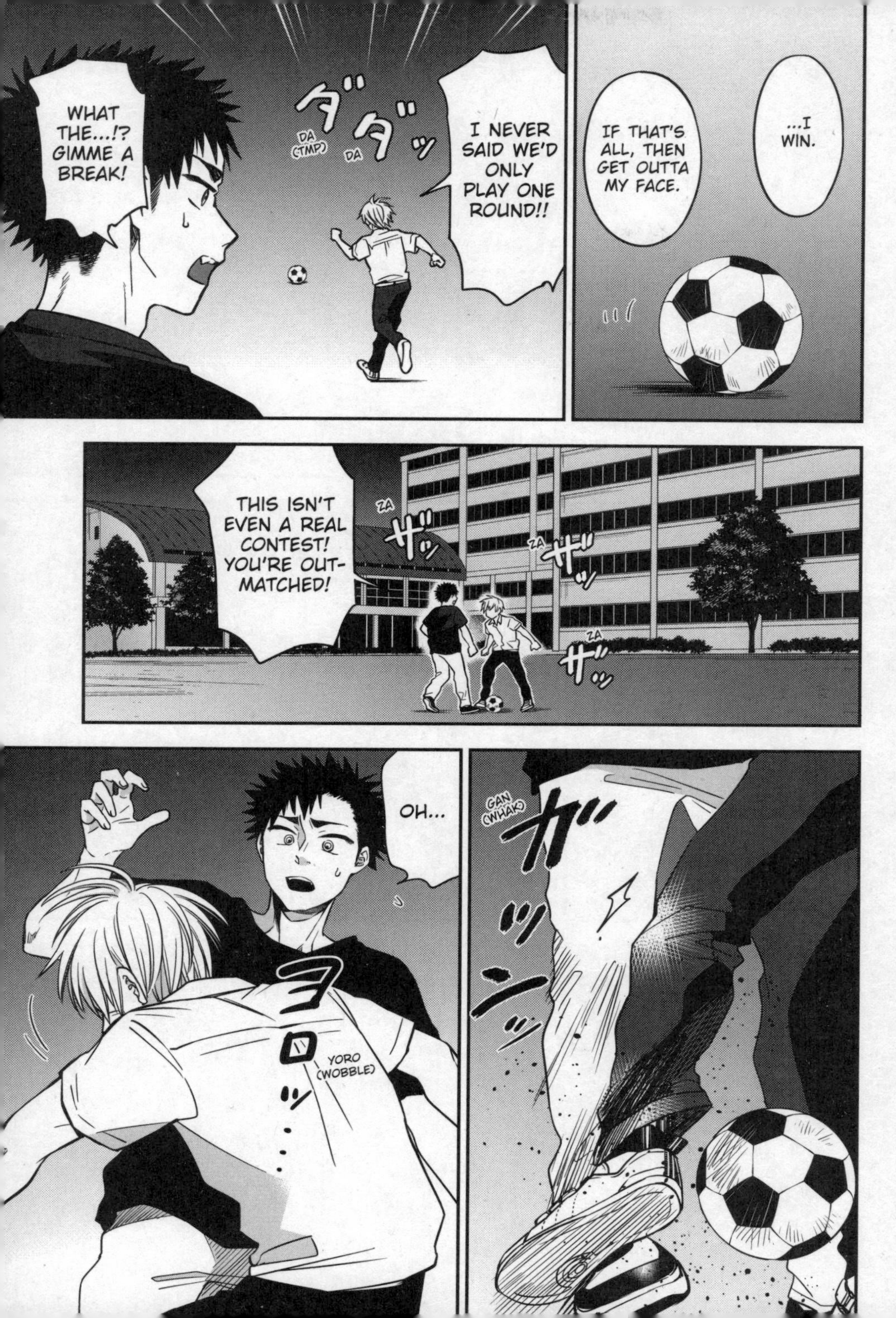

...I WIN.
IF THAT'S ALL, THEN GET OUTTA MY FACE.
I NEVER SAID WE'D ONLY PLAY ONE ROUND!!
DA (TMP) DA
WHAT THE...!? GIMME A BREAK!
ZA ZA ZA
THIS ISN'T EVEN A REAL CONTEST! YOU'RE OUT-MATCHED!
GAN (WHAK)
OH...
YORO (WOBBLE)

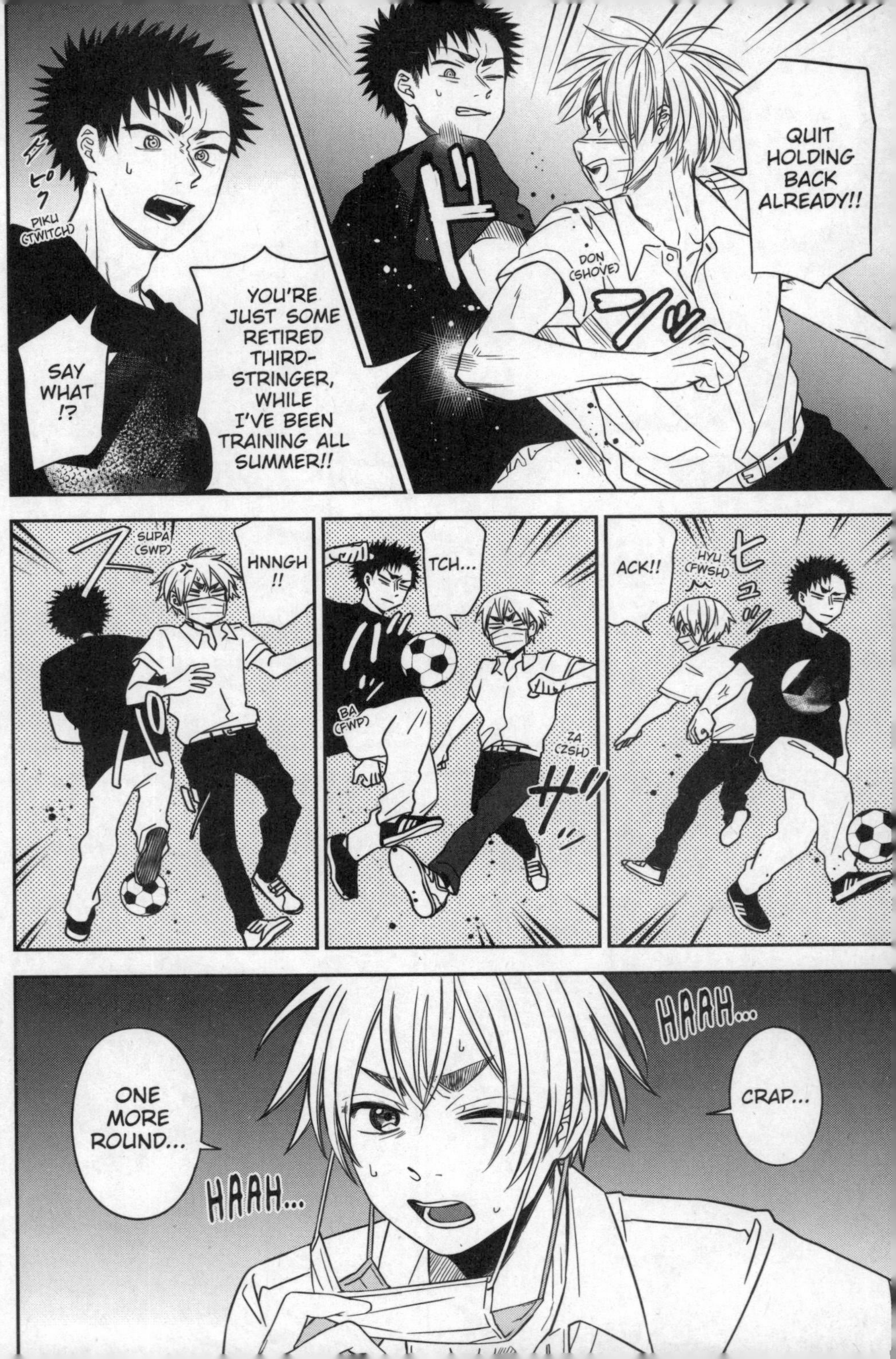
DON
(SHOVE)
QUIT HOLDING BACK ALREADY!!
YOU'RE JUST SOME RETIRED THIRD-STRINGER, WHILE I'VE BEEN TRAINING ALL SUMMER!!
PIKU
(TWITCH)
SAY WHAT!?
HYU
(FWSH)
ACK!!
TCH...
BA
(FWP)
ZA
(ZSH)
HNNGH!!
SUPA
(SWP)
HAAAH...
CRAP...
ONE MORE ROUND...
HAAAH...

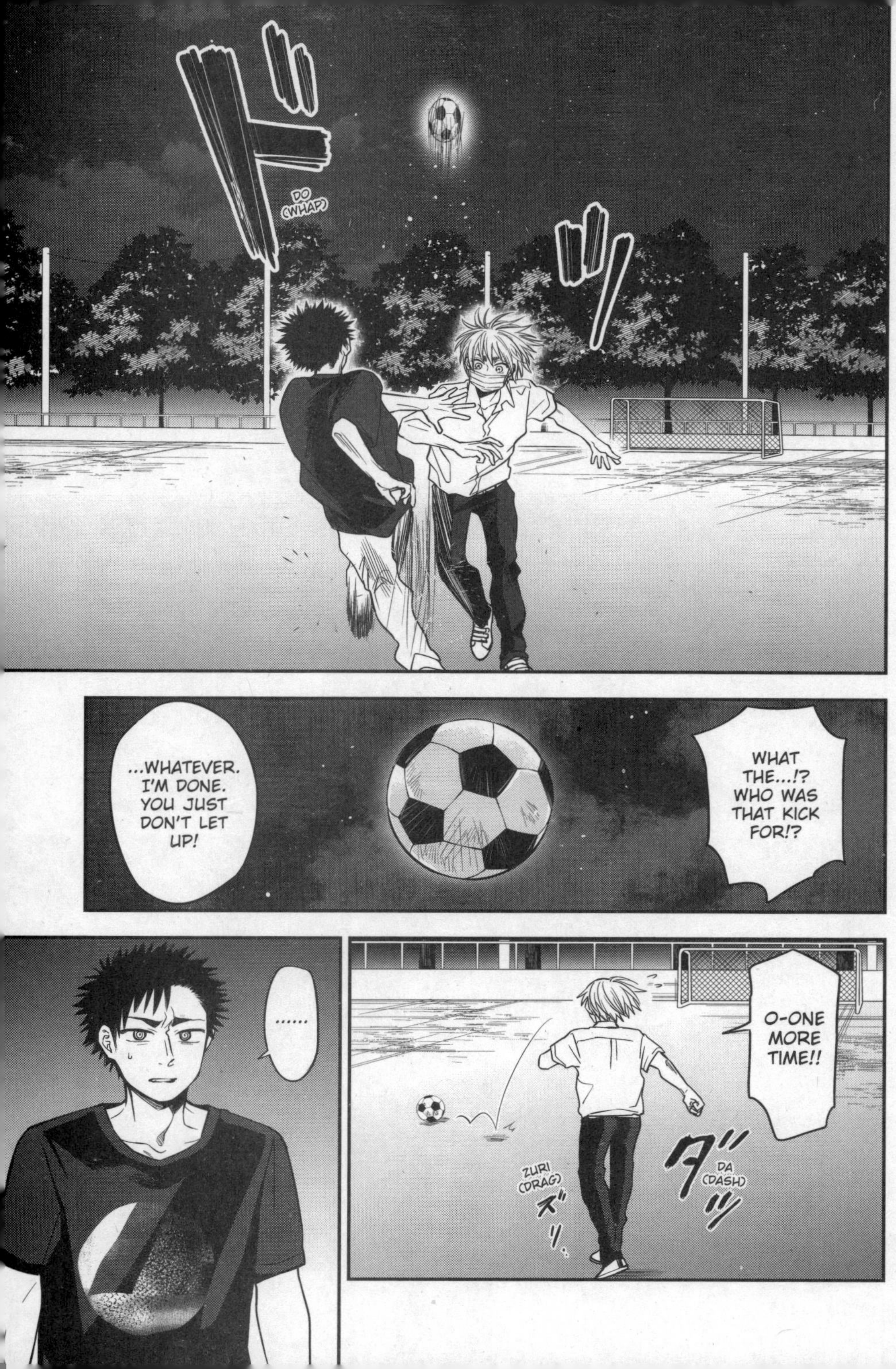
DO (WHAP)
WHAT THE...!? WHO WAS THAT KICK FOR!?
...WHATEVER. I'M DONE. YOU JUST DON'T LET UP!
O-ONE MORE TIME!!
DA (DASH)
ZURI (DRAG)
......

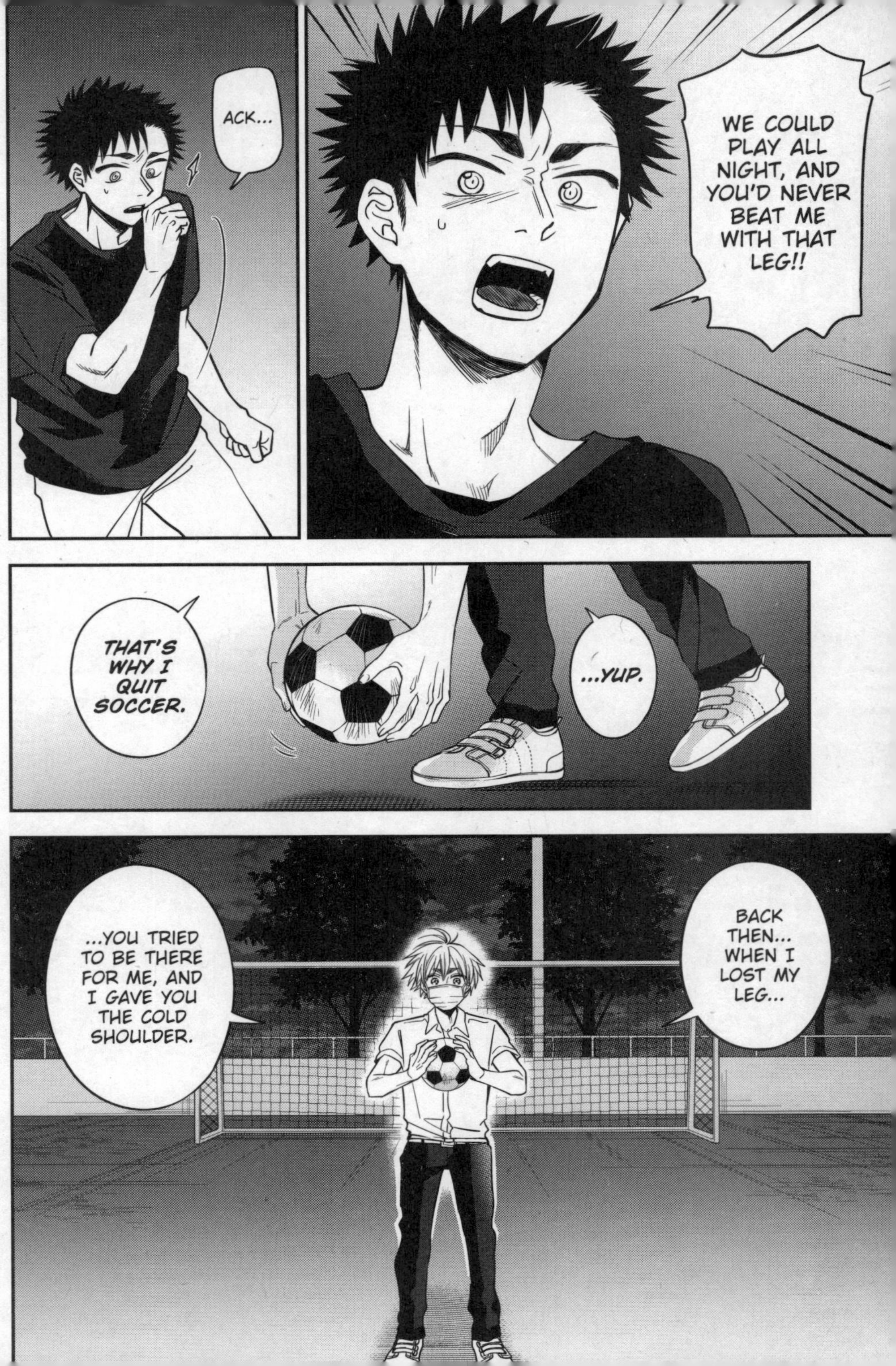
WE COULD PLAY ALL NIGHT, AND YOU'D NEVER BEAT ME WITH THAT LEG!!
ACK...
...YUP.
THAT'S WHY I QUIT SOCCER.
BACK THEN... WHEN I LOST MY LEG...
...YOU TRIED TO BE THERE FOR ME, AND I GAVE YOU THE COLD SHOULDER.

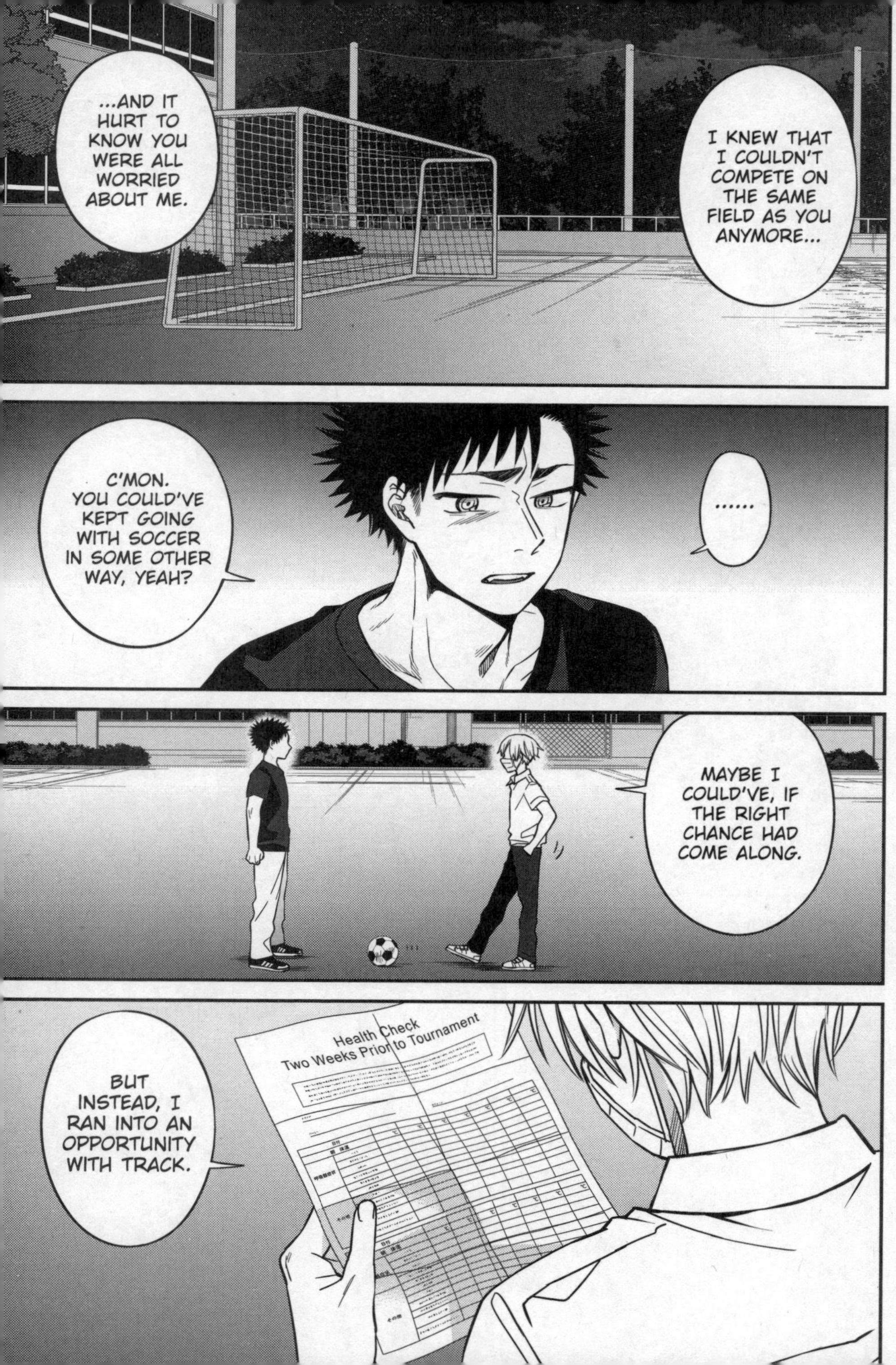
I KNEW THAT I COULDN'T COMPETE ON THE SAME FIELD AS YOU ANYMORE...
...AND IT HURT TO KNOW YOU WERE ALL WORRIED ABOUT ME.
......
C'MON. YOU COULD'VE KEPT GOING WITH SOCCER IN SOME OTHER WAY, YEAH?
MAYBE I COULD'VE, IF THE RIGHT CHANCE HAD COME ALONG.
Health Check Two Weeks Prior to Tournament
BUT INSTEAD, I RAN INTO AN OPPORTUNITY WITH TRACK.

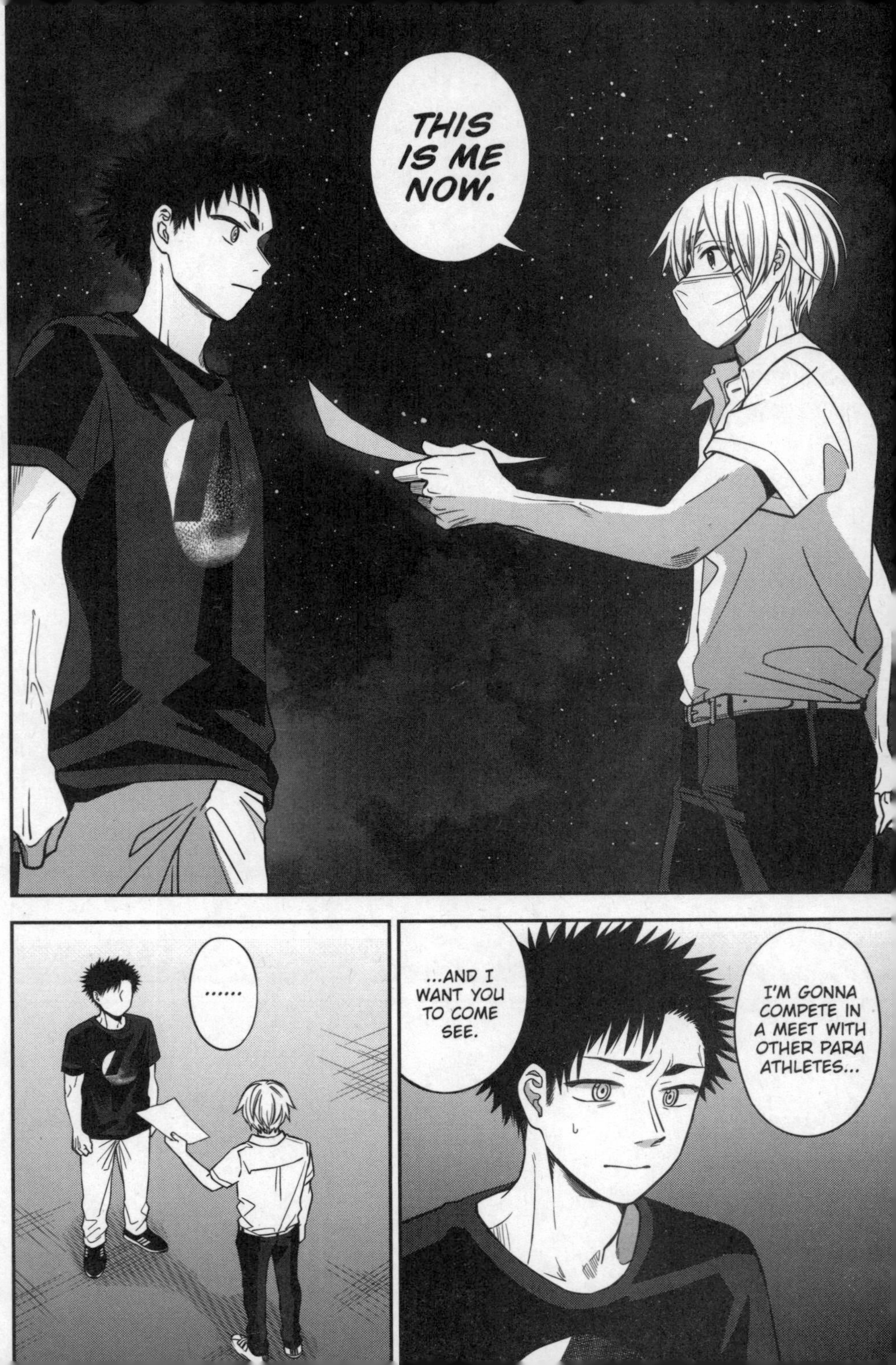
THIS IS ME NOW.
I'M GONNA COMPETE IN A MEET WITH OTHER PARA ATHLETES...
...AND I WANT YOU TO COME SEE.
......

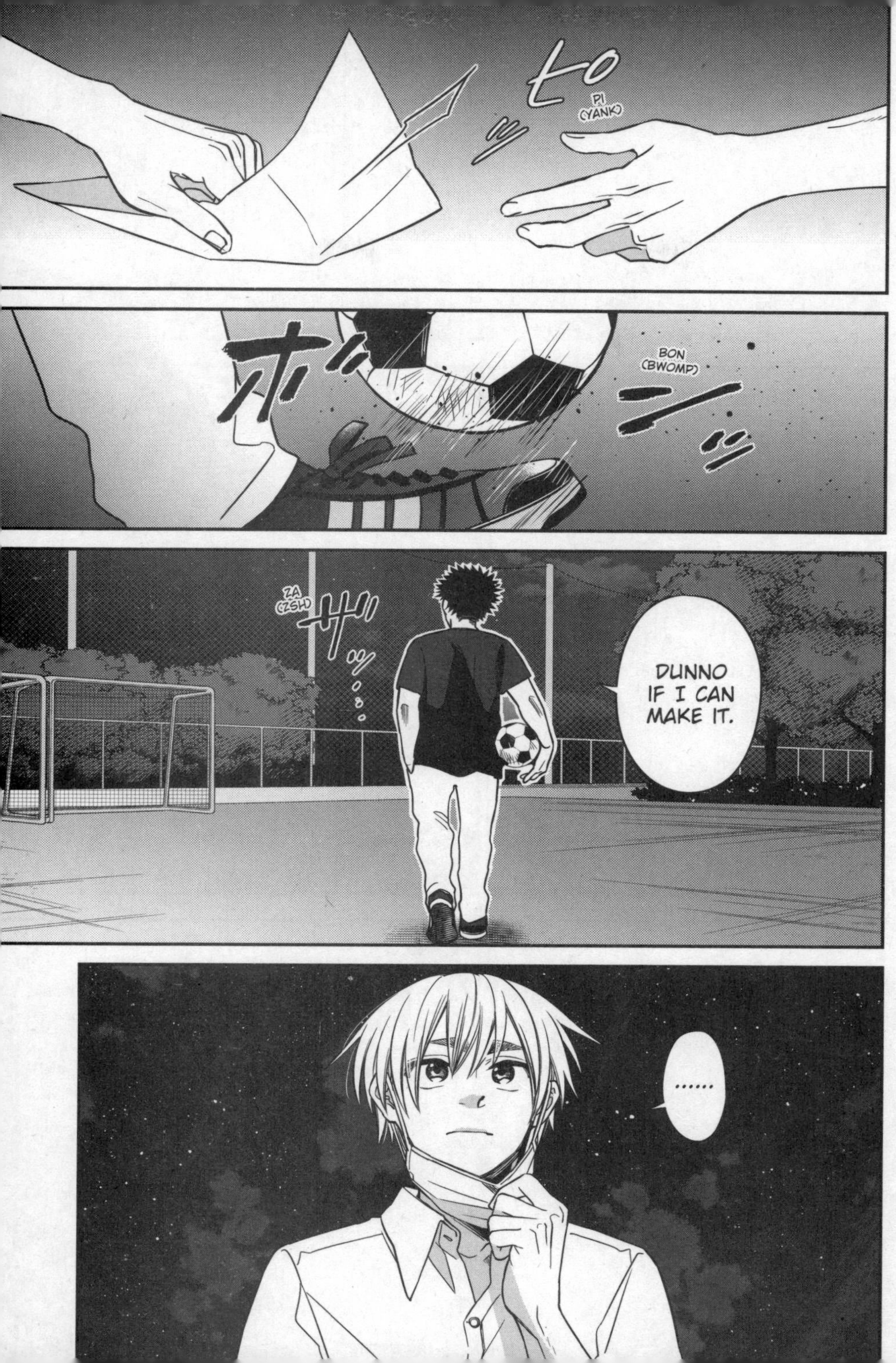
PI (YANK)
BON (BWOMP)
ZA (ZSH)
DUNNO IF I CAN MAKE IT.
......

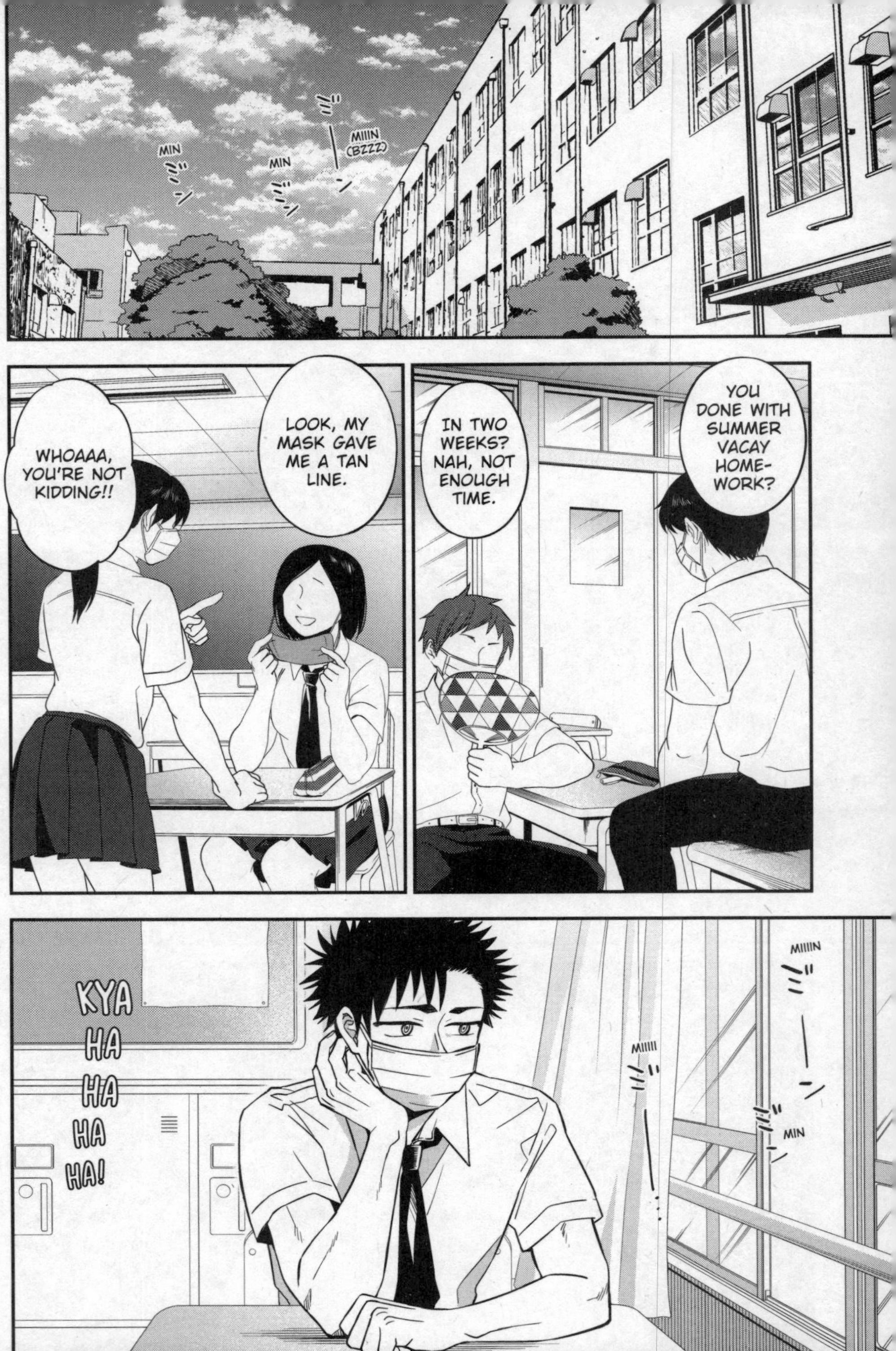
MIIIN (BZZZ)
MIN
MIN
YOU DONE WITH SUMMER VACAY HOME-WORK?
IN TWO WEEKS? NAH, NOT ENOUGH TIME.
LOOK, MY MASK GAVE ME A TAN LINE.
WHOAAA, YOU'RE NOT KIDDING!!
MIIIIN
MIIIII
MIN
KYA HA HA HA HA HA!

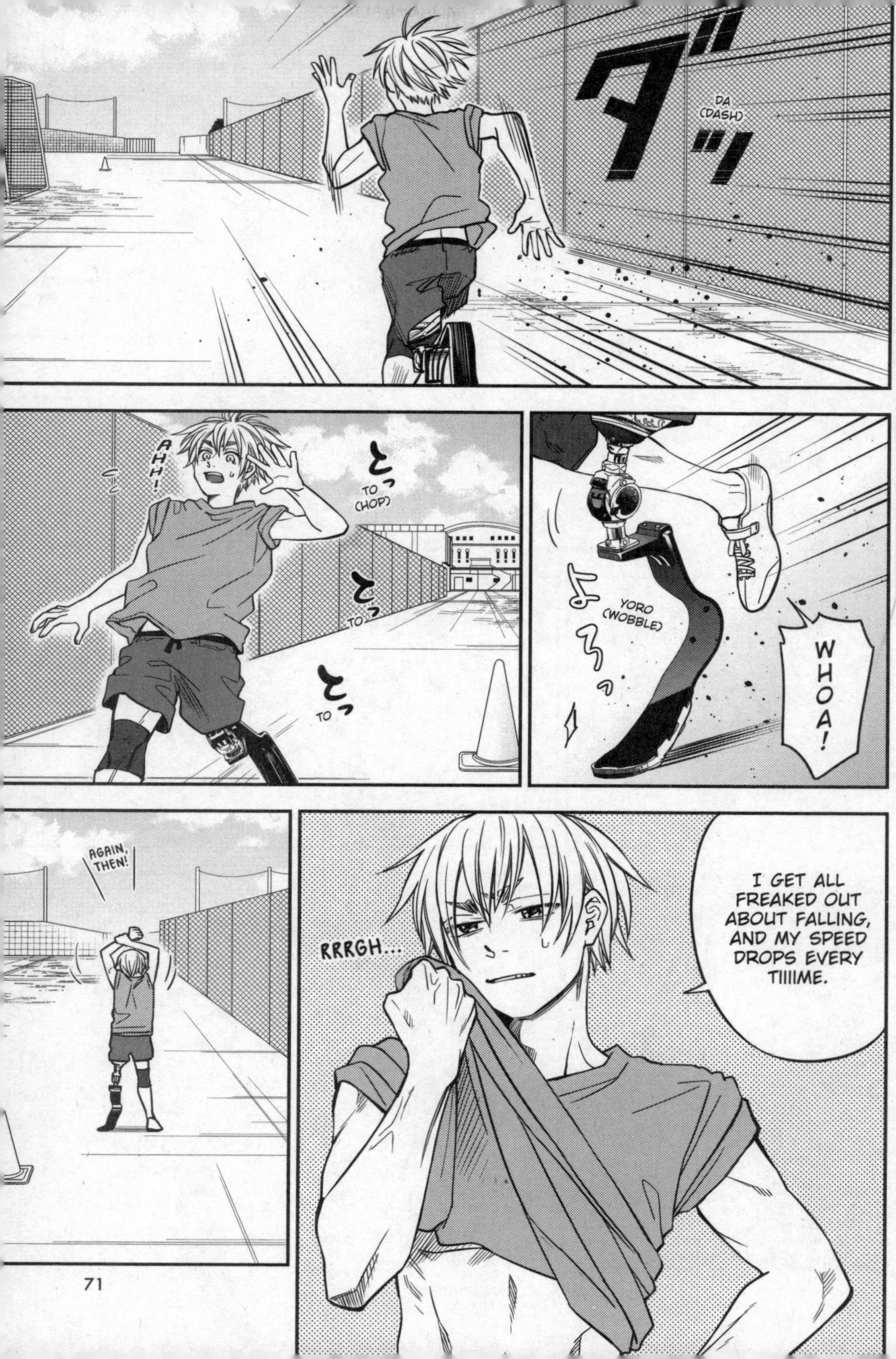
ダッ
DA (DASH)
よろっ
YORO (WOBBLE)
WHOA!
AHH!
とっ
TO (HOP)
とっ
TO
とっ
TO
I GET ALL FREAKED OUT ABOUT FALLING, AND MY SPEED DROPS EVERY TIIIIME.
RRRGH...
AGAIN, THEN!

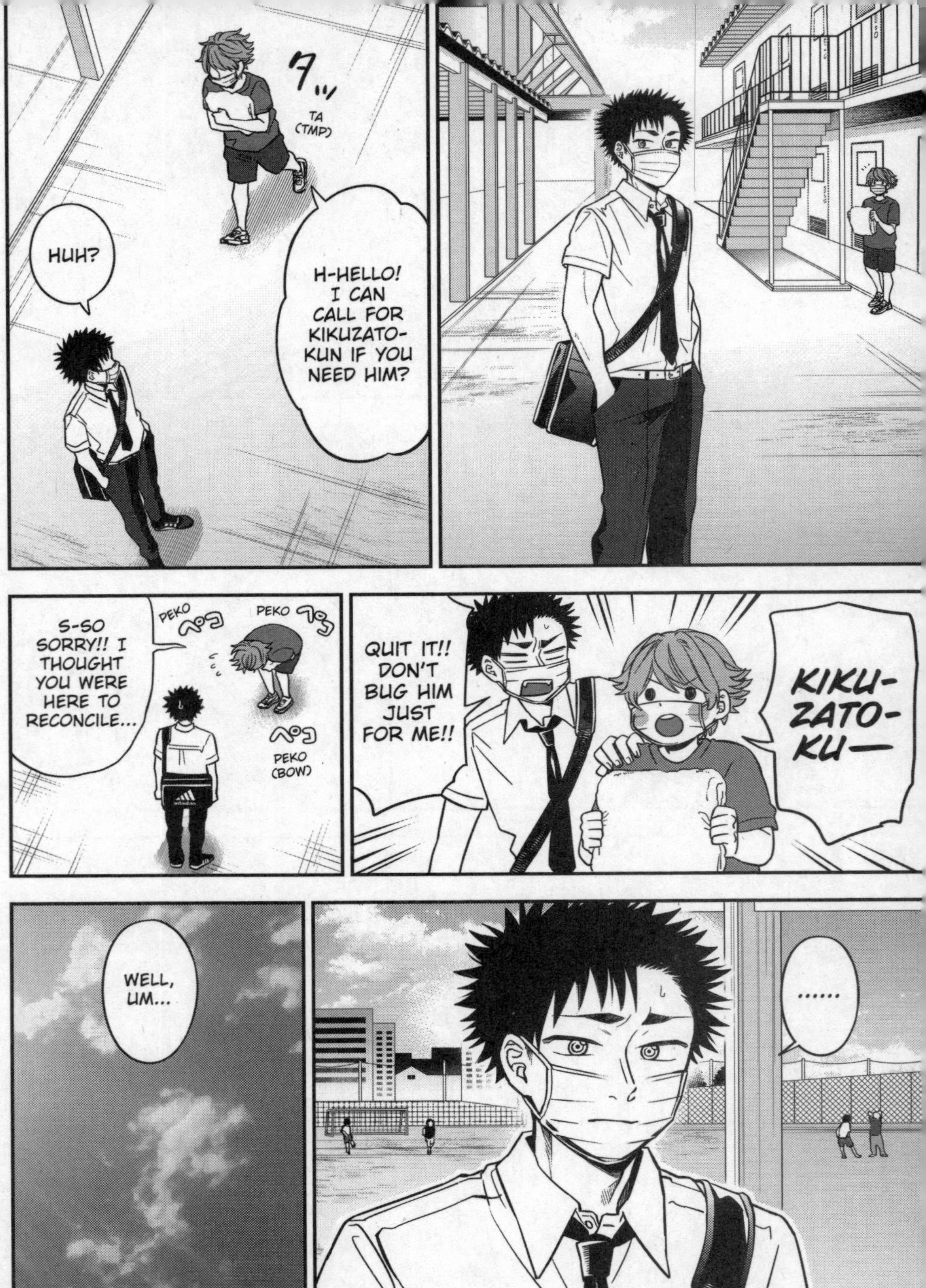

タッ
TA (TMP)
H-HELLO! I CAN CALL FOR KIKUZATO-KUN IF YOU NEED HIM?
HUH?
KIKU-ZATO-KU—
QUIT IT!! DON'T BUG HIM JUST FOR ME!!
PEKO ぺこ
PEKO ぺこ
S-SO SORRY!! I THOUGHT YOU WERE HERE TO RECONCILE...
ぺこ PEKO (BOW)
......
WELL, UM...

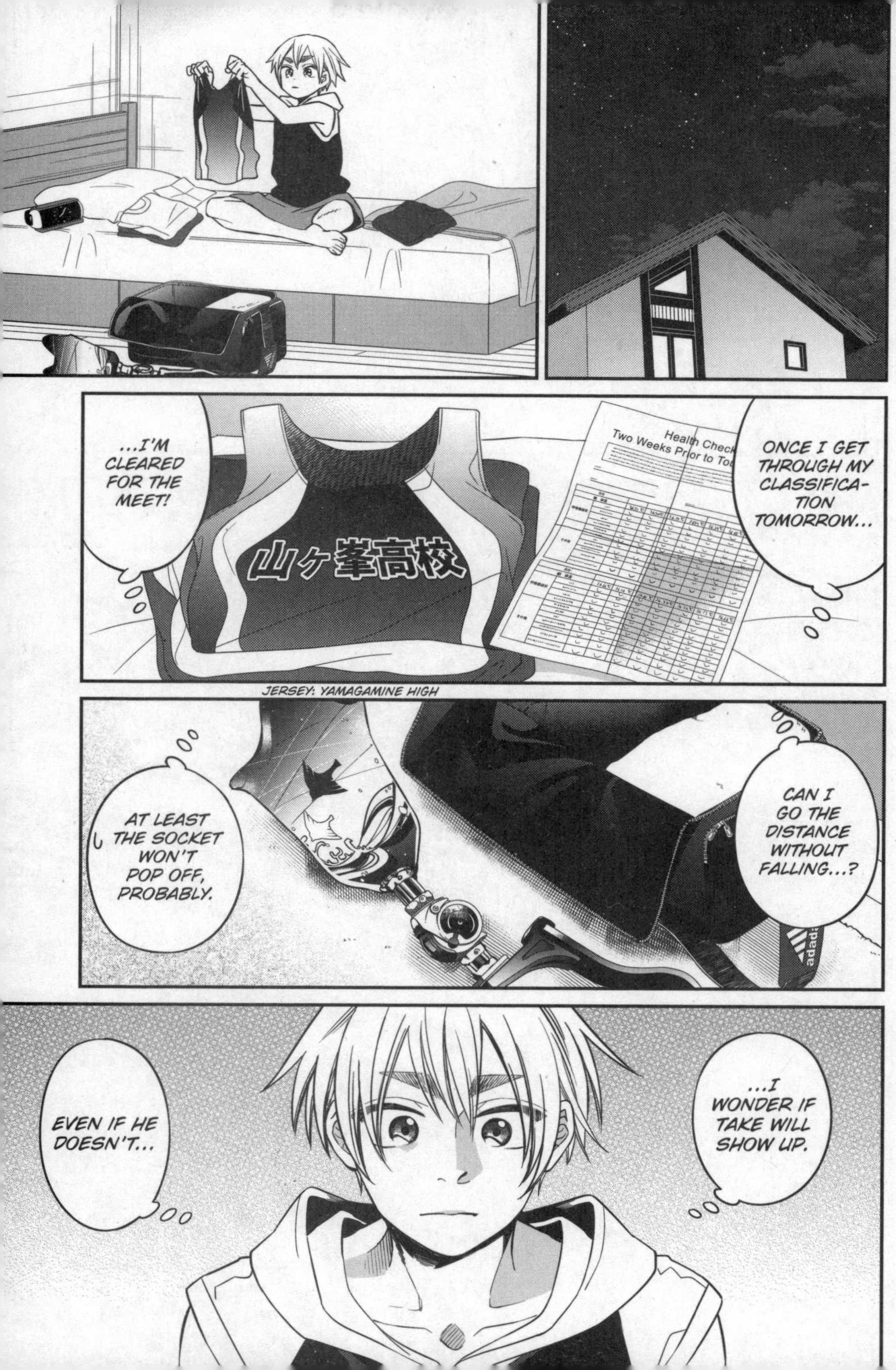
ONCE I GET THROUGH MY CLASSIFICATION TOMORROW...
...I'M CLEARED FOR THE MEET!
Health Check
山ヶ峯高校
JERSEY: YAMAGAMINE HIGH
CAN I GO THE DISTANCE WITHOUT FALLING...?
AT LEAST THE SOCKET WON'T POP OFF, PROBABLY.
...I WONDER IF TAKE WILL SHOW UP.
EVEN IF HE DOESN'T...

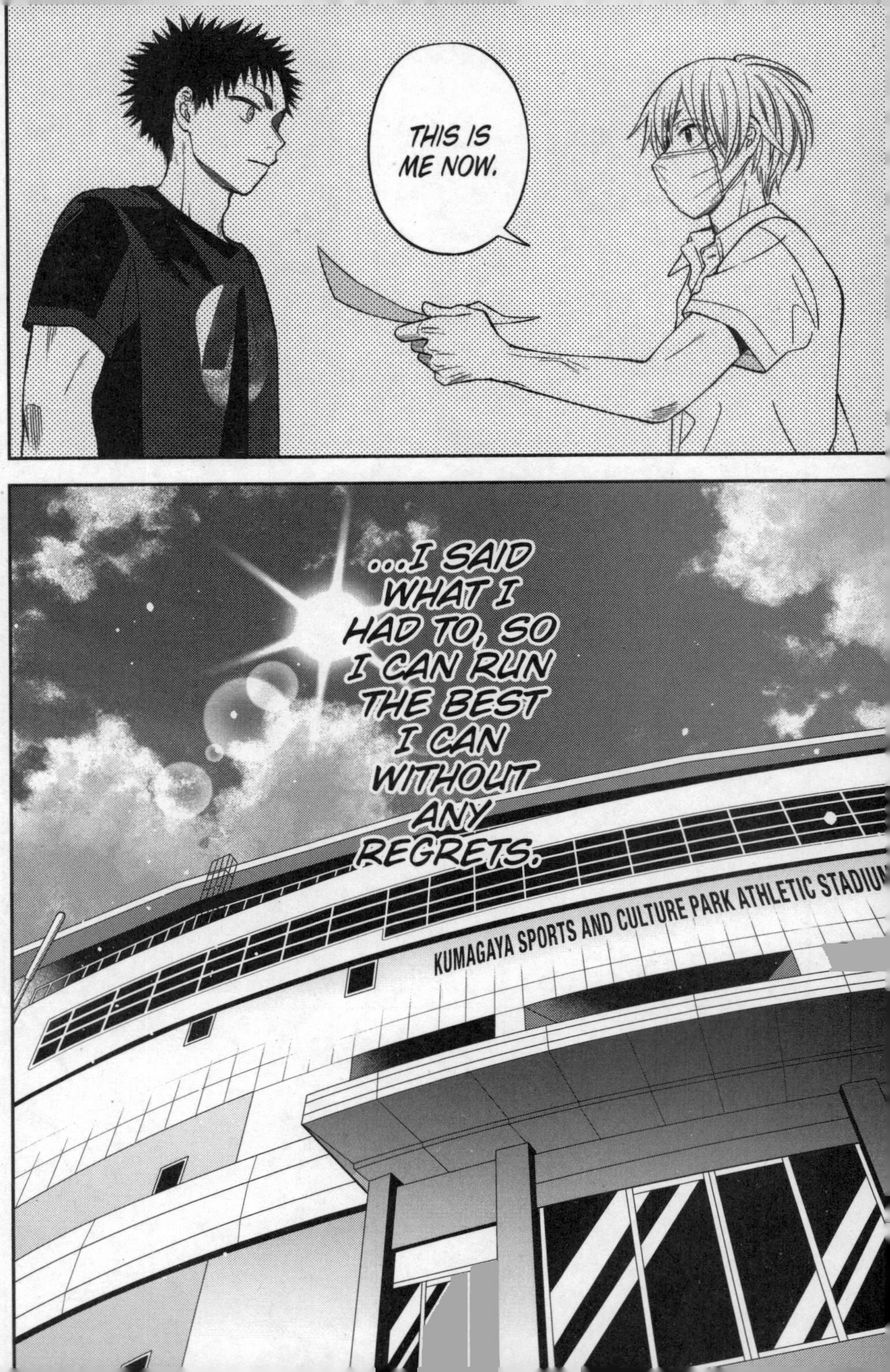
THIS IS ME NOW.
...I SAID WHAT I HAD TO, SO I CAN RUN THE BEST I CAN WITHOUT ANY REGRETS.
KUMAGAYA SPORTS AND CULTURE PARK ATHLETIC STADIUM

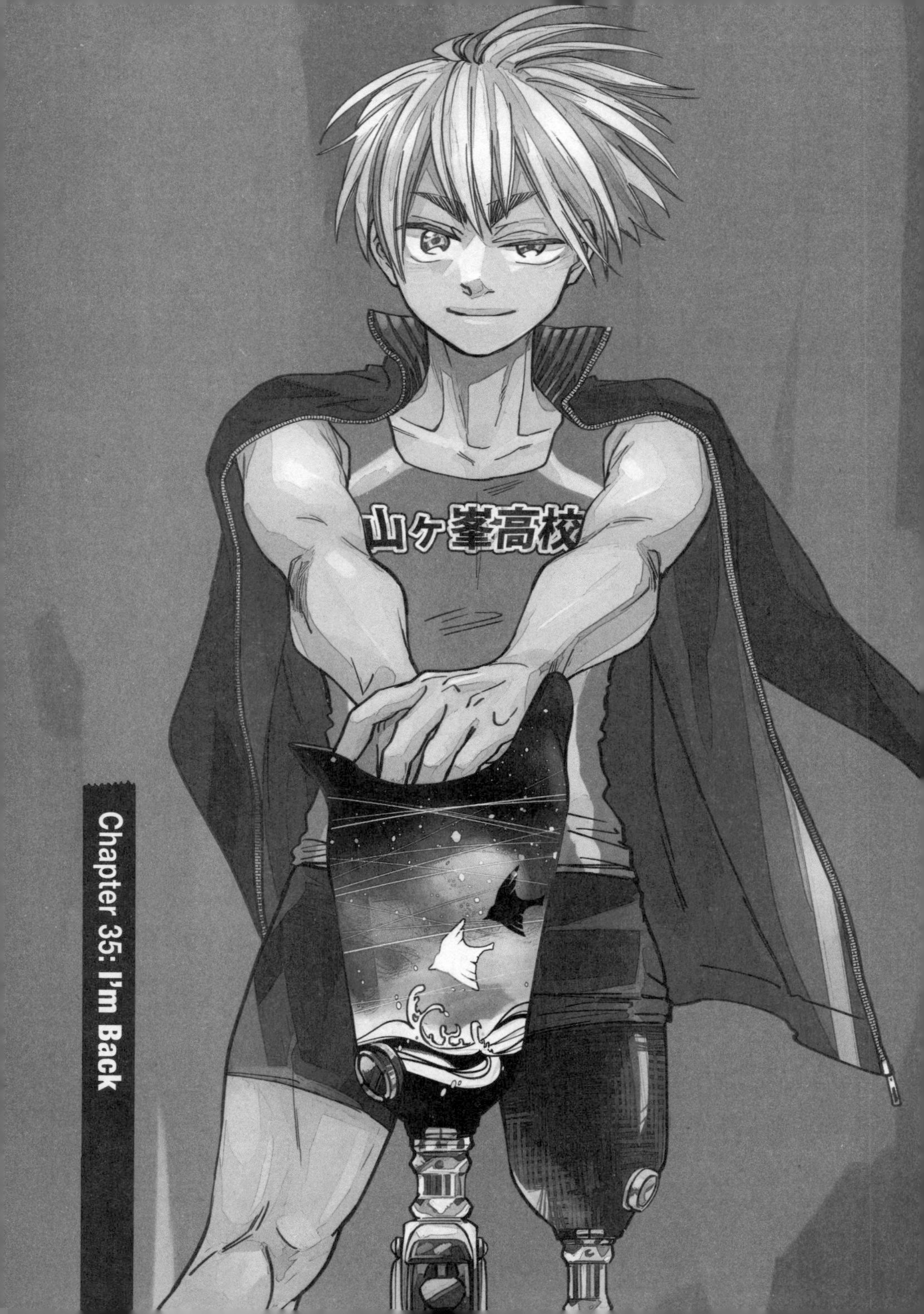
Chapter 35: I'm Back
山ヶ峯高校

RUN ON YOUR
NEW LEGS

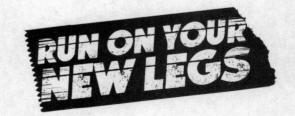

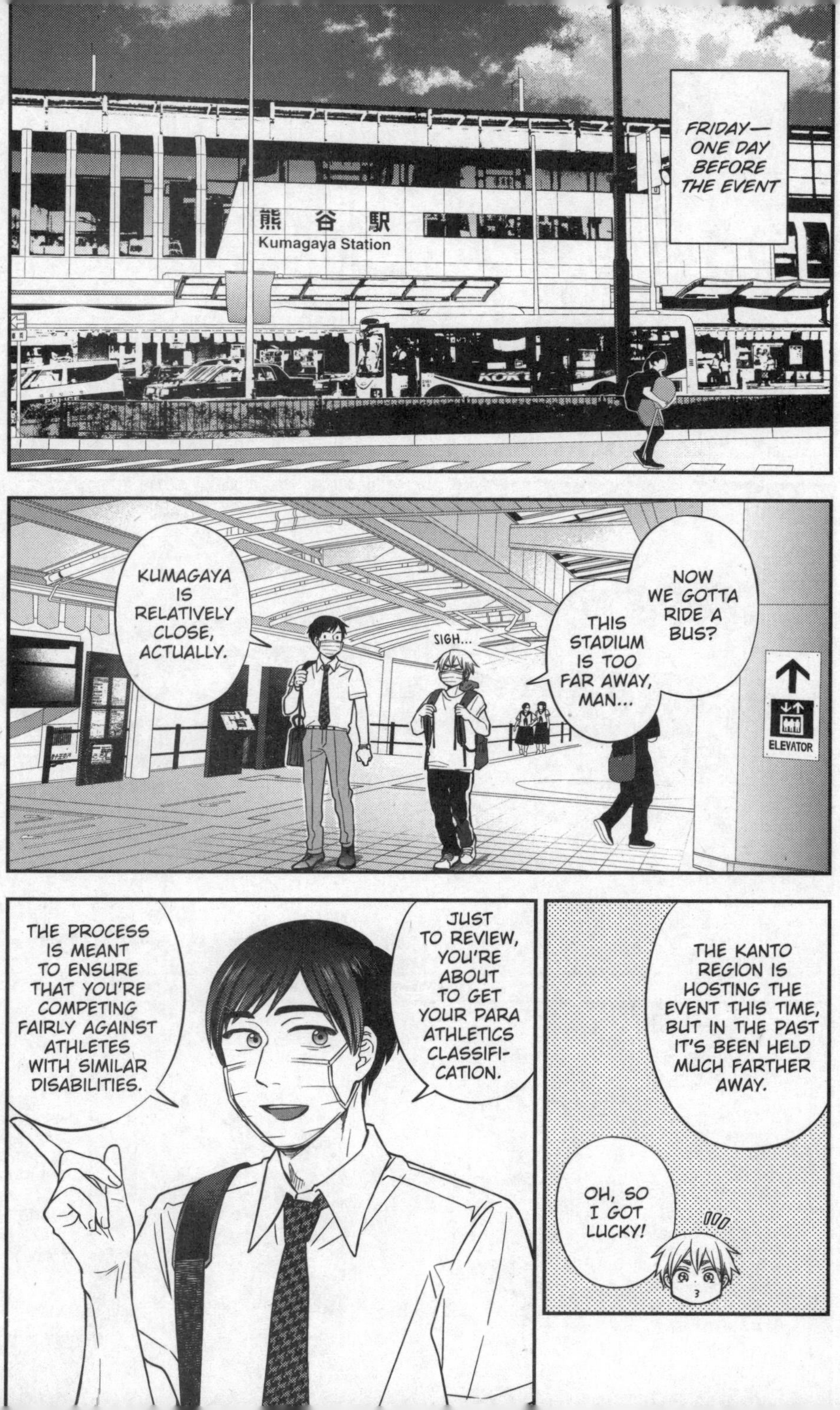
FRIDAY— ONE DAY BEFORE THE EVENT
熊谷駅
Kumagaya Station
POLICE
NOW WE GOTTA RIDE A BUS?
THIS STADIUM IS TOO FAR AWAY, MAN...
SIGH...
KUMAGAYA IS RELATIVELY CLOSE, ACTUALLY.
ELEVATOR
THE KANTO REGION IS HOSTING THE EVENT THIS TIME, BUT IN THE PAST IT'S BEEN HELD MUCH FARTHER AWAY.
OH, SO I GOT LUCKY!
JUST TO REVIEW, YOU'RE ABOUT TO GET YOUR PARA ATHLETICS CLASSIFI-CATION.
THE PROCESS IS MEANT TO ENSURE THAT YOU'RE COMPETING FAIRLY AGAINST ATHLETES WITH SIMILAR DISABILITIES.

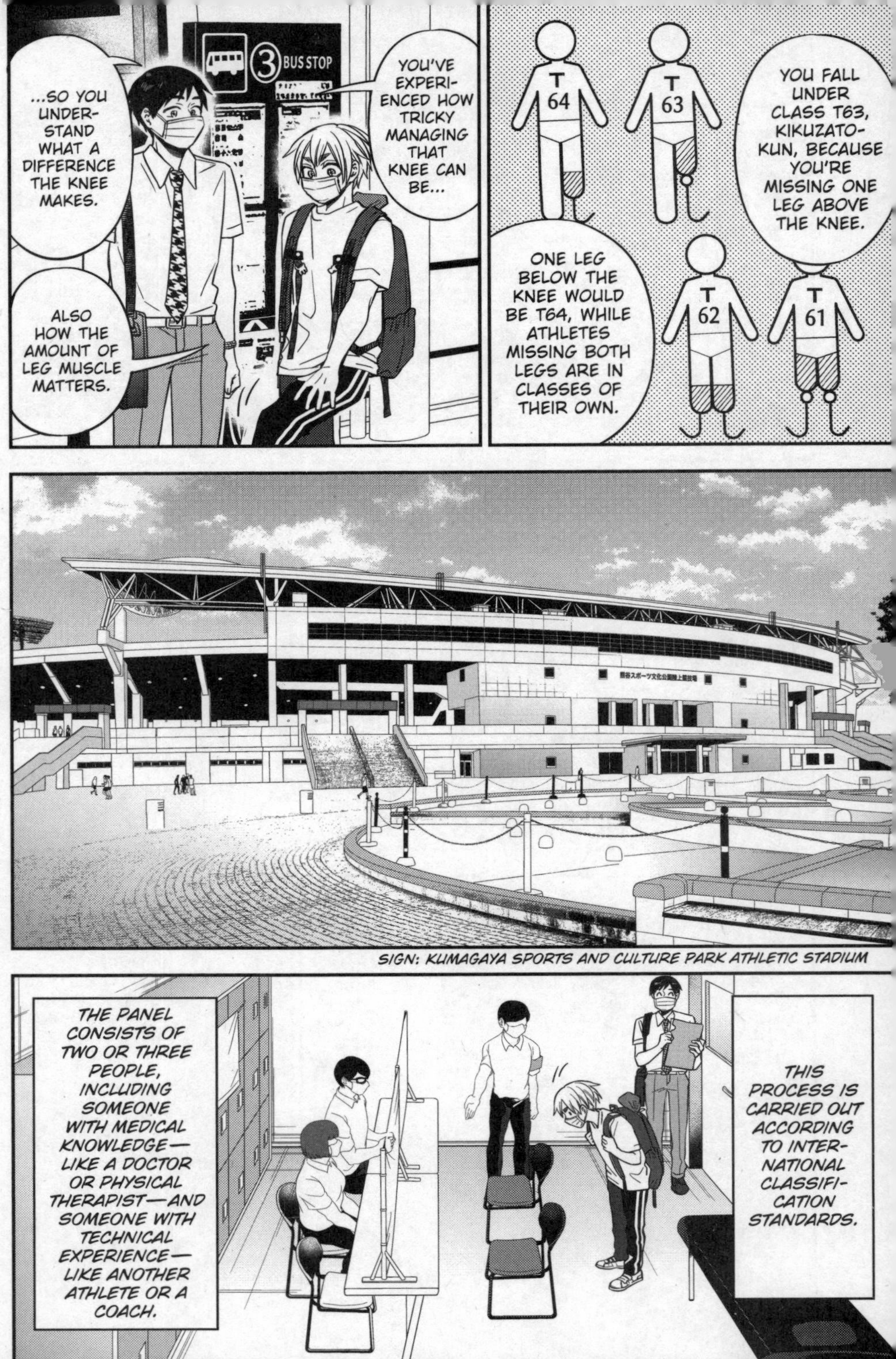
YOU FALL UNDER CLASS T63, KIKUZATO-KUN, BECAUSE YOU'RE MISSING ONE LEG ABOVE THE KNEE.
T 64
T 63
ONE LEG BELOW THE KNEE WOULD BE T64, WHILE ATHLETES MISSING BOTH LEGS ARE IN CLASSES OF THEIR OWN.
T 61
T 62
3 BUS STOP
YOU'VE EXPERIENCED HOW TRICKY MANAGING THAT KNEE CAN BE...
...SO YOU UNDERSTAND WHAT A DIFFERENCE THE KNEE MAKES.
ALSO HOW THE AMOUNT OF LEG MUSCLE MATTERS.
SIGN: KUMAGAYA SPORTS AND CULTURE PARK ATHLETIC STADIUM
THIS PROCESS IS CARRIED OUT ACCORDING TO INTERNATIONAL CLASSIFICATION STANDARDS.
THE PANEL CONSISTS OF TWO OR THREE PEOPLE, INCLUDING SOMEONE WITH MEDICAL KNOWLEDGE—LIKE A DOCTOR OR PHYSICAL THERAPIST—AND SOMEONE WITH TECHNICAL EXPERIENCE—LIKE ANOTHER ATHLETE OR A COACH.

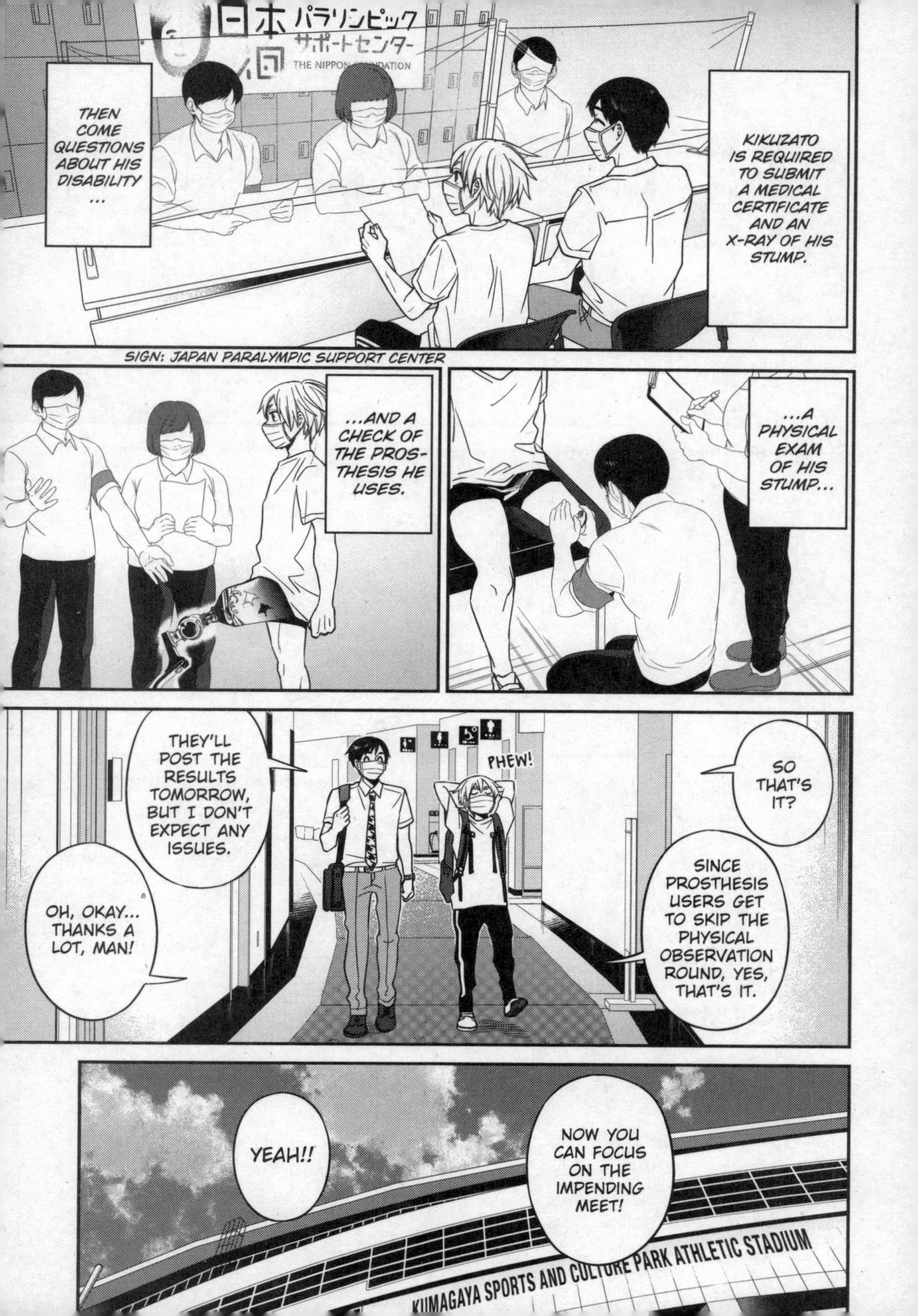
日本 パラリンピック
サポートセンター
THE NIPPON FOUNDATION
KIKUZATO IS REQUIRED TO SUBMIT A MEDICAL CERTIFICATE AND AN X-RAY OF HIS STUMP.
THEN COME QUESTIONS ABOUT HIS DISABILITY...
SIGN: JAPAN PARALYMPIC SUPPORT CENTER
...A PHYSICAL EXAM OF HIS STUMP...
...AND A CHECK OF THE PROSTHESIS HE USES.
SO THAT'S IT?
THEY'LL POST THE RESULTS TOMORROW, BUT I DON'T EXPECT ANY ISSUES.
PHEW!
SINCE PROSTHESIS USERS GET TO SKIP THE PHYSICAL OBSERVATION ROUND, YES, THAT'S IT.
OH, OKAY... THANKS A LOT, MAN!
NOW YOU CAN FOCUS ON THE IMPENDING MEET!
YEAH!!
KUMAGAYA SPORTS AND CULTURE PARK ATHLETIC STADIUM

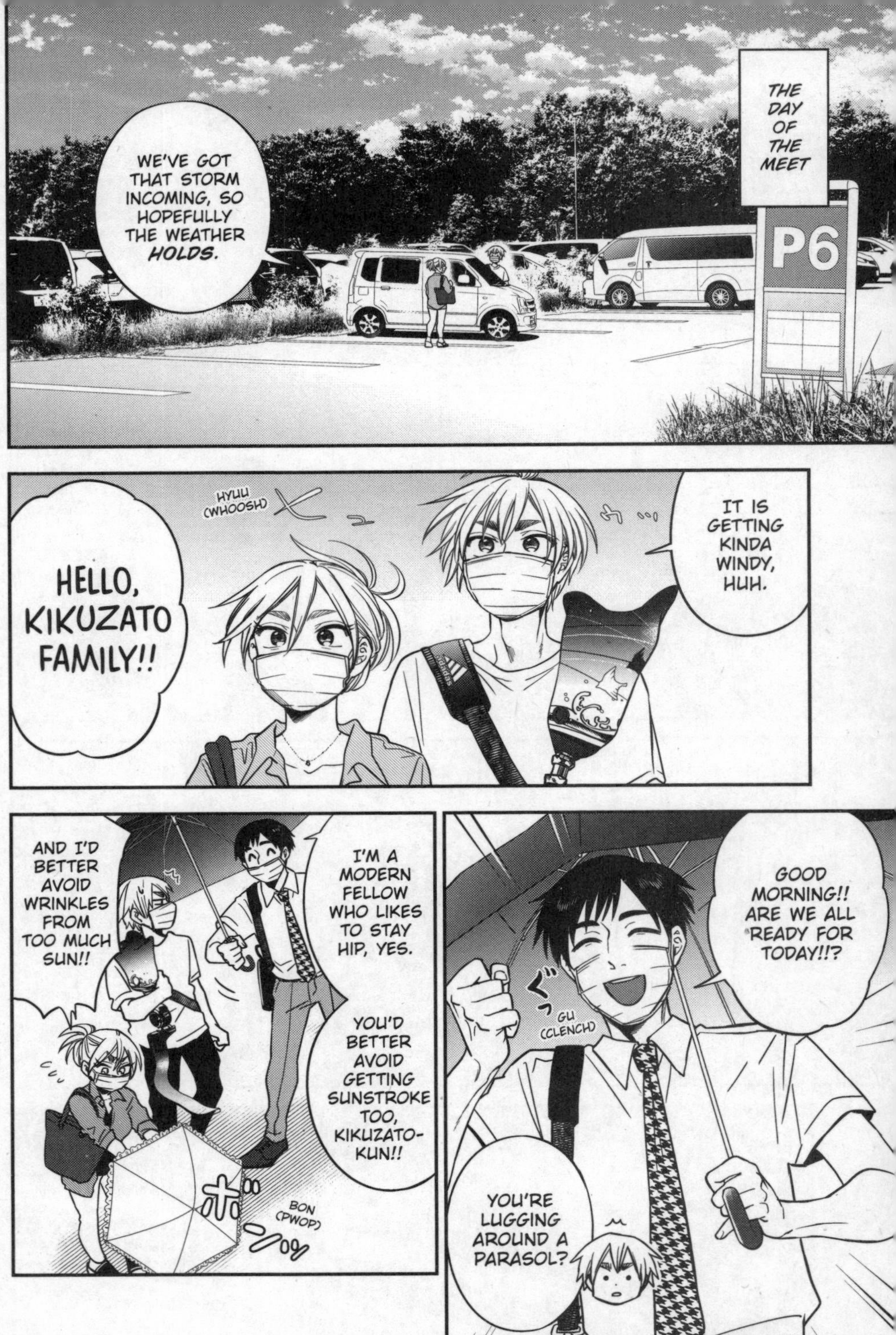
THE DAY OF THE MEET
WE'VE GOT THAT STORM INCOMING, SO HOPEFULLY THE WEATHER *HOLDS.*
IT IS GETTING KINDA WINDY, HUH.
HYUU (WHOOSH)
HELLO, KIKUZATO FAMILY!!
GOOD MORNING!! ARE WE ALL READY FOR TODAY!!?
GU (CLENCH)
YOU'RE LUGGING AROUND A PARASOL?
I'M A MODERN FELLOW WHO LIKES TO STAY HIP, YES.
AND I'D BETTER AVOID WRINKLES FROM TOO MUCH SUN!!
YOU'D BETTER AVOID GETTING SUNSTROKE TOO, KIKUZATO-KUN!!
BON (PWOP)

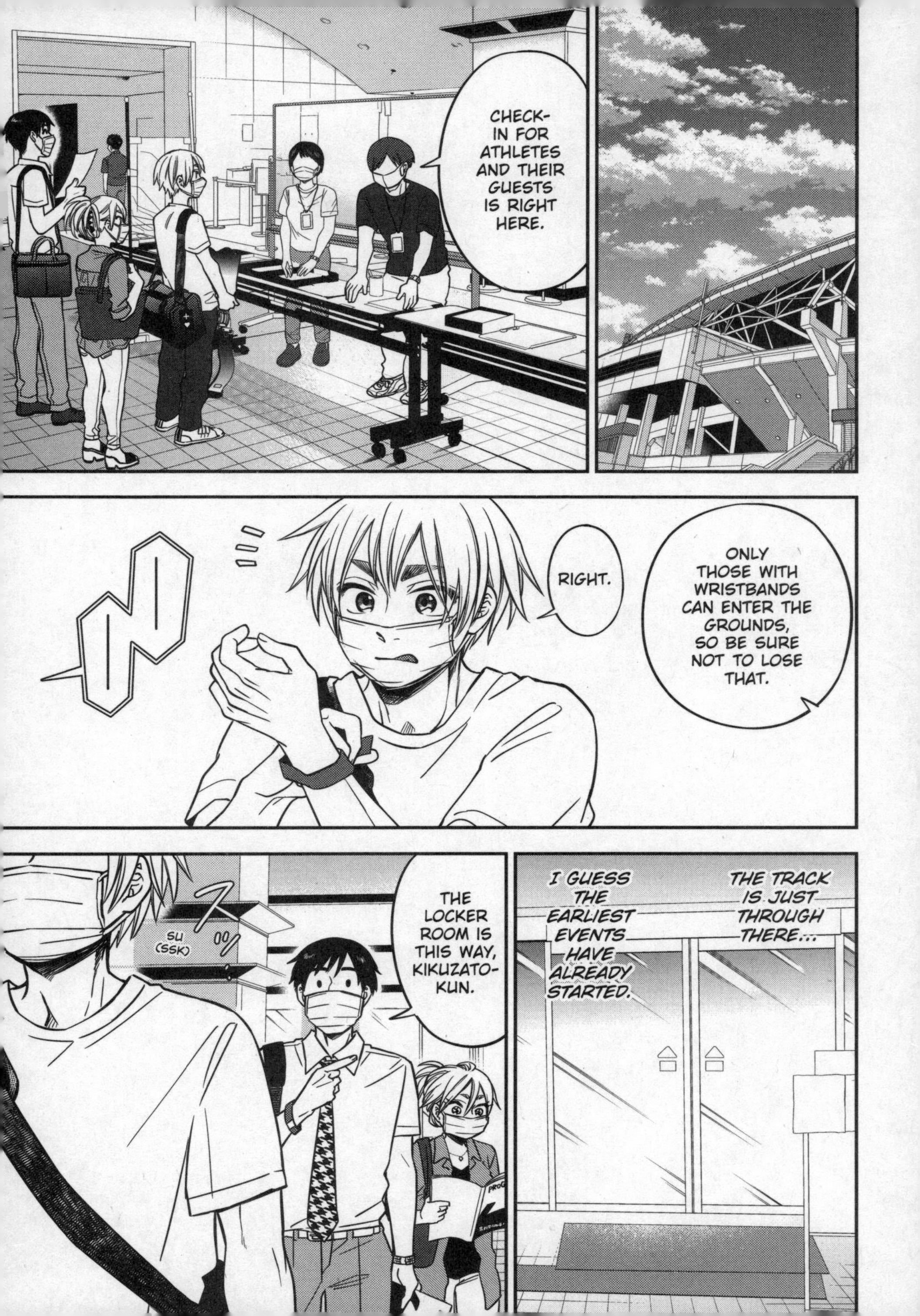
CHECK-IN FOR ATHLETES AND THEIR GUESTS IS RIGHT HERE.
ONLY THOSE WITH WRISTBANDS CAN ENTER THE GROUNDS, SO BE SURE NOT TO LOSE THAT.
RIGHT.
THE TRACK IS JUST THROUGH THERE...
I GUESS THE EARLIEST EVENTS HAVE ALREADY STARTED.
THE LOCKER ROOM IS THIS WAY, KIKUZATO-KUN.
SU (SSK)

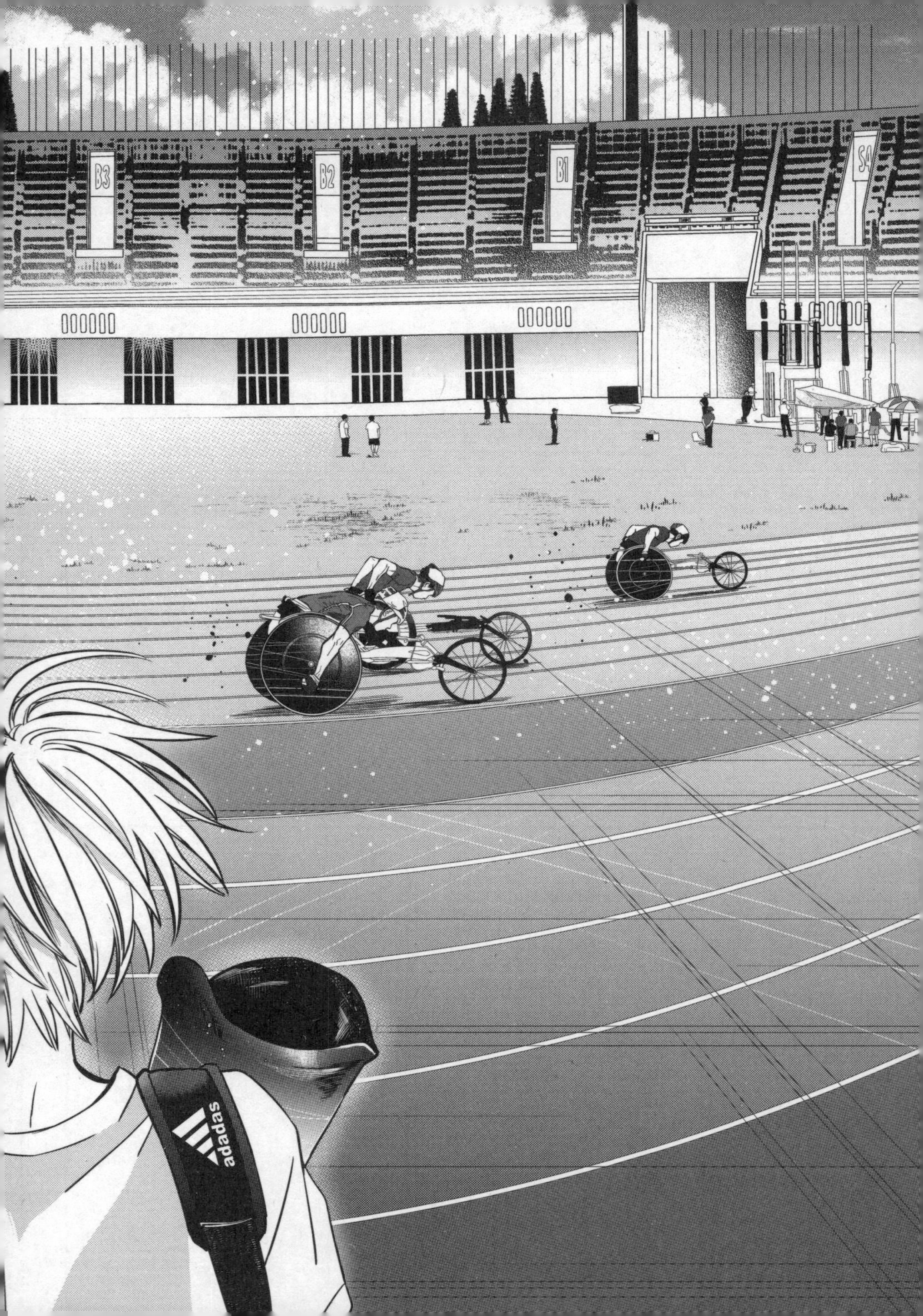
S4
B1
B2
B3
adadas

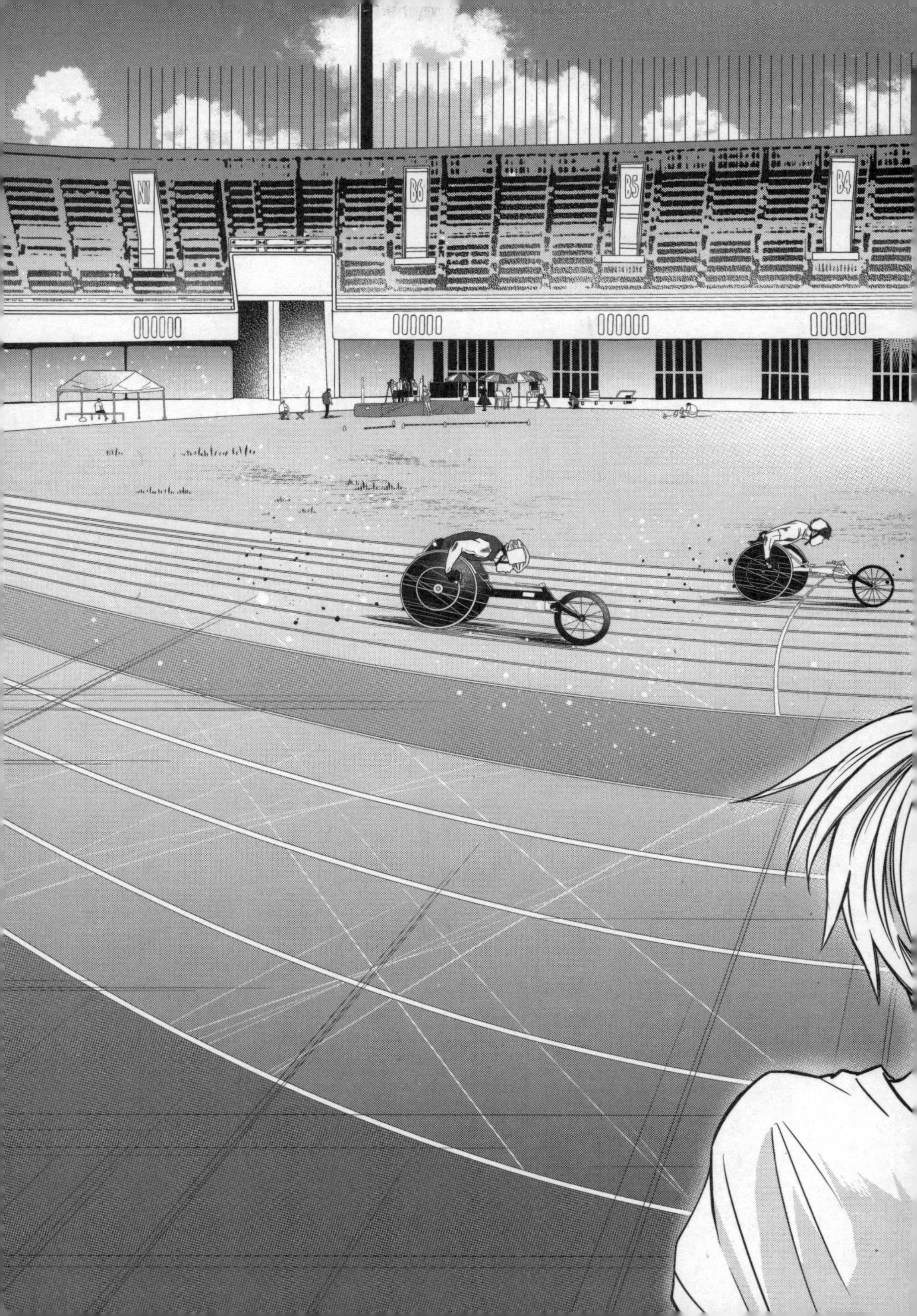
N1
B6
B5
B4

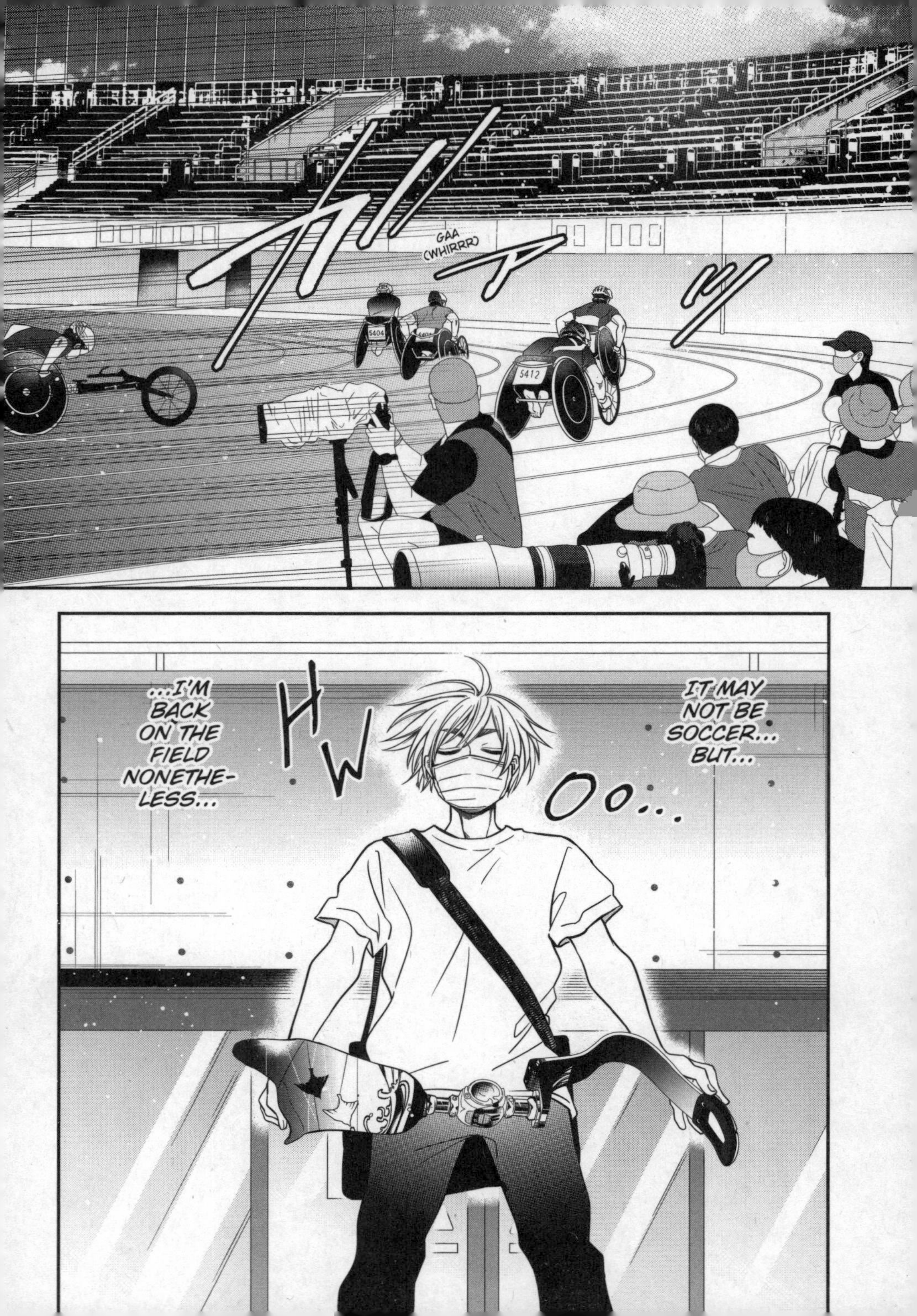
GAA (WHIRRR)
5404
5412
IT MAY NOT BE SOCCER... BUT...
...I'M BACK ON THE FIELD NONETHE-LESS...
HWOO...

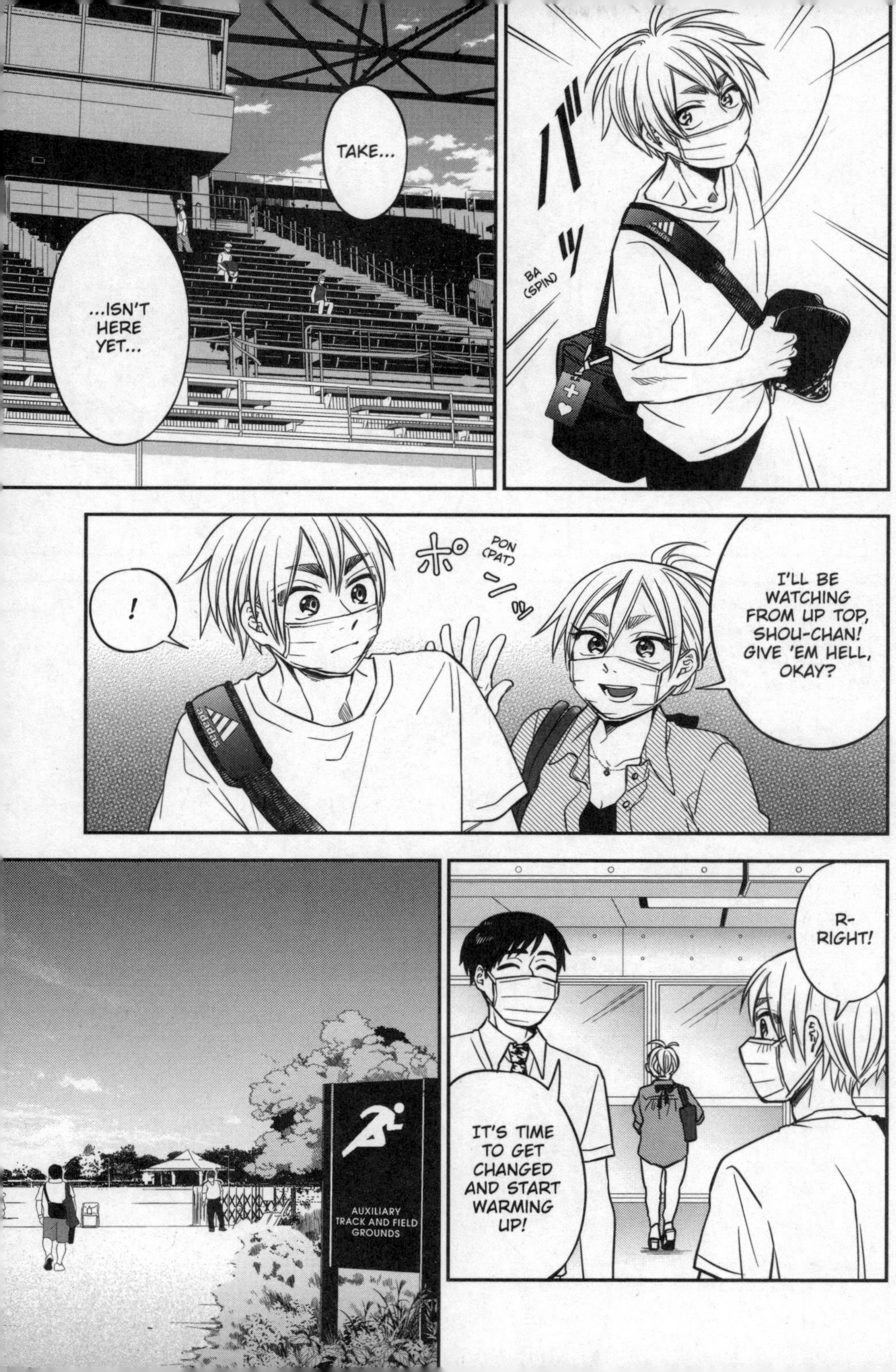
BA (SPIN)
TAKE...
...ISN'T HERE YET...
I'LL BE WATCHING FROM UP TOP, SHOU-CHAN! GIVE 'EM HELL, OKAY?
PON (PAT)
!
R-RIGHT!
IT'S TIME TO GET CHANGED AND START WARMING UP!
AUXILIARY TRACK AND FIELD GROUNDS

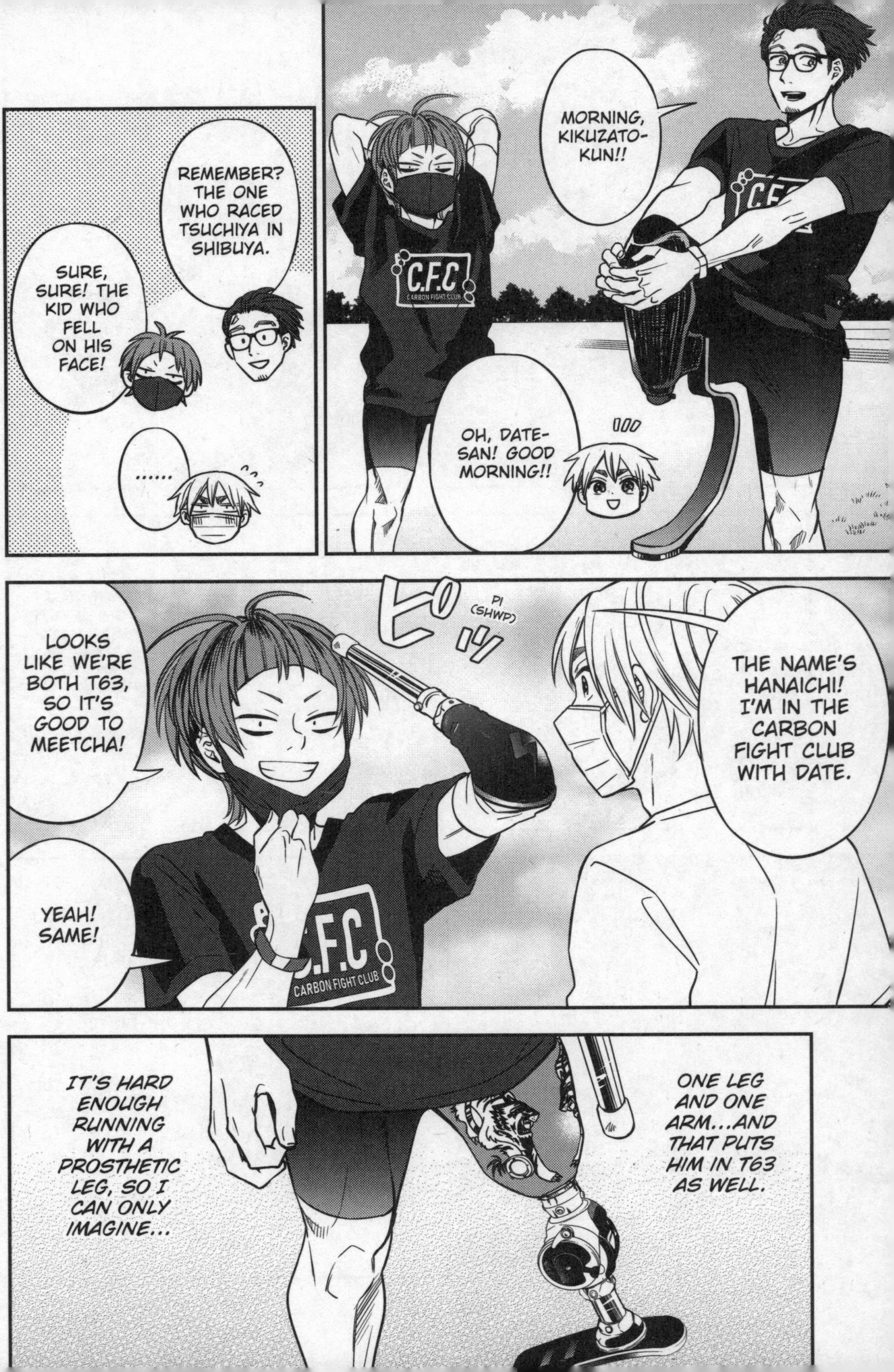
MORNING, KIKUZATO-KUN!!
OH, DATE-SAN! GOOD MORNING!!
REMEMBER? THE ONE WHO RACED TSUCHIYA IN SHIBUYA.
SURE, SURE! THE KID WHO FELL ON HIS FACE!
......
THE NAME'S HANAICHI! I'M IN THE CARBON FIGHT CLUB WITH DATE.
PI (SHWD)
LOOKS LIKE WE'RE BOTH T63, SO IT'S GOOD TO MEETCHA!
YEAH! SAME!
ONE LEG AND ONE ARM...AND THAT PUTS HIM IN T63 AS WELL.
IT'S HARD ENOUGH RUNNING WITH A PROSTHETIC LEG, SO I CAN ONLY IMAGINE...

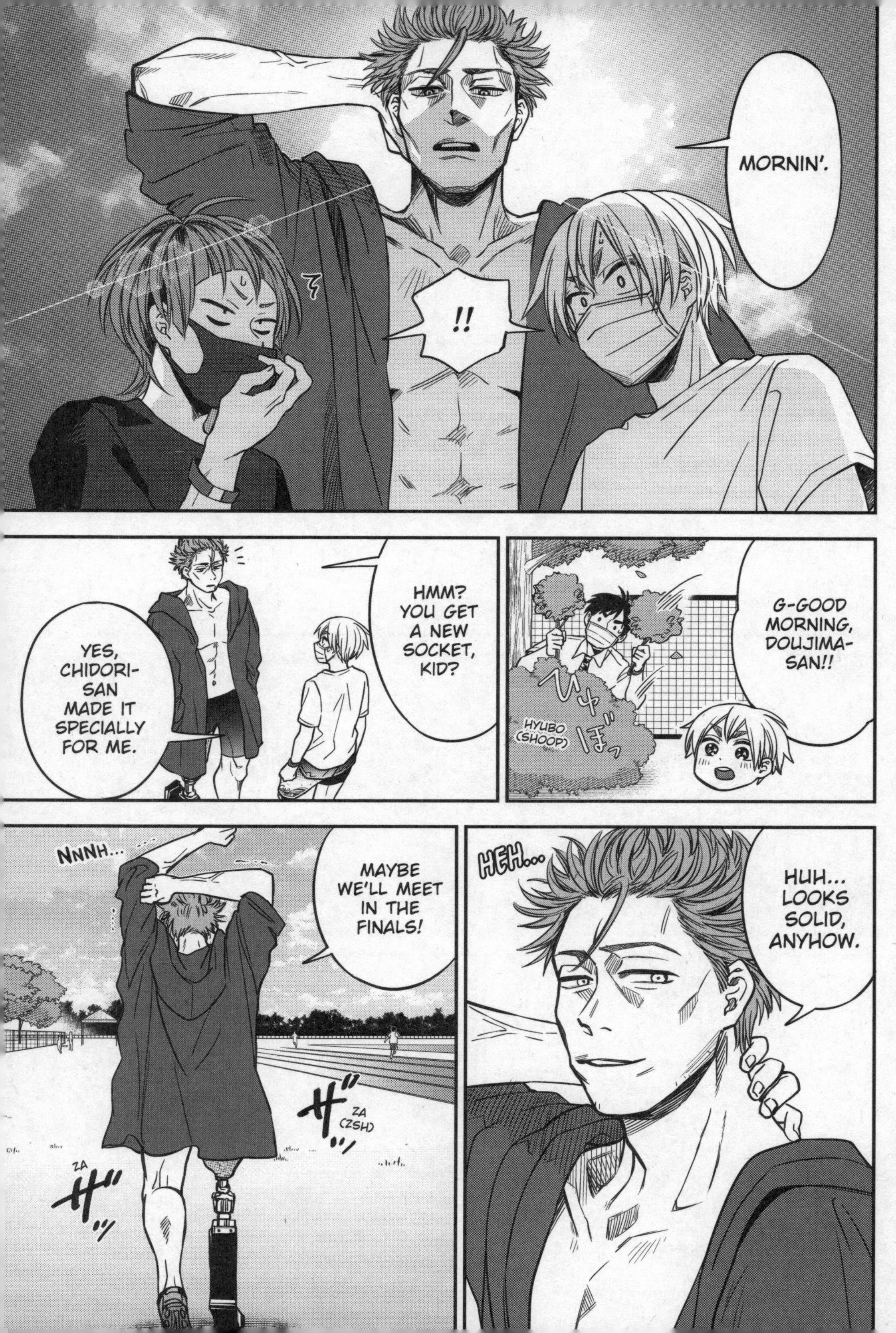
MORNIN'.
!!
て
G-GOOD MORNING, DOUJIMA-SAN!!
ひゅぼっ
HYUBO (SHOOP)
HMM? YOU GET A NEW SOCKET, KID?
YES, CHIDORI-SAN MADE IT SPECIALLY FOR ME.
HEH...
HUH... LOOKS SOLID, ANYHOW.
NNNH...
MAYBE WE'LL MEET IN THE FINALS!
ZA (ZSH)
ZA

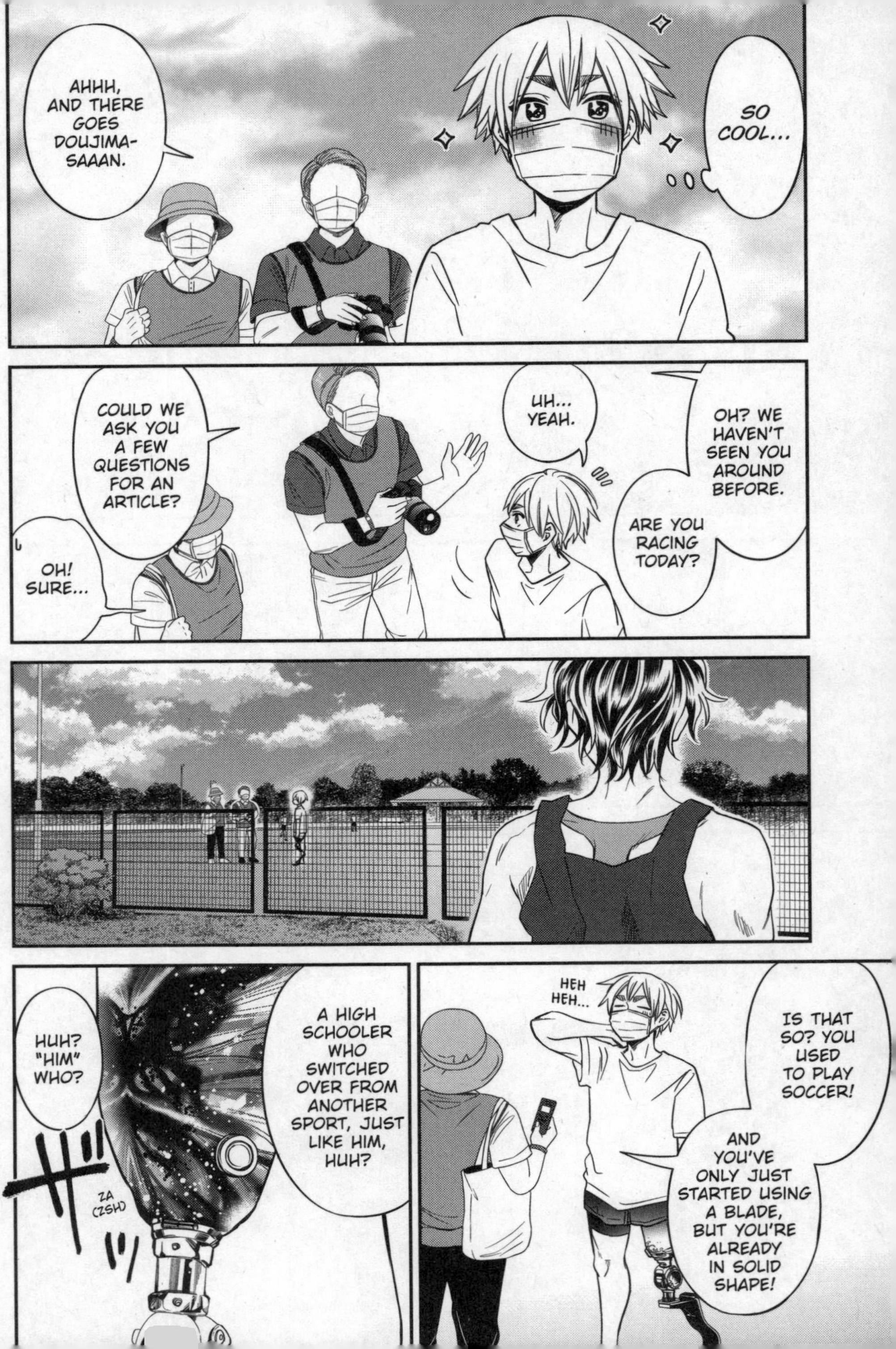
SO COOL...
AHHH, AND THERE GOES DOUJIMA-SAAAN.
OH? WE HAVEN'T SEEN YOU AROUND BEFORE.
ARE YOU RACING TODAY?
UH... YEAH.
COULD WE ASK YOU A FEW QUESTIONS FOR AN ARTICLE?
OH! SURE...
IS THAT SO? YOU USED TO PLAY SOCCER!
HEH HEH...
AND YOU'VE ONLY JUST STARTED USING A BLADE, BUT YOU'RE ALREADY IN SOLID SHAPE!
A HIGH SCHOOLER WHO SWITCHED OVER FROM ANOTHER SPORT, JUST LIKE HIM, HUH?
HUH? "HIM" WHO?
ZA (ZSH)

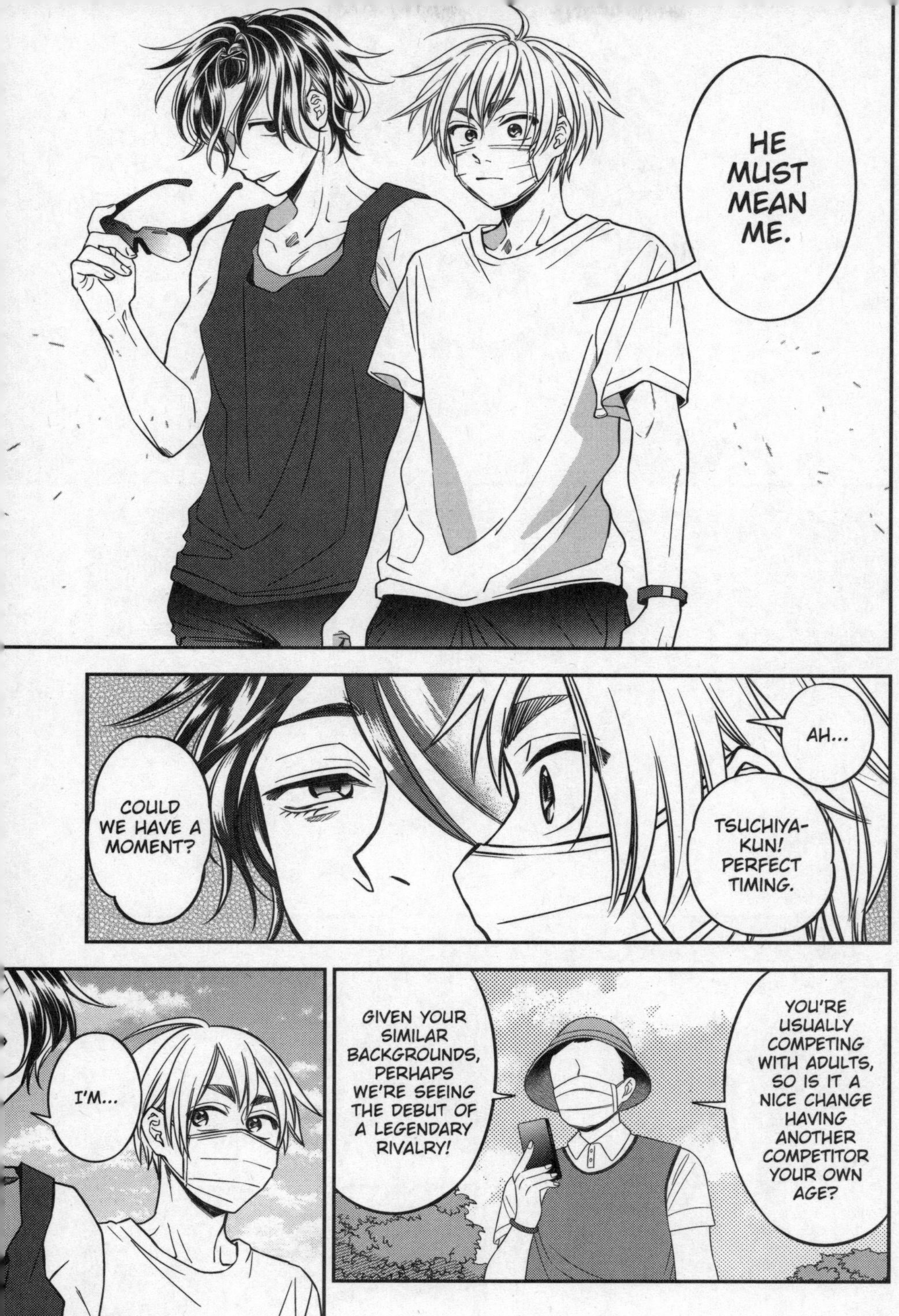
HE MUST MEAN ME.
AH...
TSUCHIYA-KUN! PERFECT TIMING.
COULD WE HAVE A MOMENT?
YOU'RE USUALLY COMPETING WITH ADULTS, SO IS IT A NICE CHANGE HAVING ANOTHER COMPETITOR YOUR OWN AGE?
GIVEN YOUR SIMILAR BACKGROUNDS, PERHAPS WE'RE SEEING THE DEBUT OF A LEGENDARY RIVALRY!
I'M...

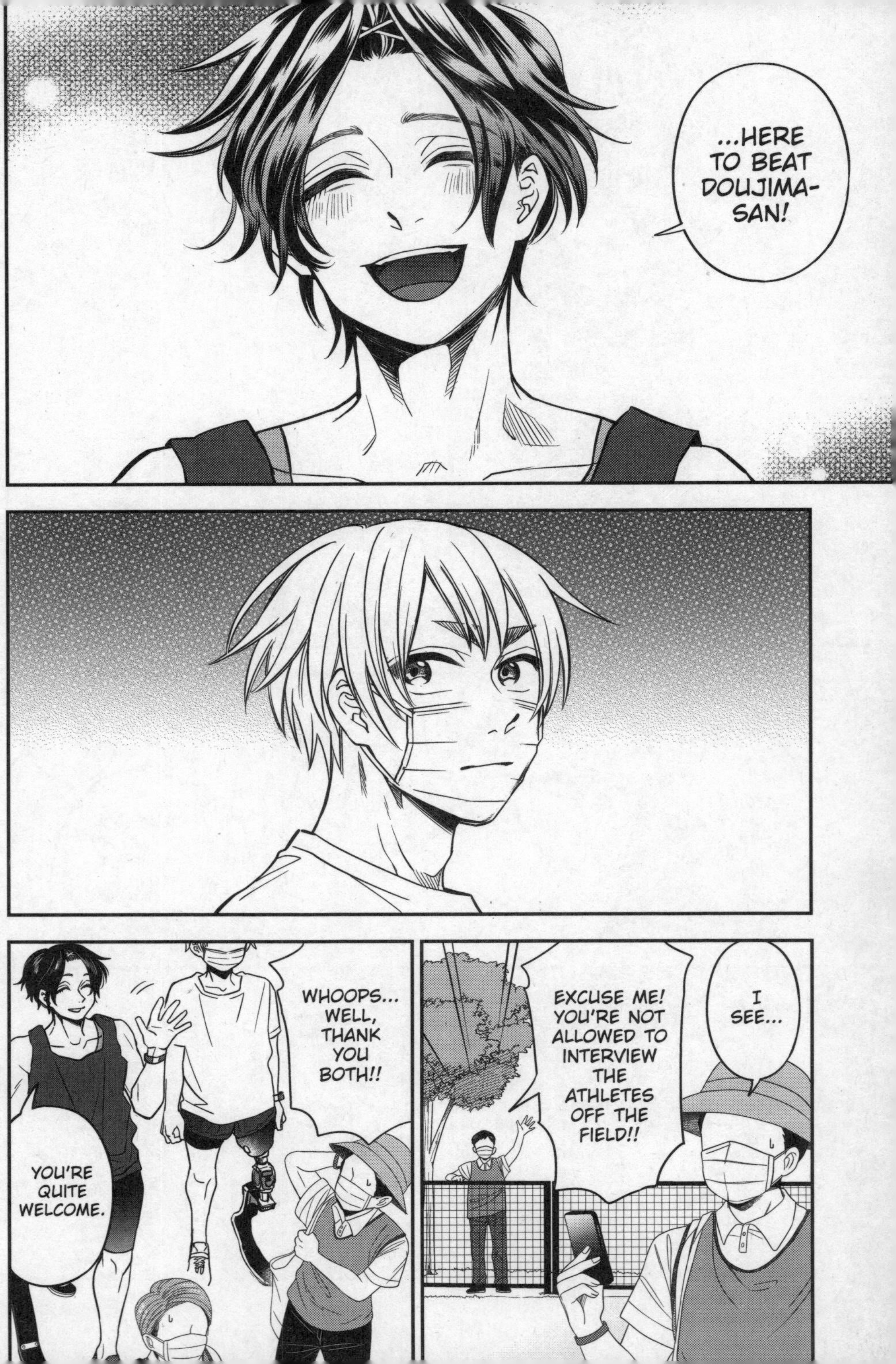
...HERE TO BEAT DOUJIMA-SAN!
I SEE...
EXCUSE ME! YOU'RE NOT ALLOWED TO INTERVIEW THE ATHLETES OFF THE FIELD!!
WHOOPS... WELL, THANK YOU BOTH!!
YOU'RE QUITE WELCOME.

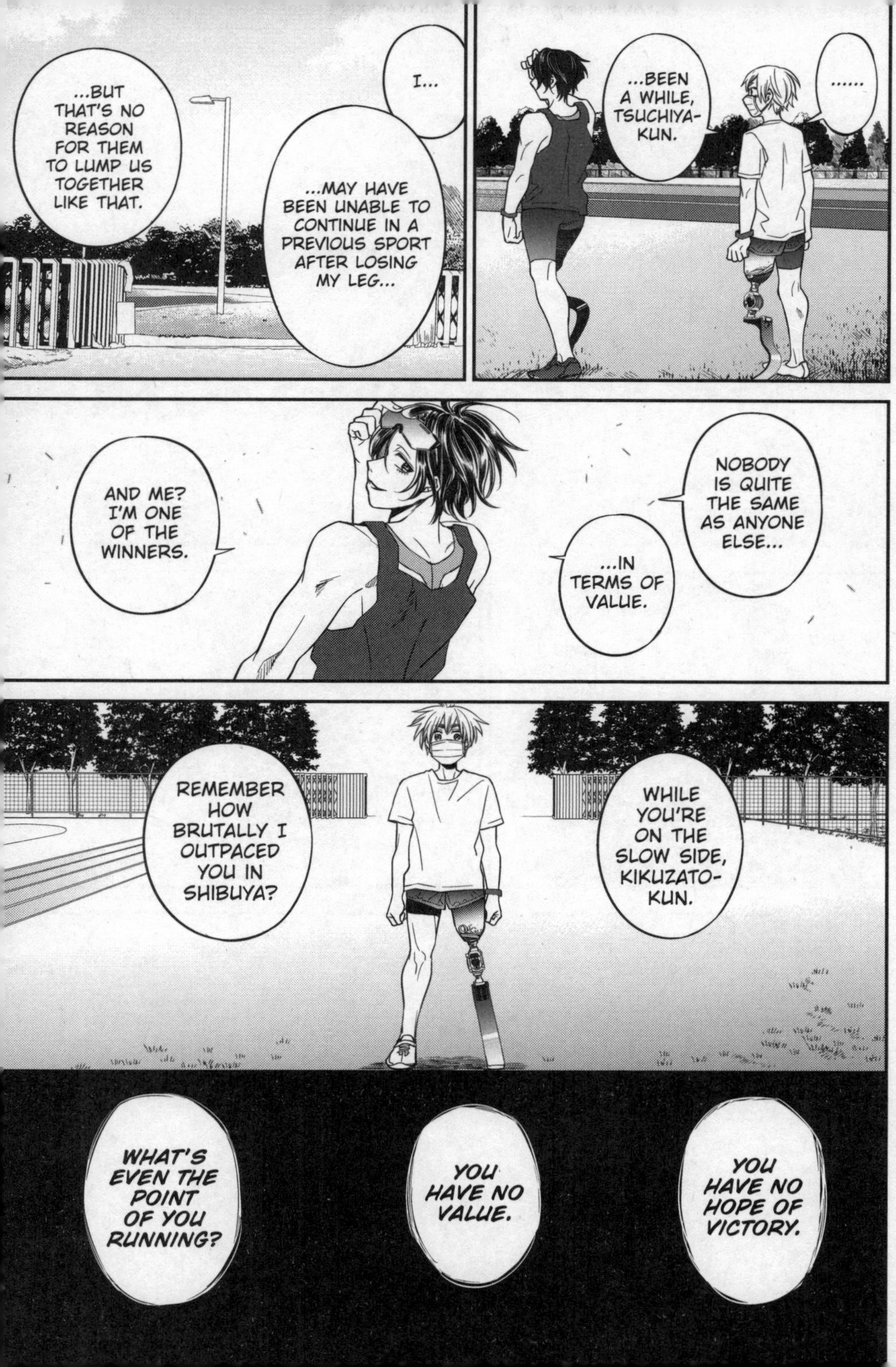
......
...BEEN A WHILE, TSUCHIYA-KUN.
I...
...MAY HAVE BEEN UNABLE TO CONTINUE IN A PREVIOUS SPORT AFTER LOSING MY LEG...
...BUT THAT'S NO REASON FOR THEM TO LUMP US TOGETHER LIKE THAT.
NOBODY IS QUITE THE SAME AS ANYONE ELSE...
...IN TERMS OF VALUE.
AND ME? I'M ONE OF THE WINNERS.
WHILE YOU'RE ON THE SLOW SIDE, KIKUZATO-KUN.
REMEMBER HOW BRUTALLY I OUTPACED YOU IN SHIBUYA?
YOU HAVE NO HOPE OF VICTORY.
YOU HAVE NO VALUE.
WHAT'S EVEN THE POINT OF YOU RUNNING?

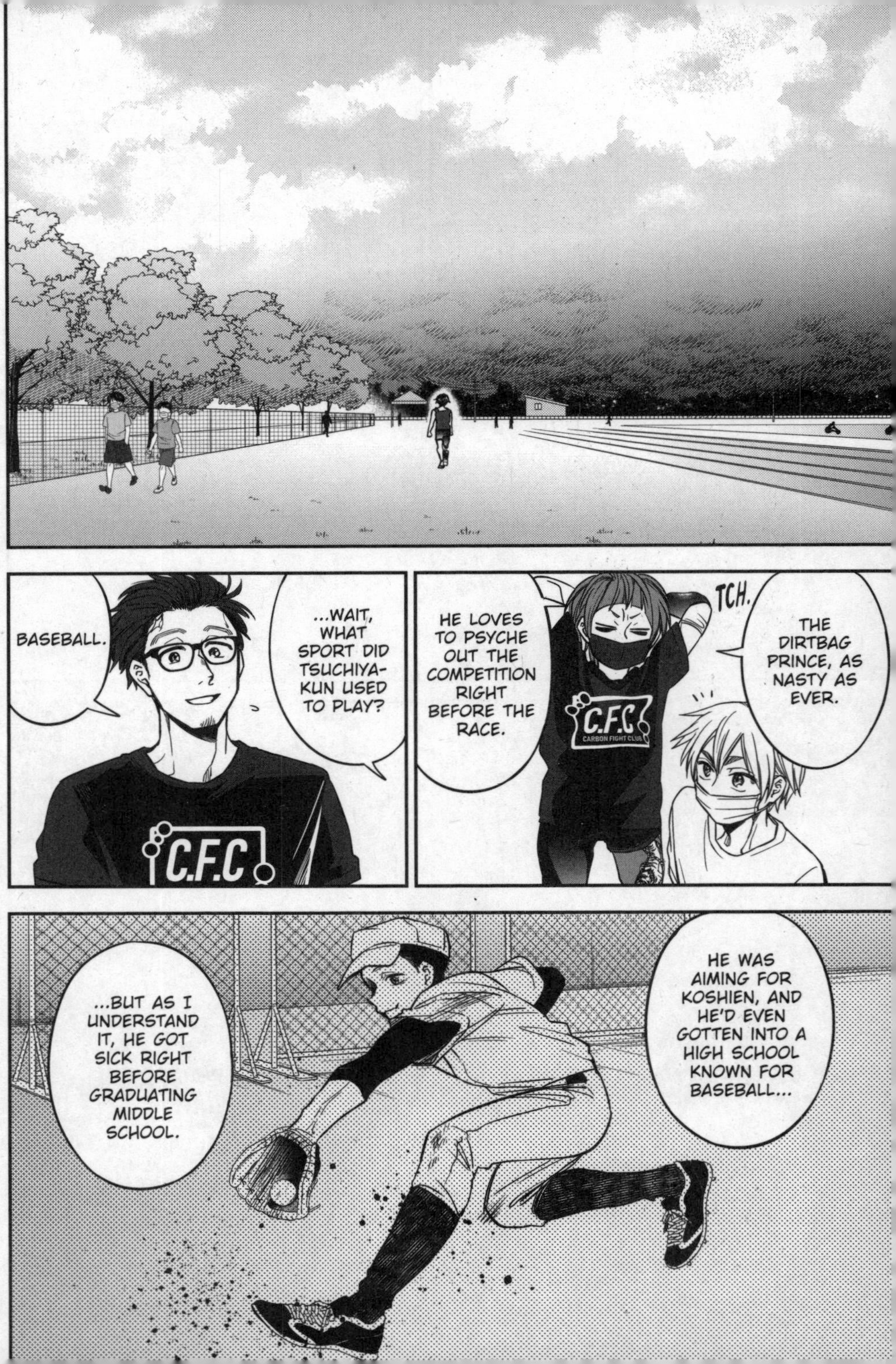
TCH.
THE DIRTBAG PRINCE, AS NASTY AS EVER.
HE LOVES TO PSYCHE OUT THE COMPETITION RIGHT BEFORE THE RACE.
C.F.C
CARBON FIGHT CLUB
...WAIT, WHAT SPORT DID TSUCHIYA-KUN USED TO PLAY?
BASEBALL.
C.F.C
HE WAS AIMING FOR KOSHIEN, AND HE'D EVEN GOTTEN INTO A HIGH SCHOOL KNOWN FOR BASEBALL...
...BUT AS I UNDERSTAND IT, HE GOT SICK RIGHT BEFORE GRADUATING MIDDLE SCHOOL.

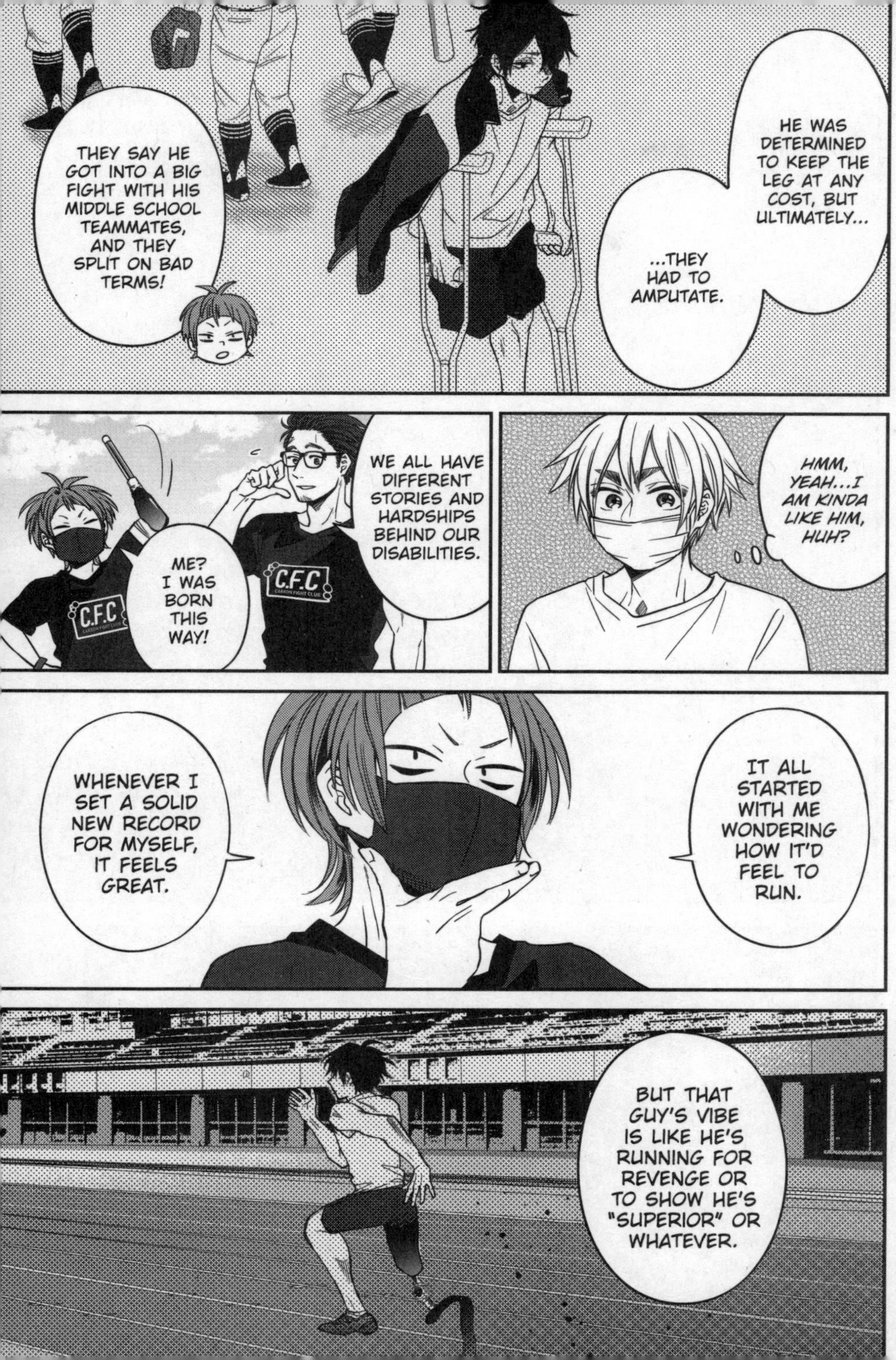
HE WAS DETERMINED TO KEEP THE LEG AT ANY COST, BUT ULTIMATELY...
...THEY HAD TO AMPUTATE.
THEY SAY HE GOT INTO A BIG FIGHT WITH HIS MIDDLE SCHOOL TEAMMATES, AND THEY SPLIT ON BAD TERMS!
HMM, YEAH...I AM KINDA LIKE HIM, HUH?
WE ALL HAVE DIFFERENT STORIES AND HARDSHIPS BEHIND OUR DISABILITIES.
C.F.C CARRON FIGHT CLUB
ME? I WAS BORN THIS WAY!
C.F.C CARRON FIGHT CLUB
IT ALL STARTED WITH ME WONDERING HOW IT'D FEEL TO RUN.
WHENEVER I SET A SOLID NEW RECORD FOR MYSELF, IT FEELS GREAT.
BUT THAT GUY'S VIBE IS LIKE HE'S RUNNING FOR REVENGE OR TO SHOW HE'S "SUPERIOR" OR WHATEVER.

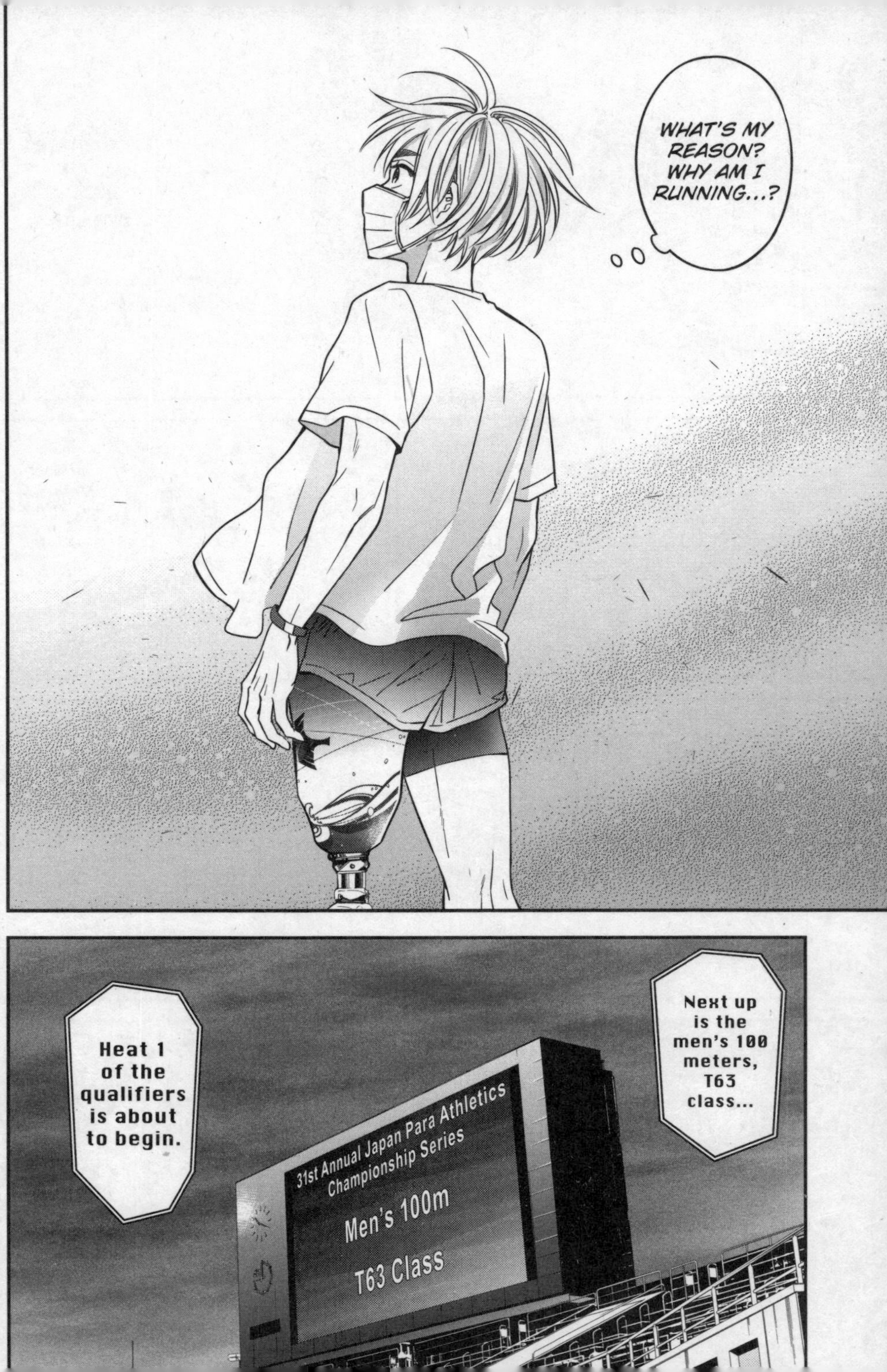
WHAT'S MY REASON? WHY AM I RUNNING...?
Next up is the men's 100 meters, T63 class...
Heat 1 of the qualifiers is about to begin.
31st Annual Japan Para Athletics Championship Series
Men's 100m
T63 Class

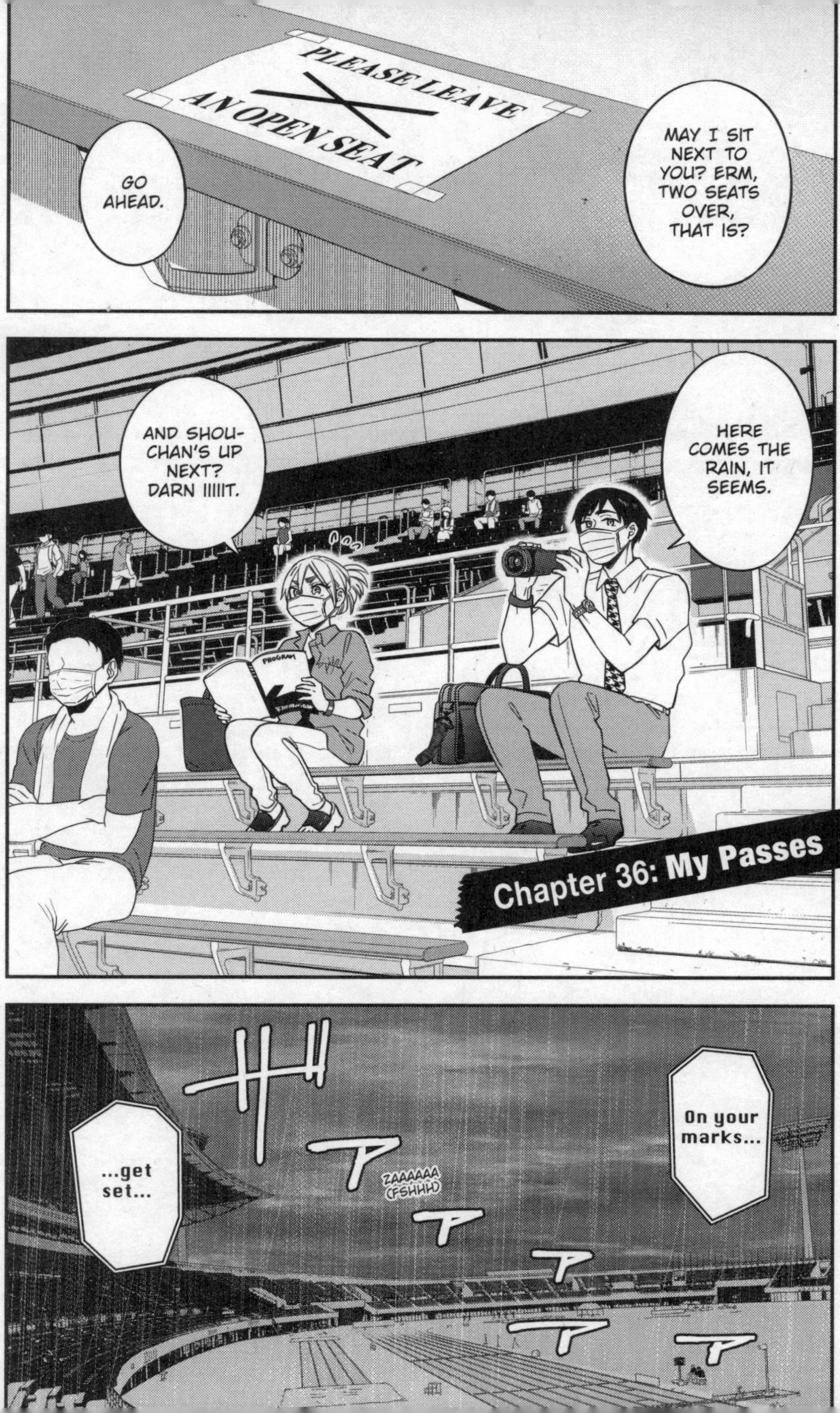
PLEASE LEAVE AN OPEN SEAT
MAY I SIT NEXT TO YOU? ERM, TWO SEATS OVER, THAT IS?
GO AHEAD.
HERE COMES THE RAIN, IT SEEMS.
AND SHOU-CHAN'S UP NEXT? DARN IIIIIT.
PROGRAM
Chapter 36: My Passes
On your marks...
...get set...
ZAAAAAA (FSHHH)

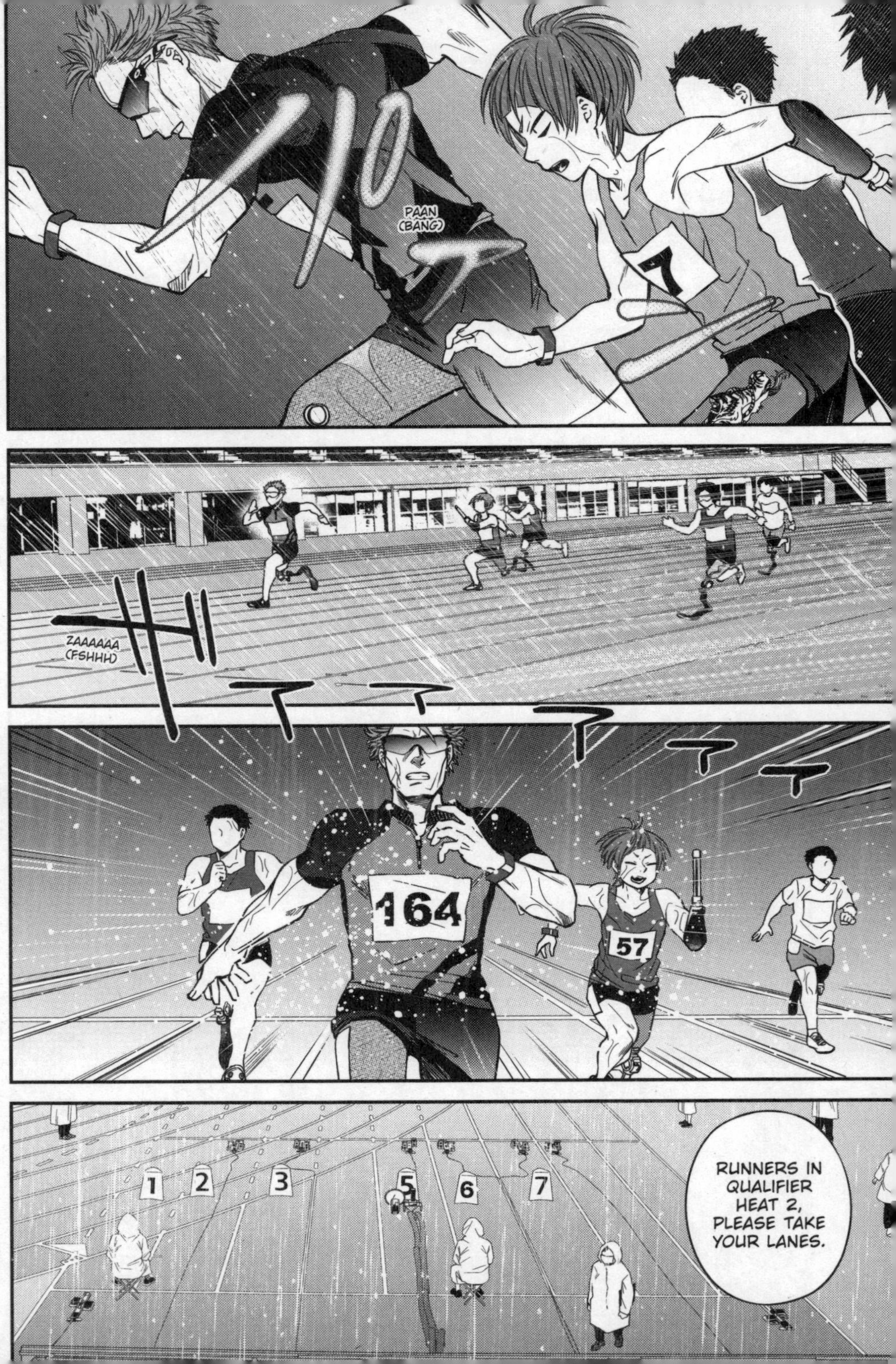
PAAN (BANG)
ZAAAAAA (FSHHH)
164
57
7
1
2
3
5
6
7
RUNNERS IN QUALIFIER HEAT 2, PLEASE TAKE YOUR LANES.

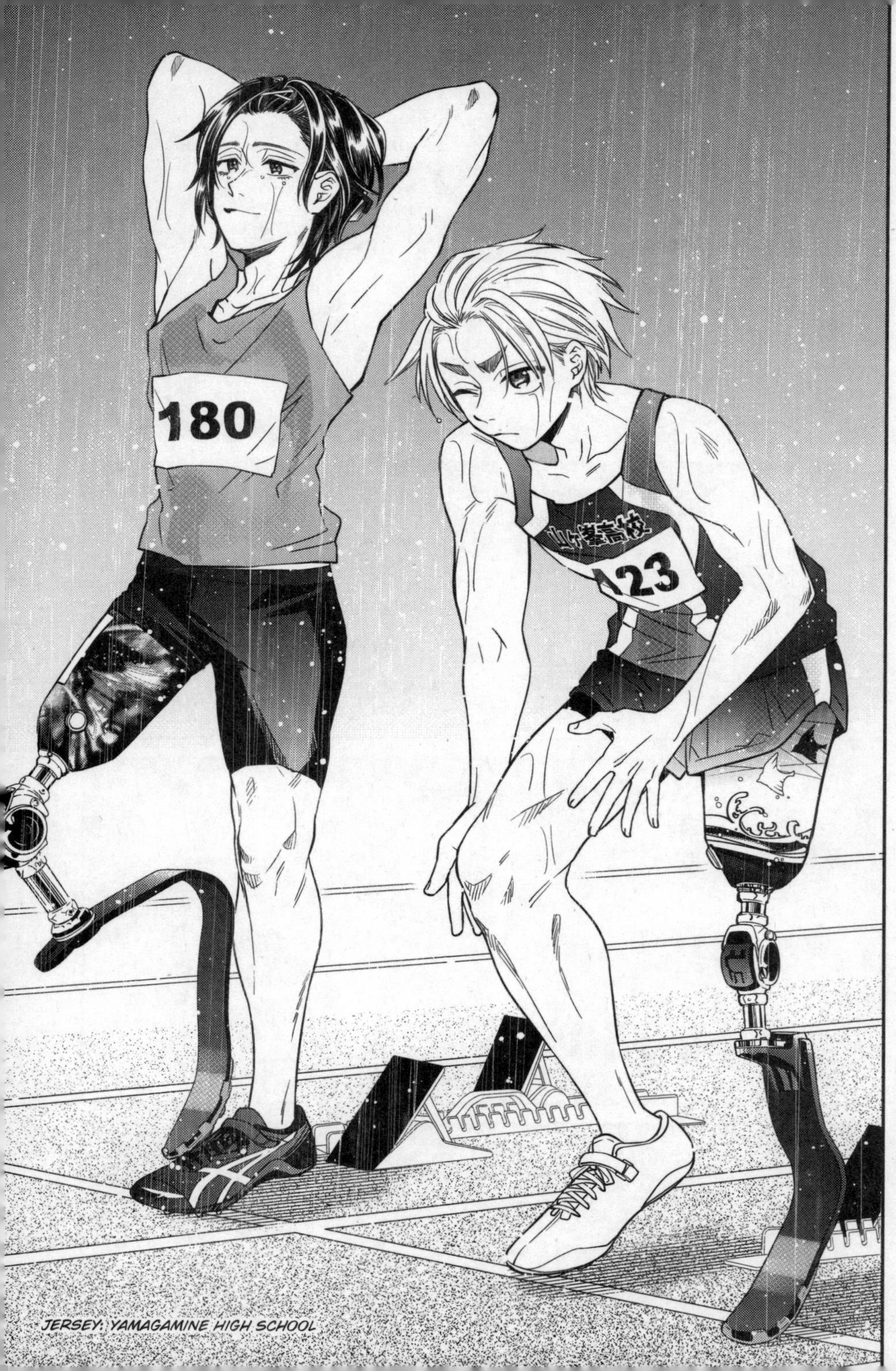
180
123
JERSEY: YAMAGAMINE HIGH SCHOOL

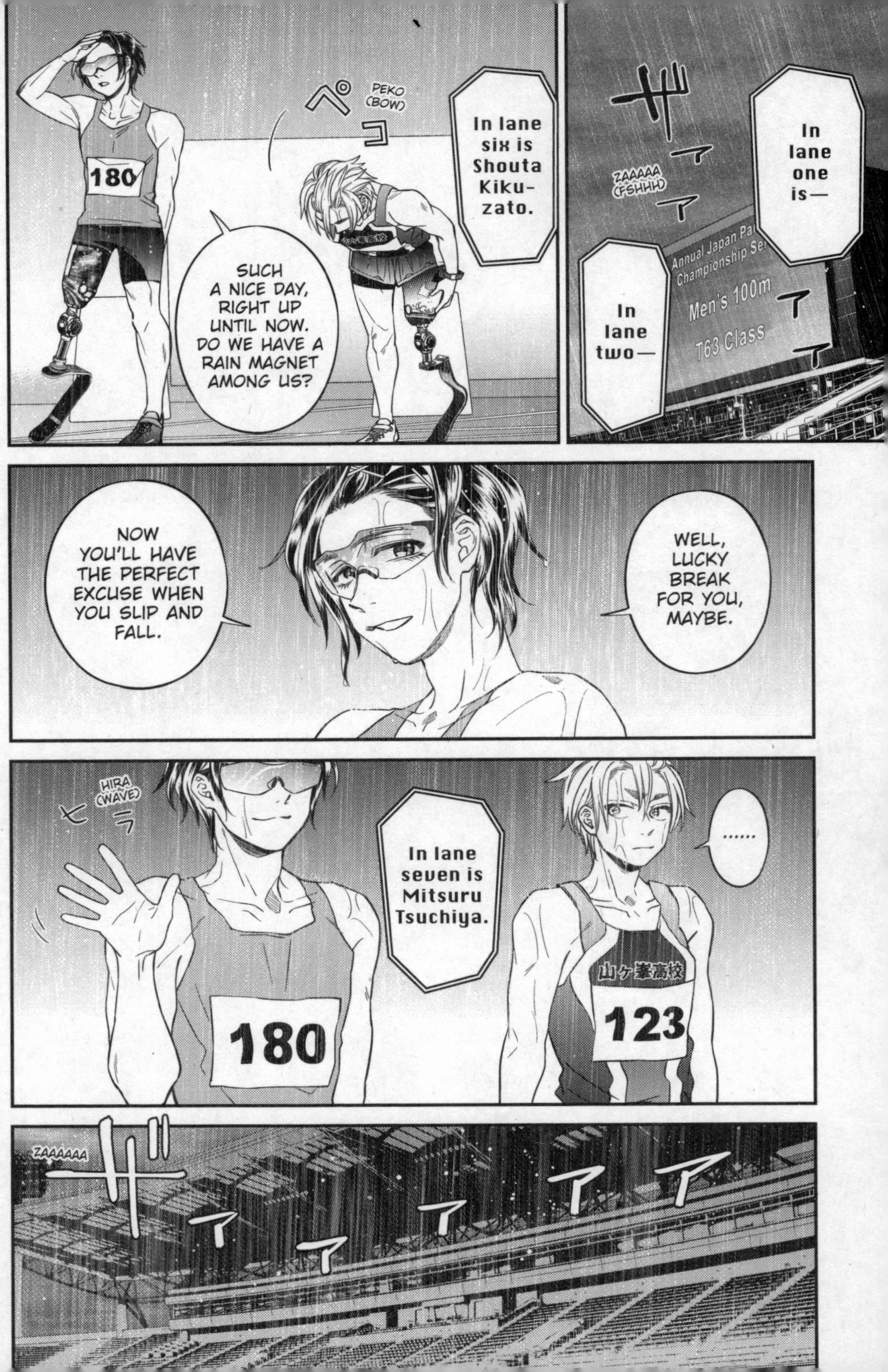
ZAAAAAA (FSHHH)
In lane one is—
In lane two—
Men's 100m
T63 Class
In lane six is Shouta Kikuzato.
PEKO (BOW)
SUCH A NICE DAY, RIGHT UP UNTIL NOW. DO WE HAVE A RAIN MAGNET AMONG US?
180
WELL, LUCKY BREAK FOR YOU, MAYBE.
NOW YOU'LL HAVE THE PERFECT EXCUSE WHEN YOU SLIP AND FALL.
......
In lane seven is Mitsuru Tsuchiya.
HIRA (WAVE)
山ヶ峯高校
123
180
ZAAAAAA

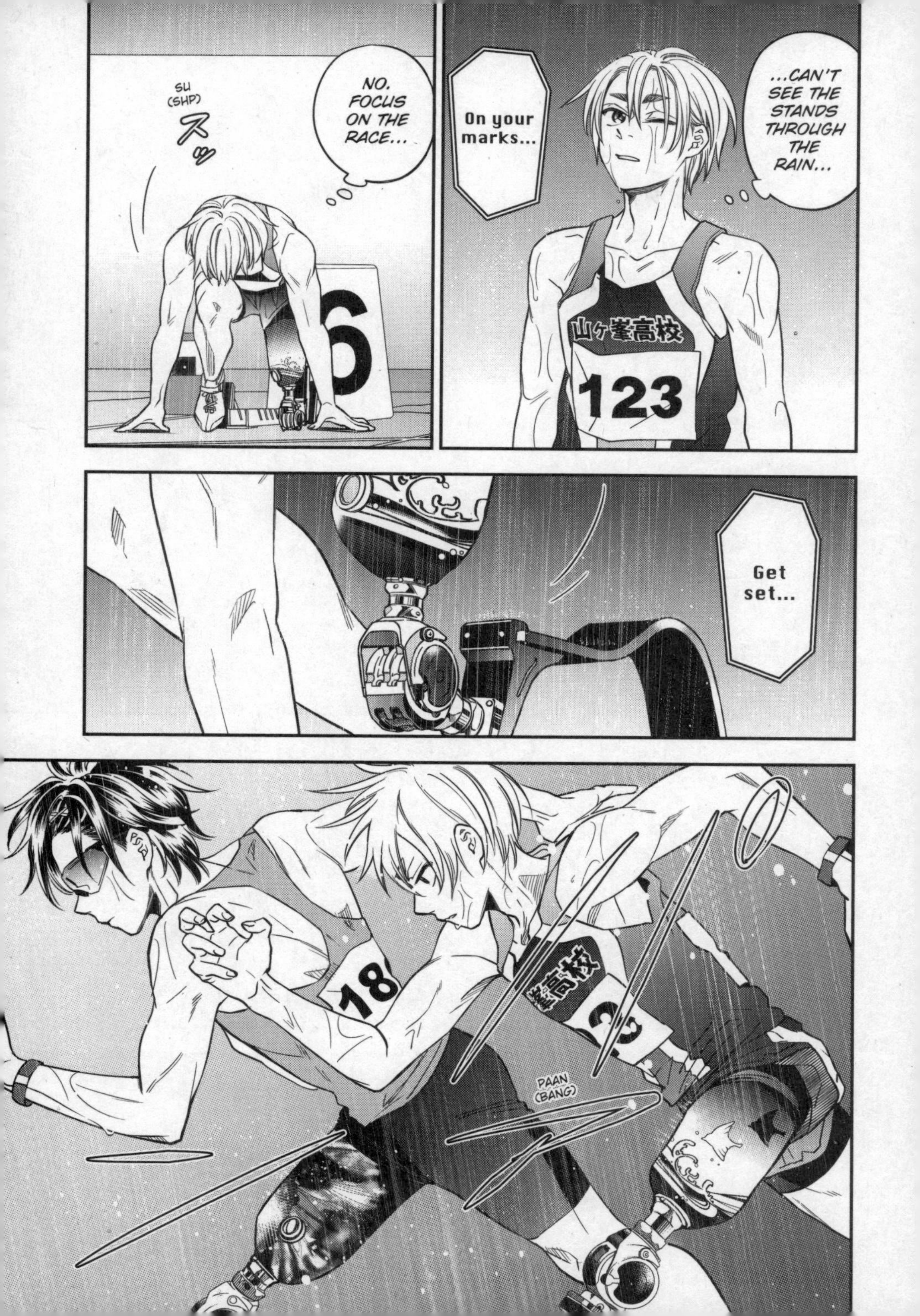
...CAN'T SEE THE STANDS THROUGH THE RAIN...
On your marks...
山ヶ峯高校
123
NO. FOCUS ON THE RACE...
SU (SHP)
スッ
Get set...
PAAN (BANG)

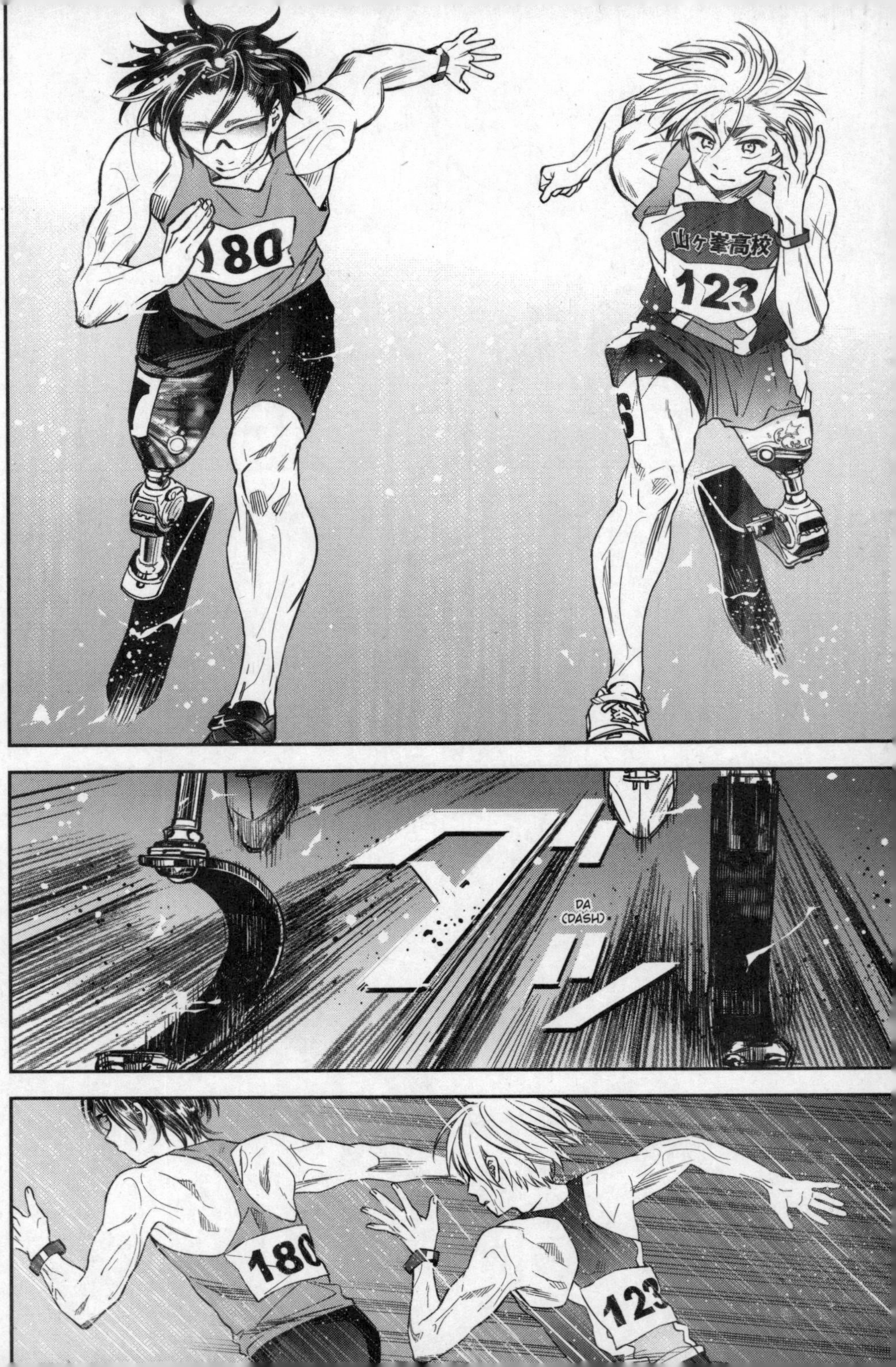

180
山ヶ峯高校
123
DA
(DASH)
180
123

BAN
(WHAM)

ビク
ッ

BIKU
(JOLT)

AH!

山ヶ峯高校

123

80

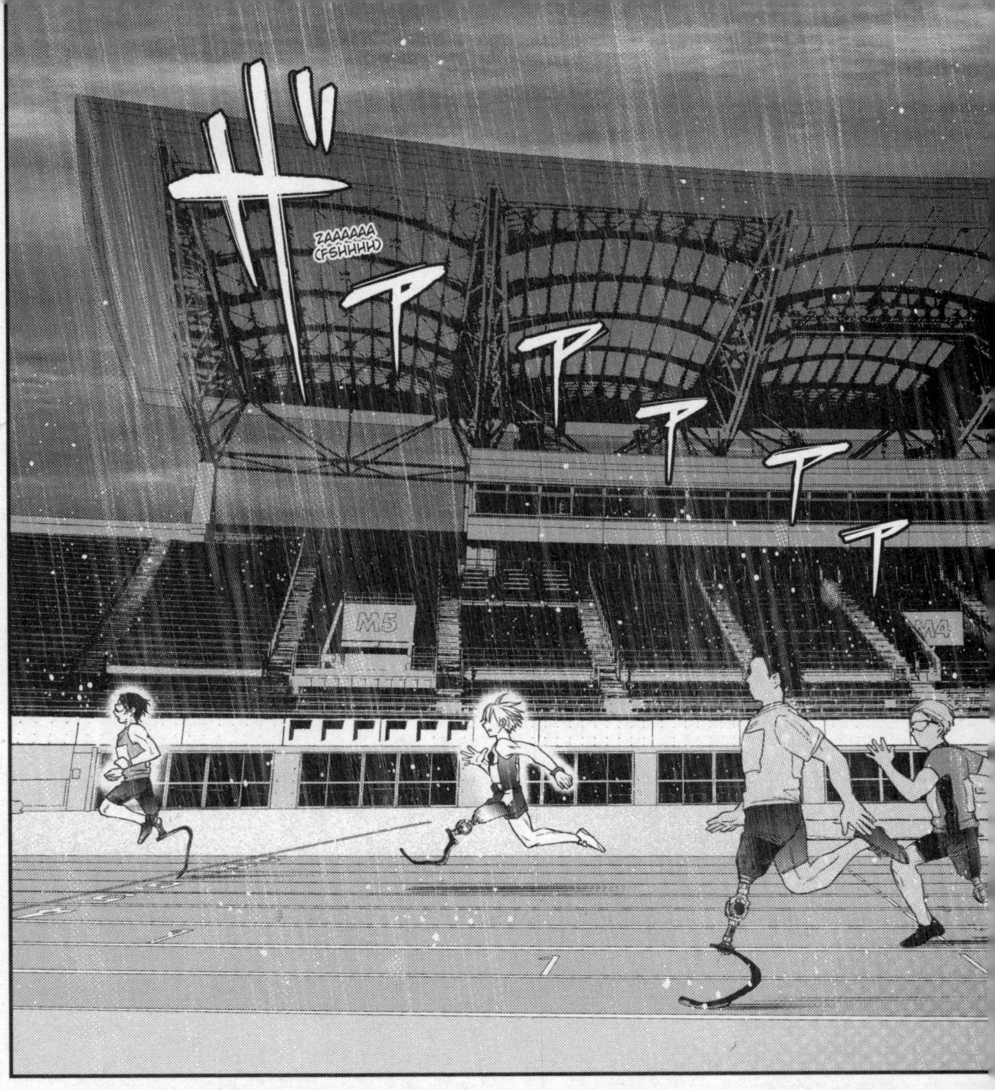
ZAAAAAA
(FSHHHHH)
M5
M4
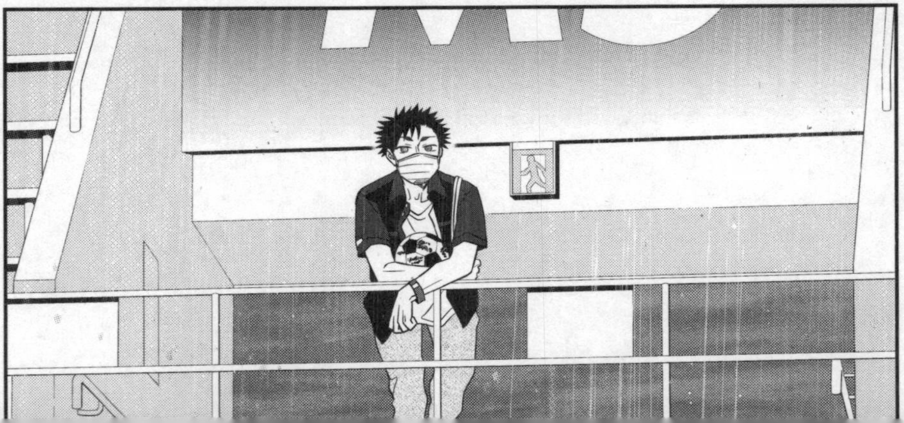

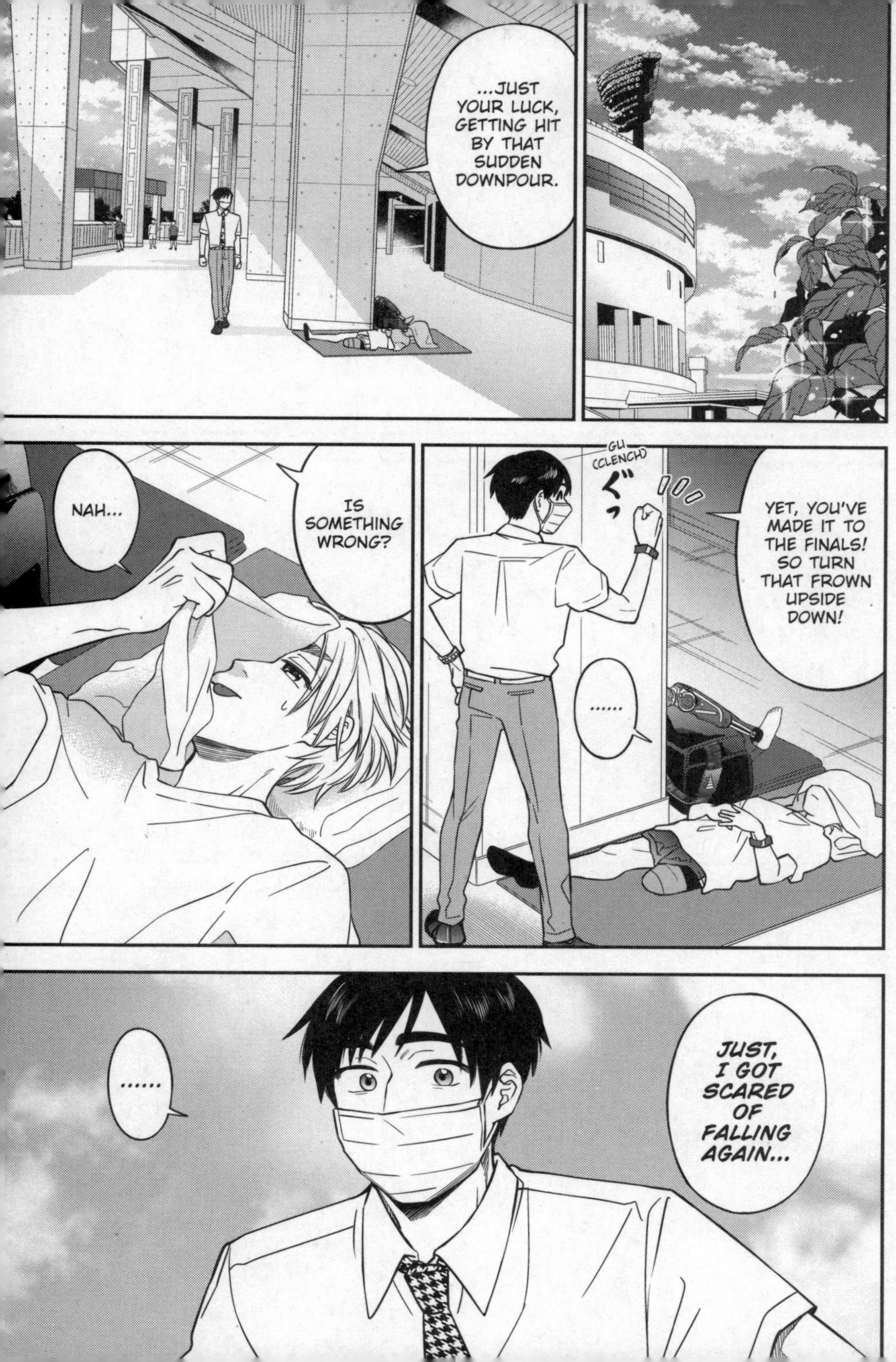
...JUST YOUR LUCK, GETTING HIT BY THAT SUDDEN DOWNPOUR.
YET, YOU'VE MADE IT TO THE FINALS! SO TURN THAT FROWN UPSIDE DOWN!
GU (CLENCH)
ぐっ
......
IS SOMETHING WRONG?
NAH...
JUST, I GOT SCARED OF FALLING AGAIN...
......

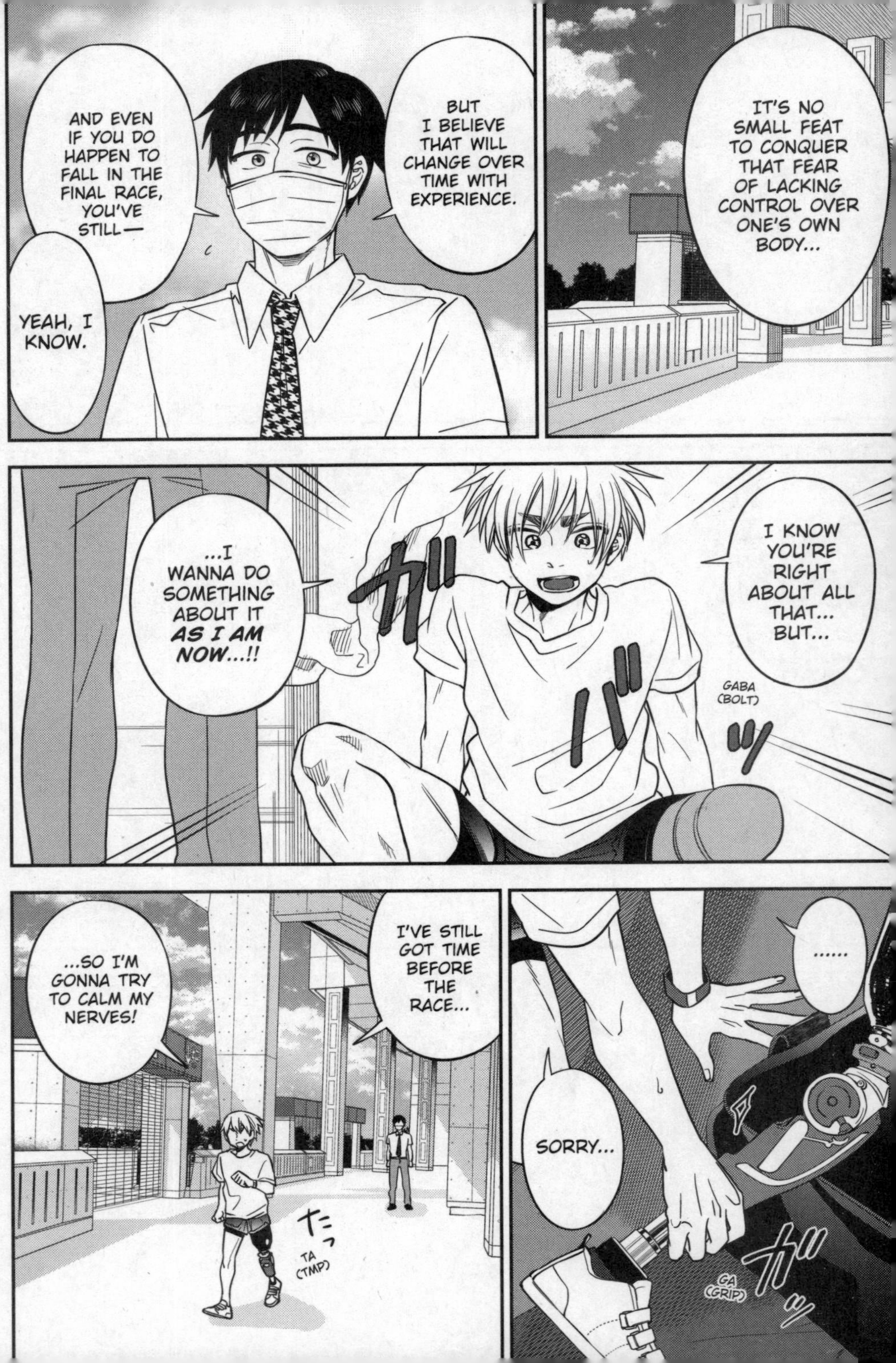
IT'S NO SMALL FEAT TO CONQUER THAT FEAR OF LACKING CONTROL OVER ONE'S OWN BODY...
BUT I BELIEVE THAT WILL CHANGE OVER TIME WITH EXPERIENCE.
AND EVEN IF YOU DO HAPPEN TO FALL IN THE FINAL RACE, YOU'VE STILL—
YEAH, I KNOW.
I KNOW YOU'RE RIGHT ABOUT ALL THAT... BUT...
GABA (BOLT)
...I WANNA DO SOMETHING ABOUT IT ***AS I AM NOW***...!!
......
SORRY...
GA (GRIP)
I'VE STILL GOT TIME BEFORE THE RACE...
...SO I'M GONNA TRY TO CALM MY NERVES!
TA (TMP)

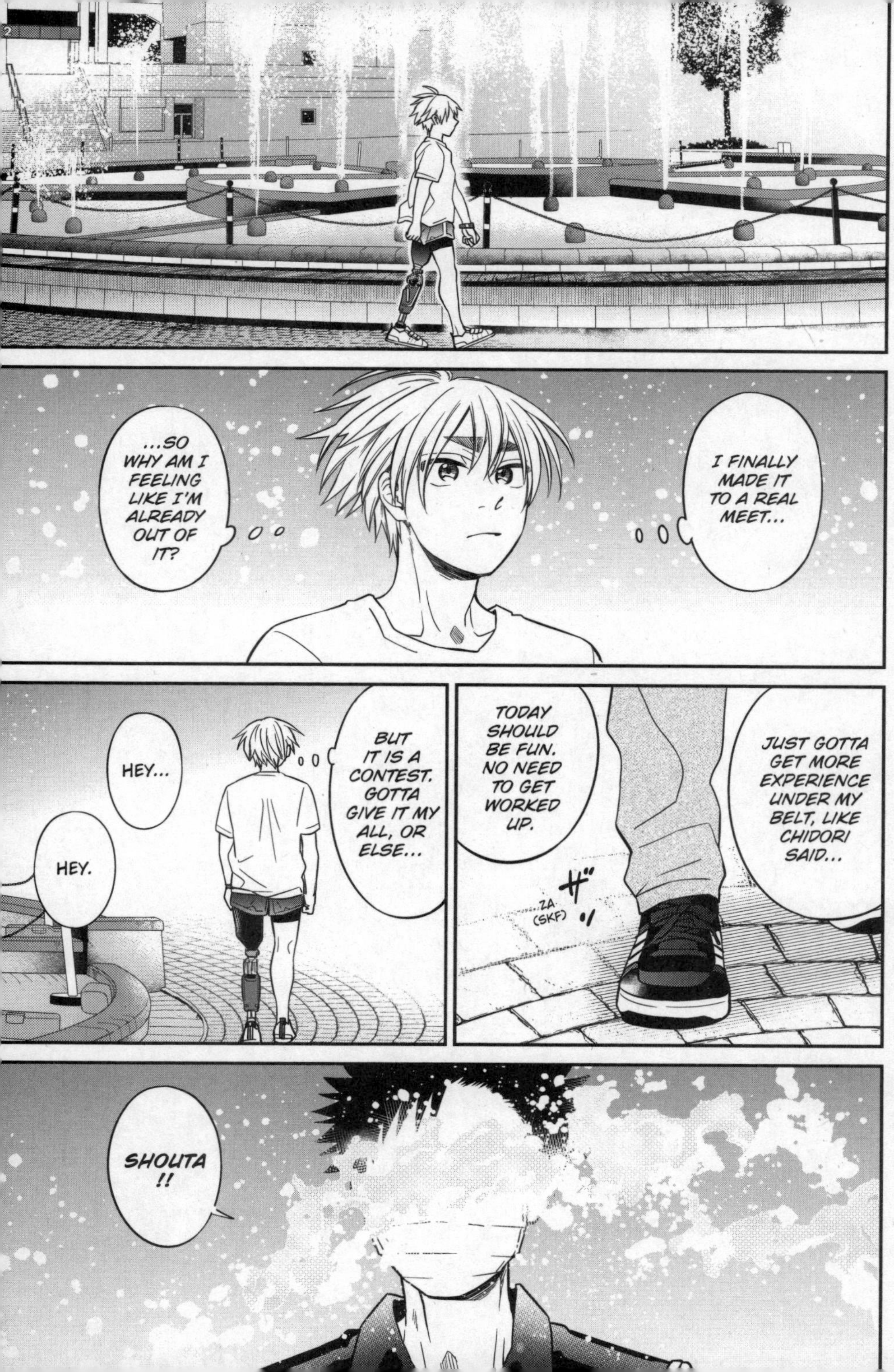
I FINALLY MADE IT TO A REAL MEET...
...SO WHY AM I FEELING LIKE I'M ALREADY OUT OF IT?
JUST GOTTA GET MORE EXPERIENCE UNDER MY BELT, LIKE CHIDORI SAID...
TODAY SHOULD BE FUN. NO NEED TO GET WORKED UP.
ZA (SKF)
BUT IT IS A CONTEST. GOTTA GIVE IT MY ALL, OR ELSE...
HEY...
HEY.
SHOUTA !!

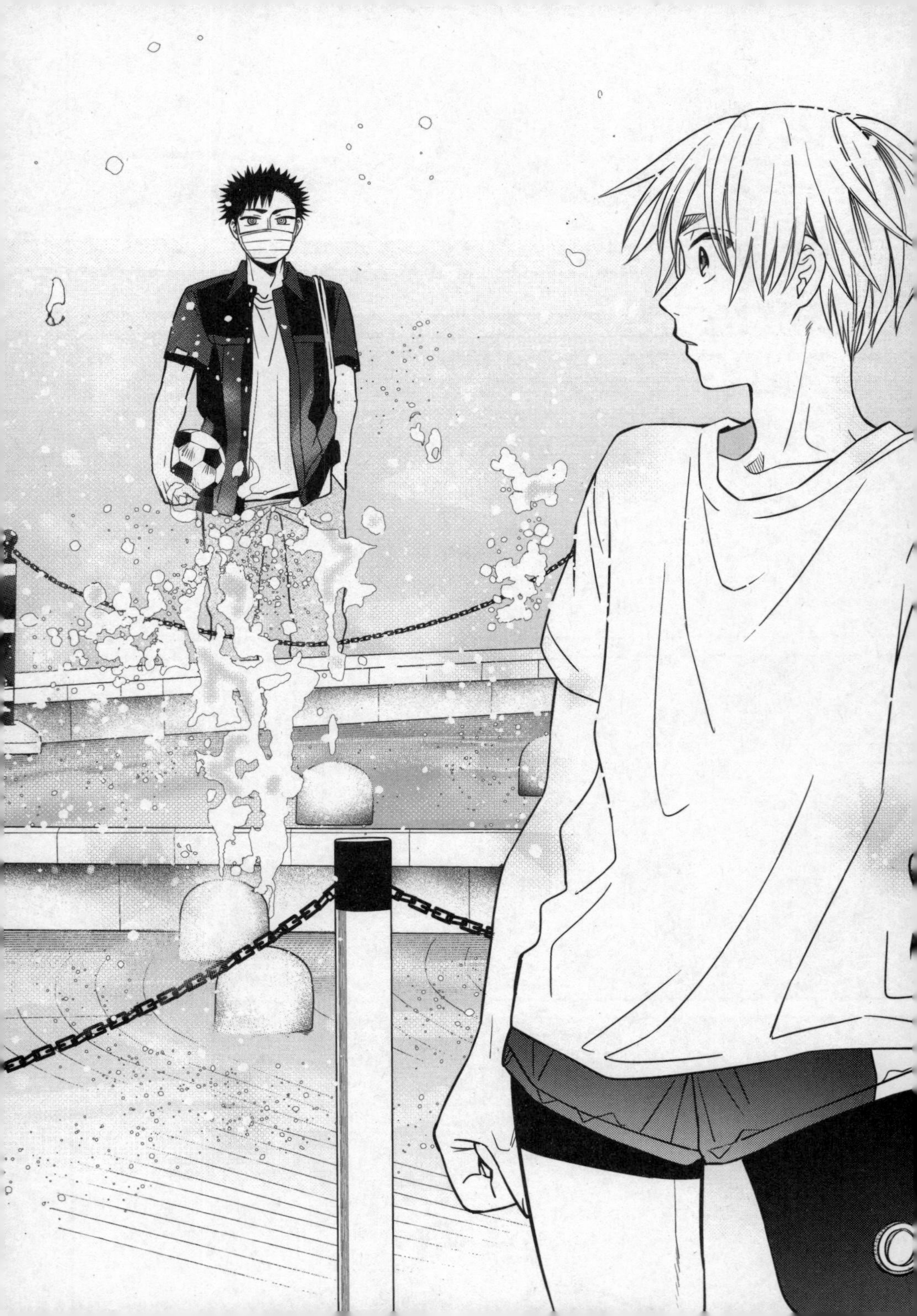

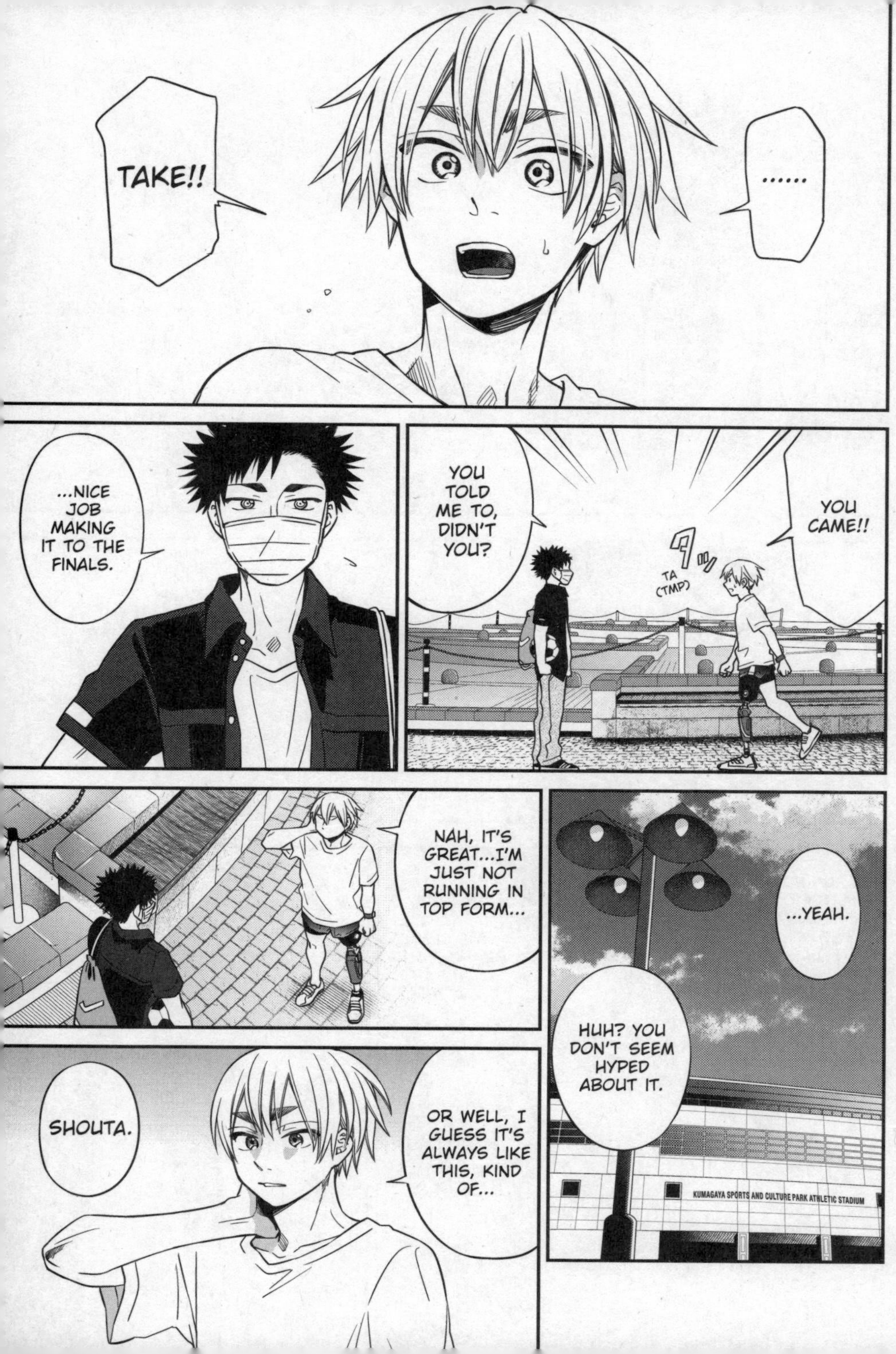
......
TAKE!!
YOU CAME!!
TA (TMP)
YOU TOLD ME TO, DIDN'T YOU?
...NICE JOB MAKING IT TO THE FINALS.
...YEAH.
HUH? YOU DON'T SEEM HYPED ABOUT IT.
KUMAGAYA SPORTS AND CULTURE PARK ATHLETIC STADIUM
NAH, IT'S GREAT...I'M JUST NOT RUNNING IN TOP FORM...
OR WELL, I GUESS IT'S ALWAYS LIKE THIS, KIND OF...
SHOUTA.

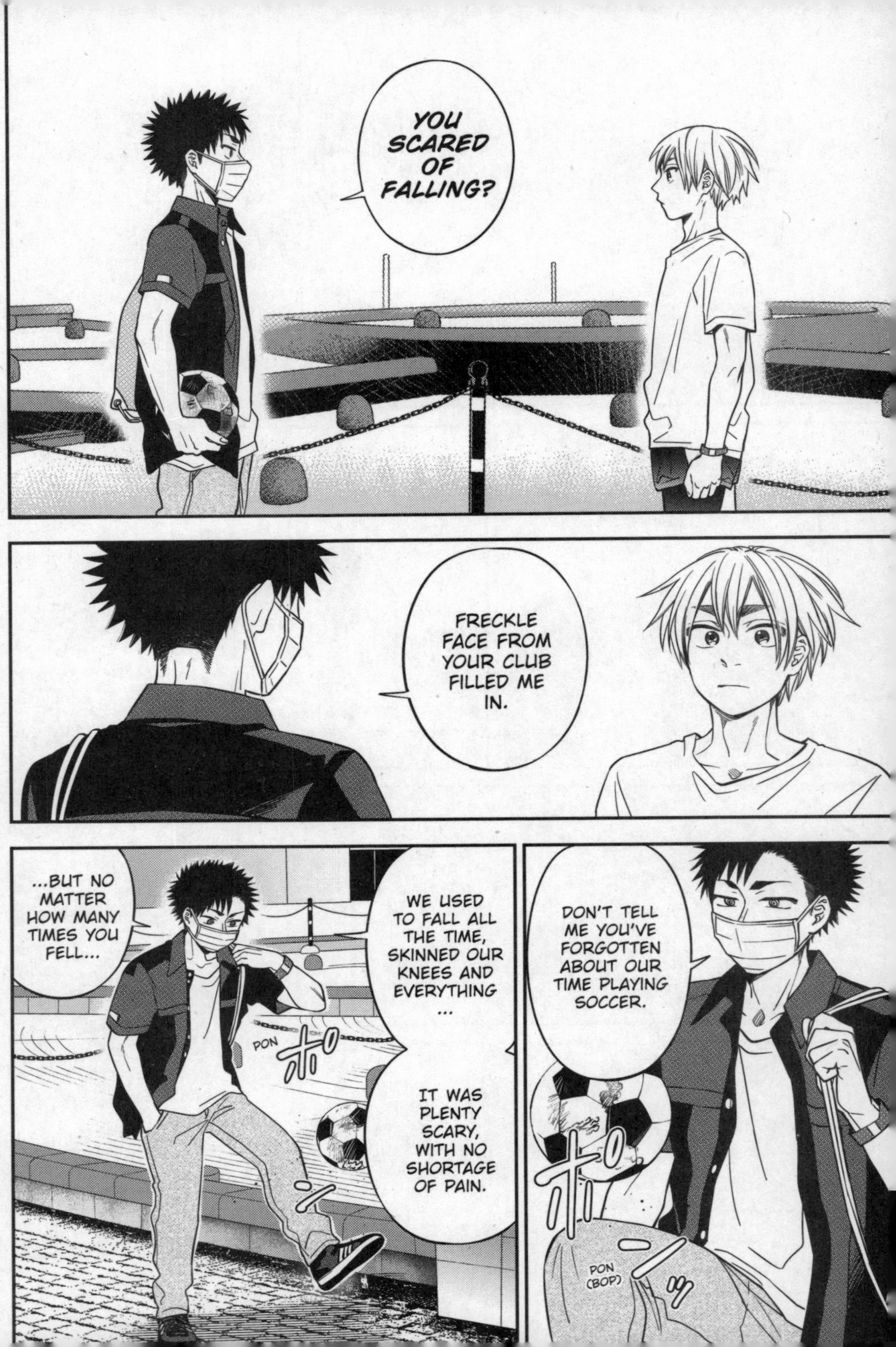
YOU SCARED OF FALLING?
FRECKLE FACE FROM YOUR CLUB FILLED ME IN.
DON'T TELL ME YOU'VE FORGOTTEN ABOUT OUR TIME PLAYING SOCCER.
PON (BOP)
WE USED TO FALL ALL THE TIME, SKINNED OUR KNEES AND EVERYTHING ...
IT WAS PLENTY SCARY, WITH NO SHORTAGE OF PAIN.
...BUT NO MATTER HOW MANY TIMES YOU FELL...
PON

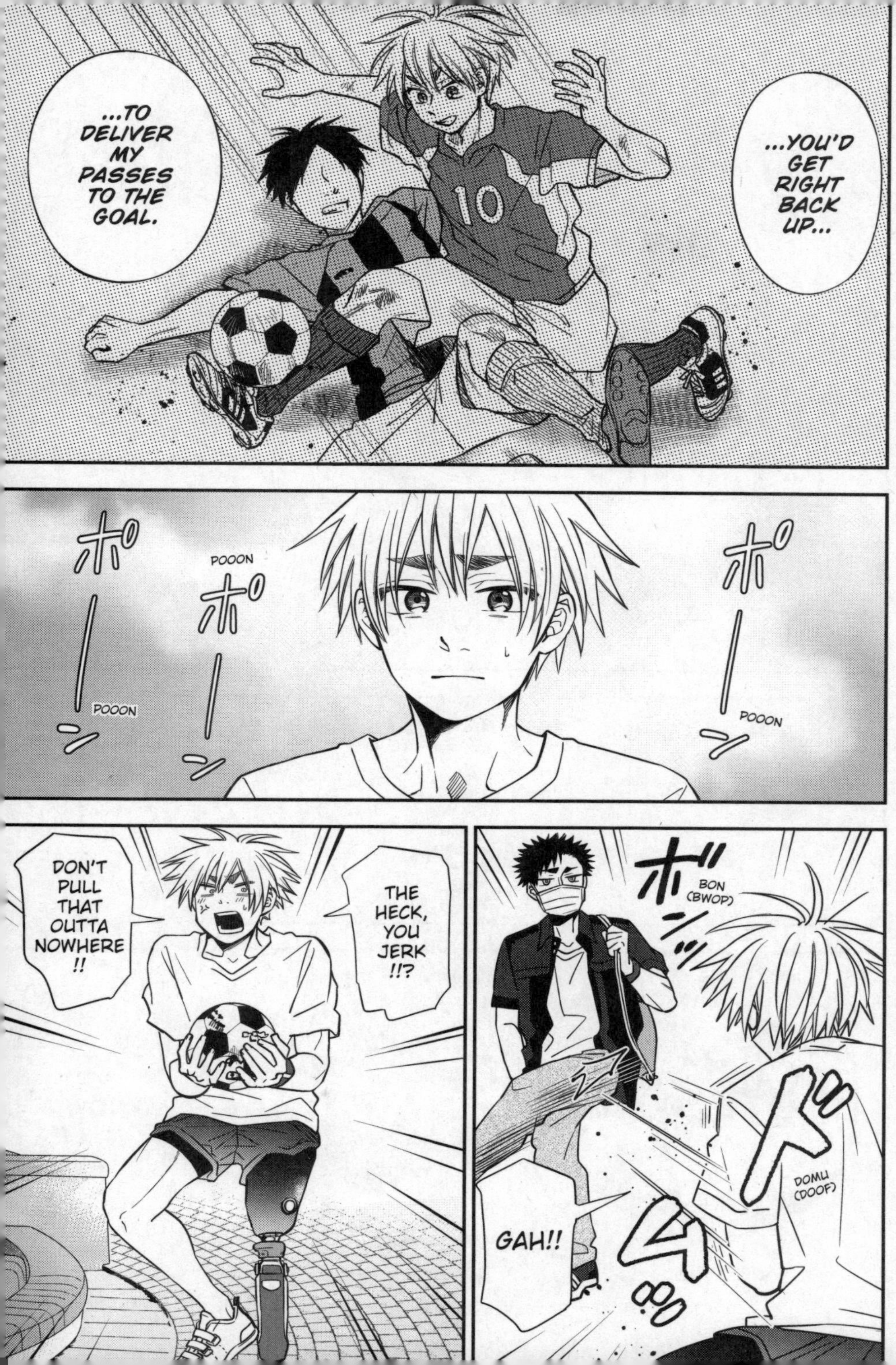
...YOU'D GET RIGHT BACK UP...
...TO DELIVER MY PASSES TO THE GOAL.
POOON
POOON
POOON
BON (BWOP)
DOMU (DOOF)
GAH!!
THE HECK, YOU JERK!!?
DON'T PULL THAT OUTTA NOWHERE!!

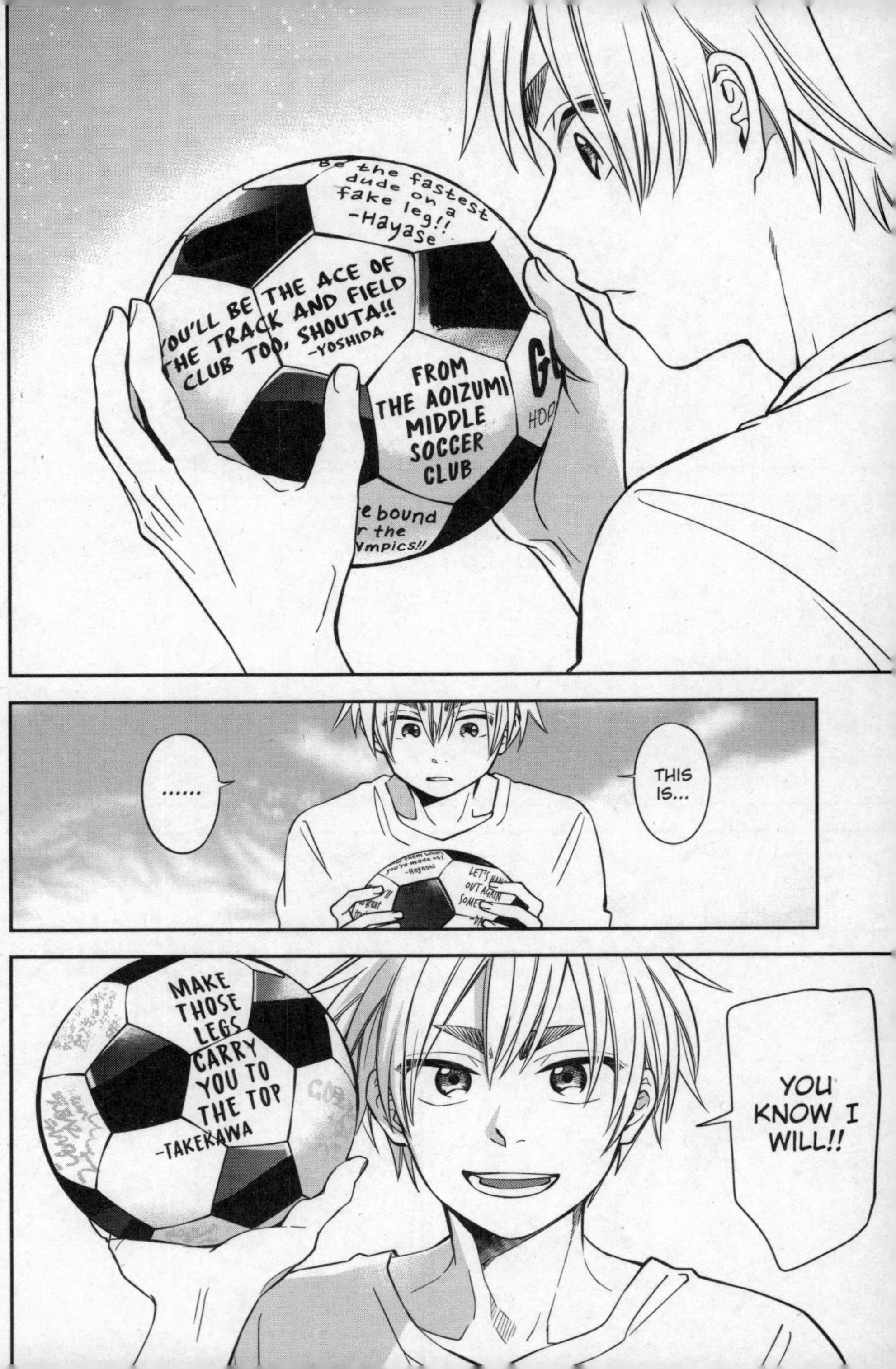
Be the fastest dude on a fake leg!! -Hayase
YOU'LL BE THE ACE OF THE TRACK AND FIELD CLUB TOO, SHOUTA!! -YOSHIDA
FROM THE AOIZUMI MIDDLE SOCCER CLUB
THIS IS...
......
MAKE THOSE LEGS CARRY YOU TO THE TOP -TAKEKAWA
YOU KNOW I WILL!!

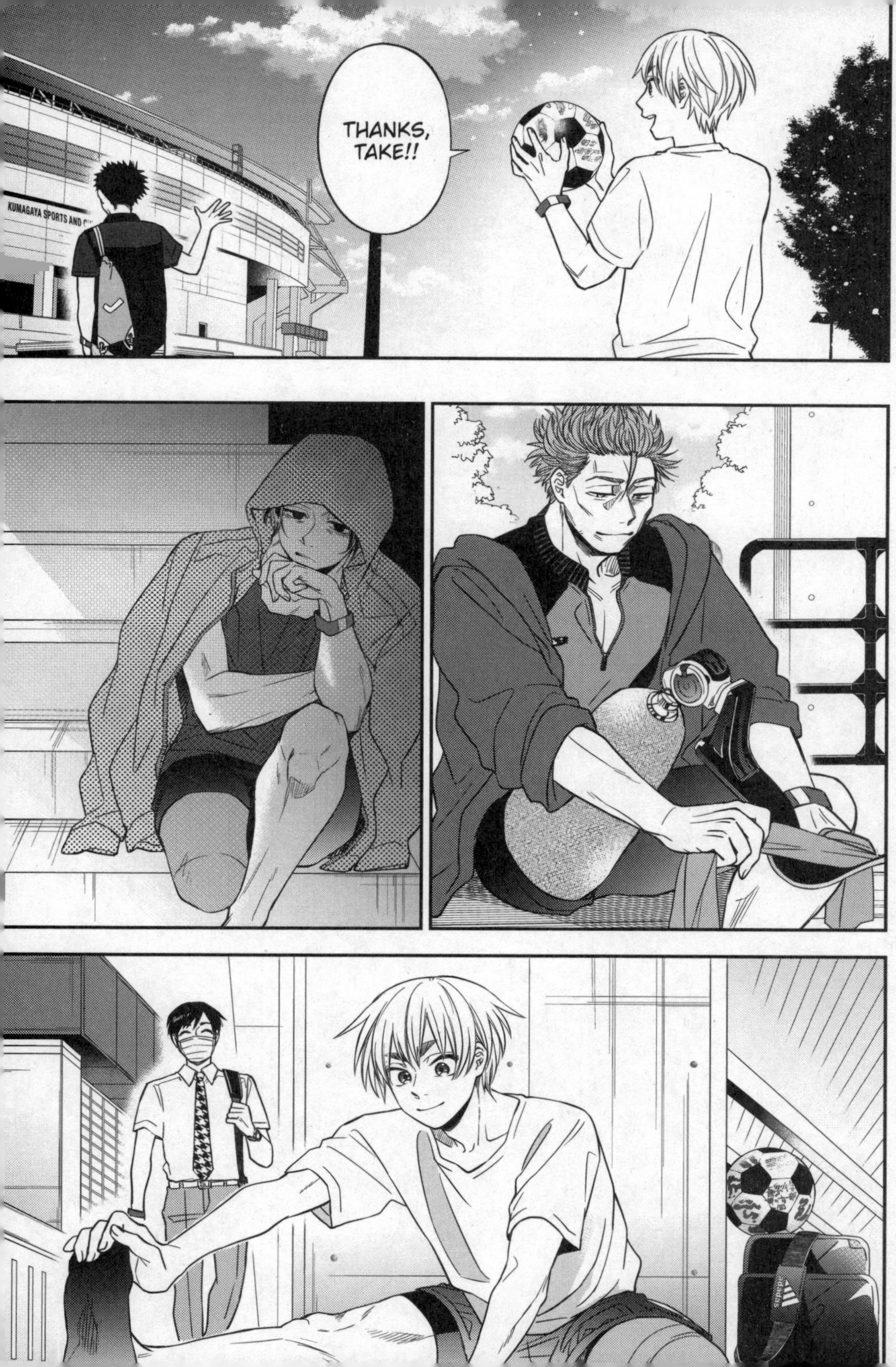
THANKS, TAKE!!

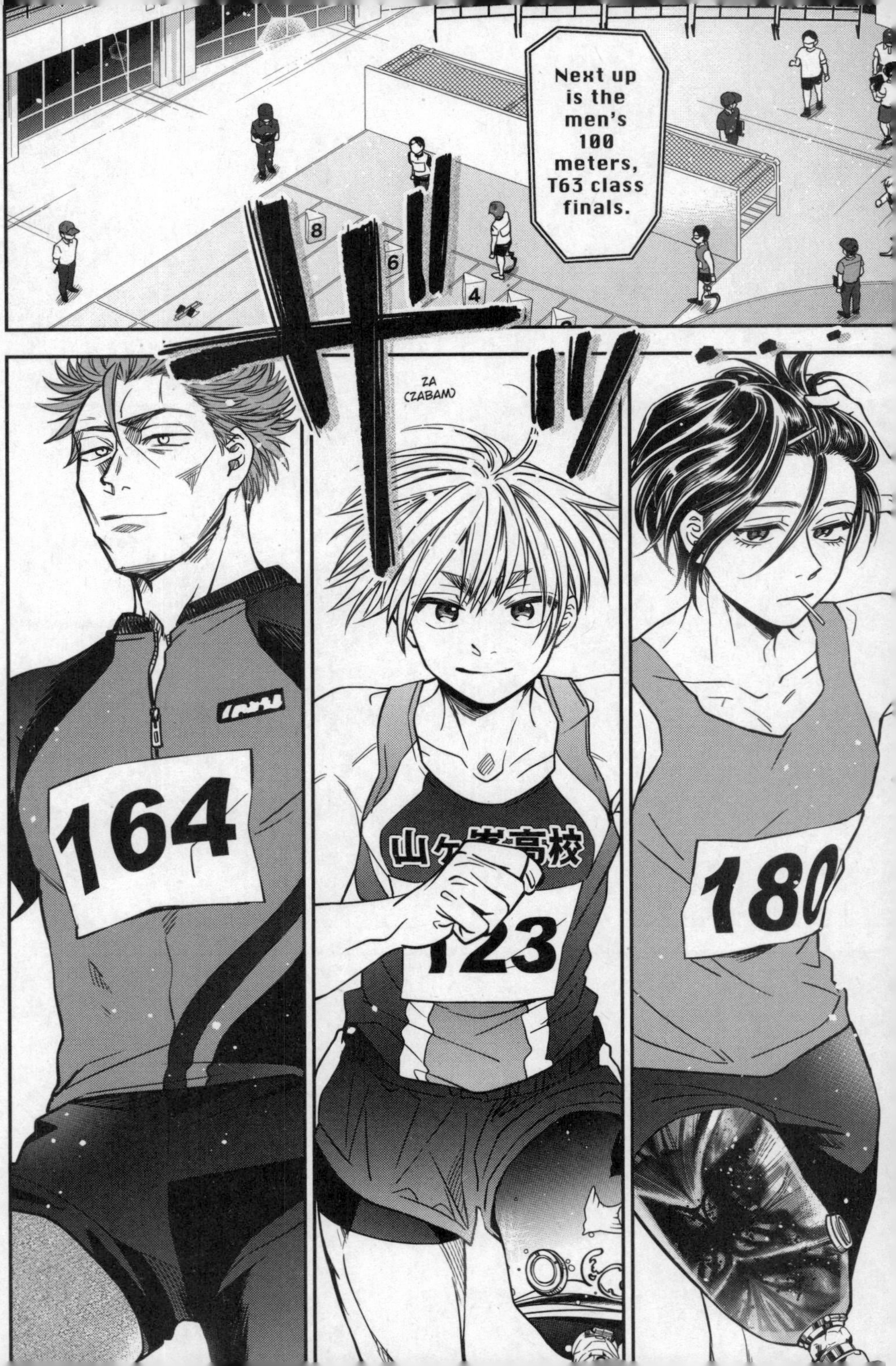
Next up is the men's 100 meters, T63 class finals.
ZA (ZABAM)
164
山ヶ岳高校
123
180

RUN ON YOUR NEW LEGS

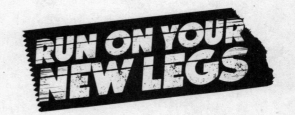

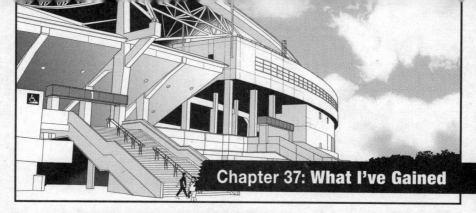

Chapter 37: What I've Gained

HA HA HA!

ZORO

ZORO
(TROMP)

—I DON'T
WANT TO
GIVE UP ON
BASEBALL!!

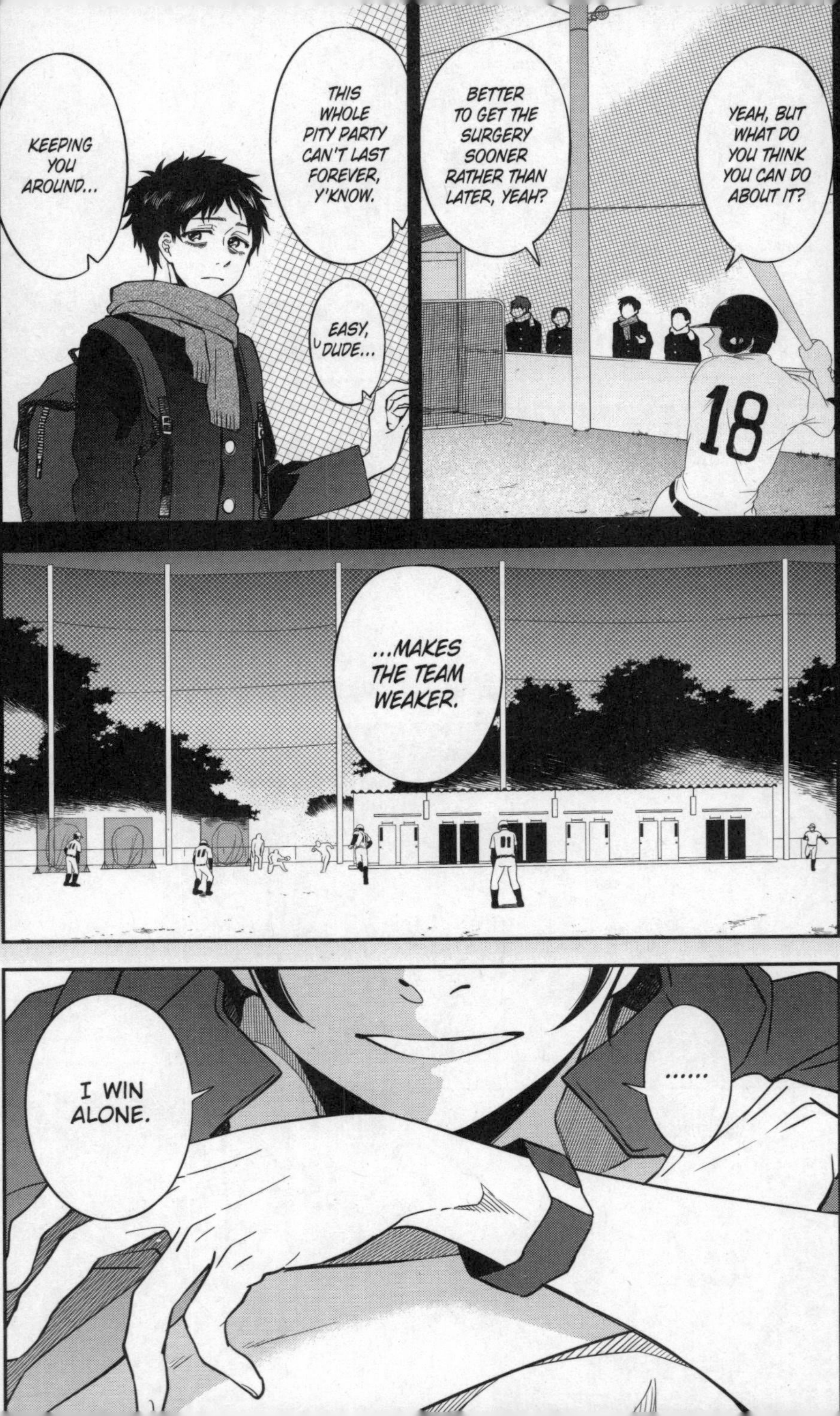
YEAH, BUT WHAT DO YOU THINK YOU CAN DO ABOUT IT?
BETTER TO GET THE SURGERY SOONER RATHER THAN LATER, YEAH?
THIS WHOLE PITY PARTY CAN'T LAST FOREVER, Y'KNOW.
EASY, DUDE...
KEEPING YOU AROUND...
18
...MAKES THE TEAM WEAKER.
......
I WIN ALONE.

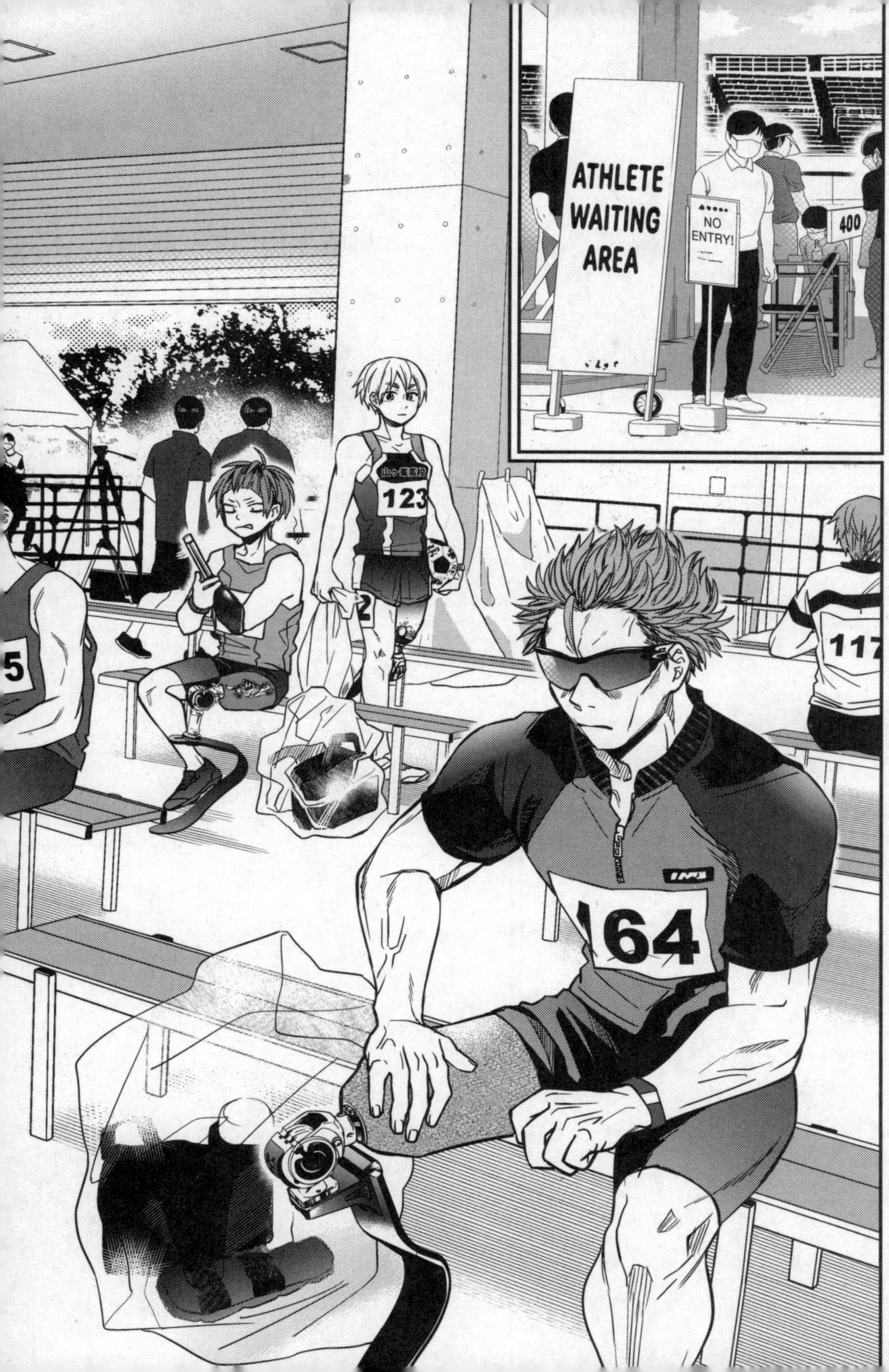
ATHLETE WAITING AREA
NO ENTRY!
400
123
117
164

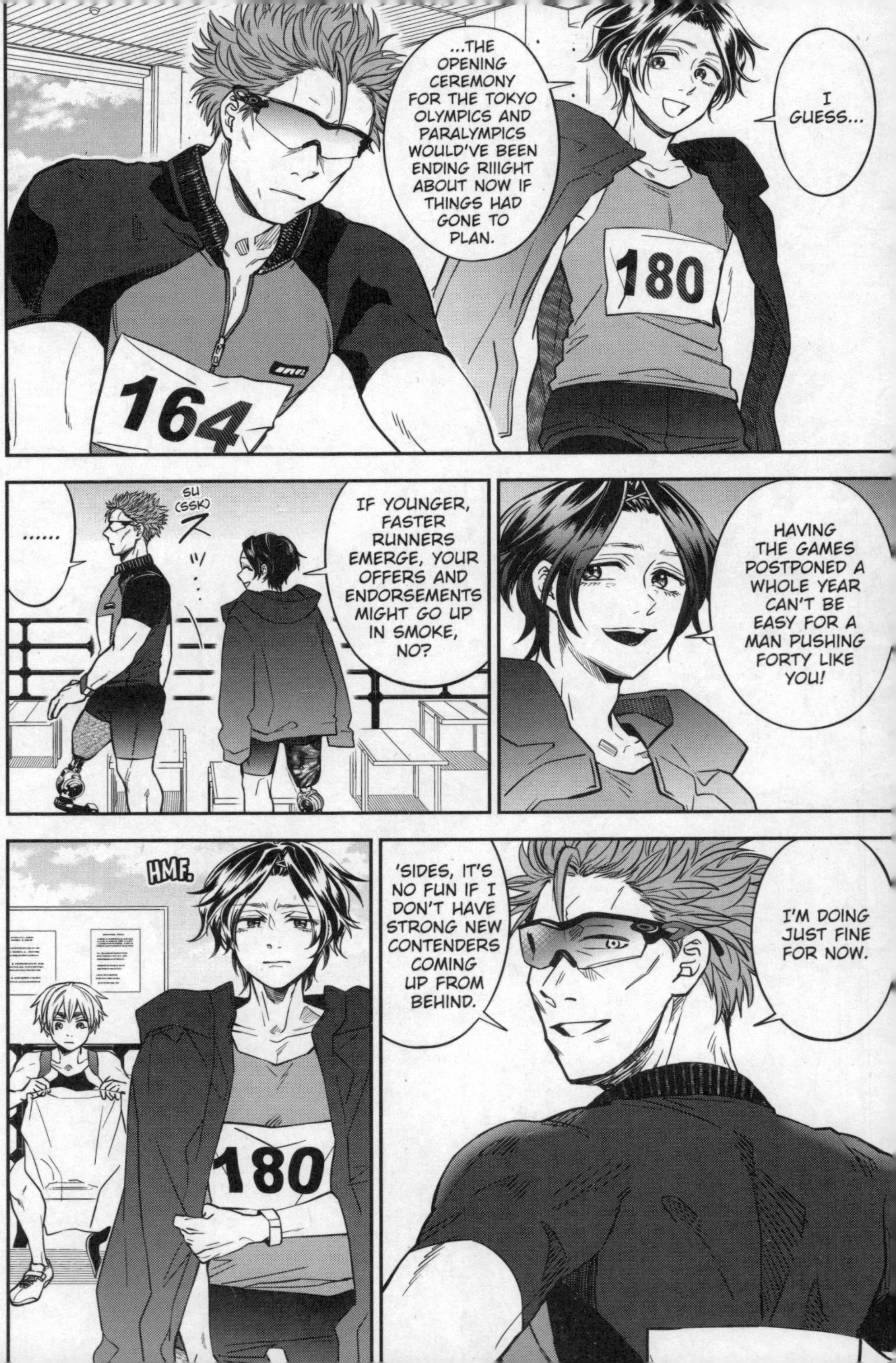
I GUESS...
...THE OPENING CEREMONY FOR THE TOKYO OLYMPICS AND PARALYMPICS WOULD'VE BEEN ENDING RIIIGHT ABOUT NOW IF THINGS HAD GONE TO PLAN.
180
164
HAVING THE GAMES POSTPONED A WHOLE YEAR CAN'T BE EASY FOR A MAN PUSHING FORTY LIKE YOU!
IF YOUNGER, FASTER RUNNERS EMERGE, YOUR OFFERS AND ENDORSEMENTS MIGHT GO UP IN SMOKE, NO?
SU (SSK)
......
I'M DOING JUST FINE FOR NOW.
'SIDES, IT'S NO FUN IF I DON'T HAVE STRONG NEW CONTENDERS COMING UP FROM BEHIND.
HMF.
180

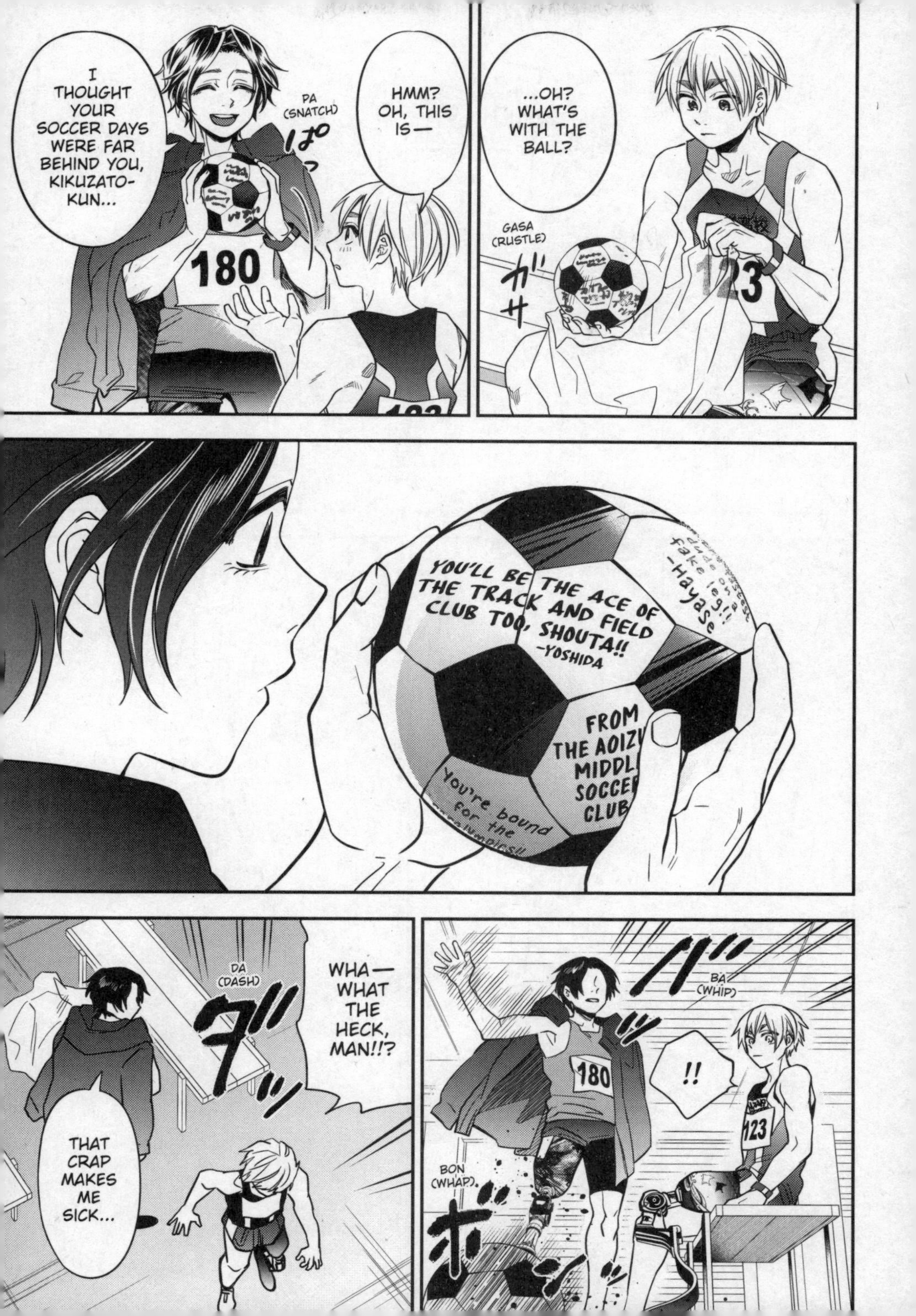
...OH? WHAT'S WITH THE BALL?
GASA (RUSTLE)
ガサ
HMM? OH, THIS IS—
PA (SNATCH)
ぱっ
I THOUGHT YOUR SOCCER DAYS WERE FAR BEHIND YOU, KIKUZATO-KUN...
180
123
fake leg!! —Hayase
YOU'LL BE THE ACE OF THE TRACK AND FIELD CLUB TOO, SHOUTA!! -YOSHIDA
FROM THE AOIZU MIDDL SOCCE CLUB
You're bound for the
BA (WHIP)
バッ
!!
BON (WHAP)
ボッ
WHA— WHAT THE HECK, MAN!!?
DA (DASH)
ダッ
THAT CRAP MAKES ME SICK...

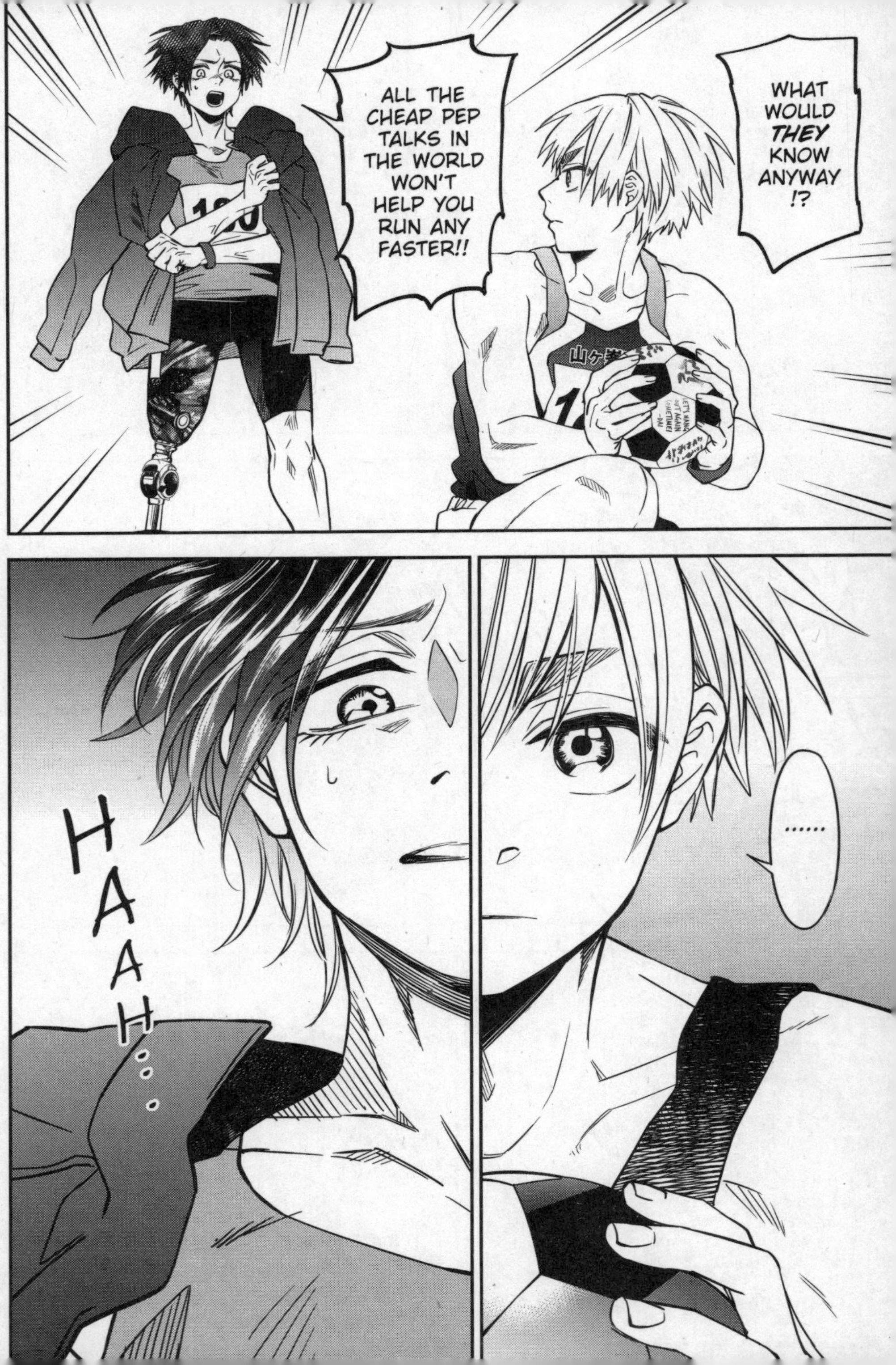
WHAT WOULD THEY KNOW ANYWAY!?
ALL THE CHEAP PEP TALKS IN THE WORLD WON'T HELP YOU RUN ANY FASTER!!
......
HAAAH...

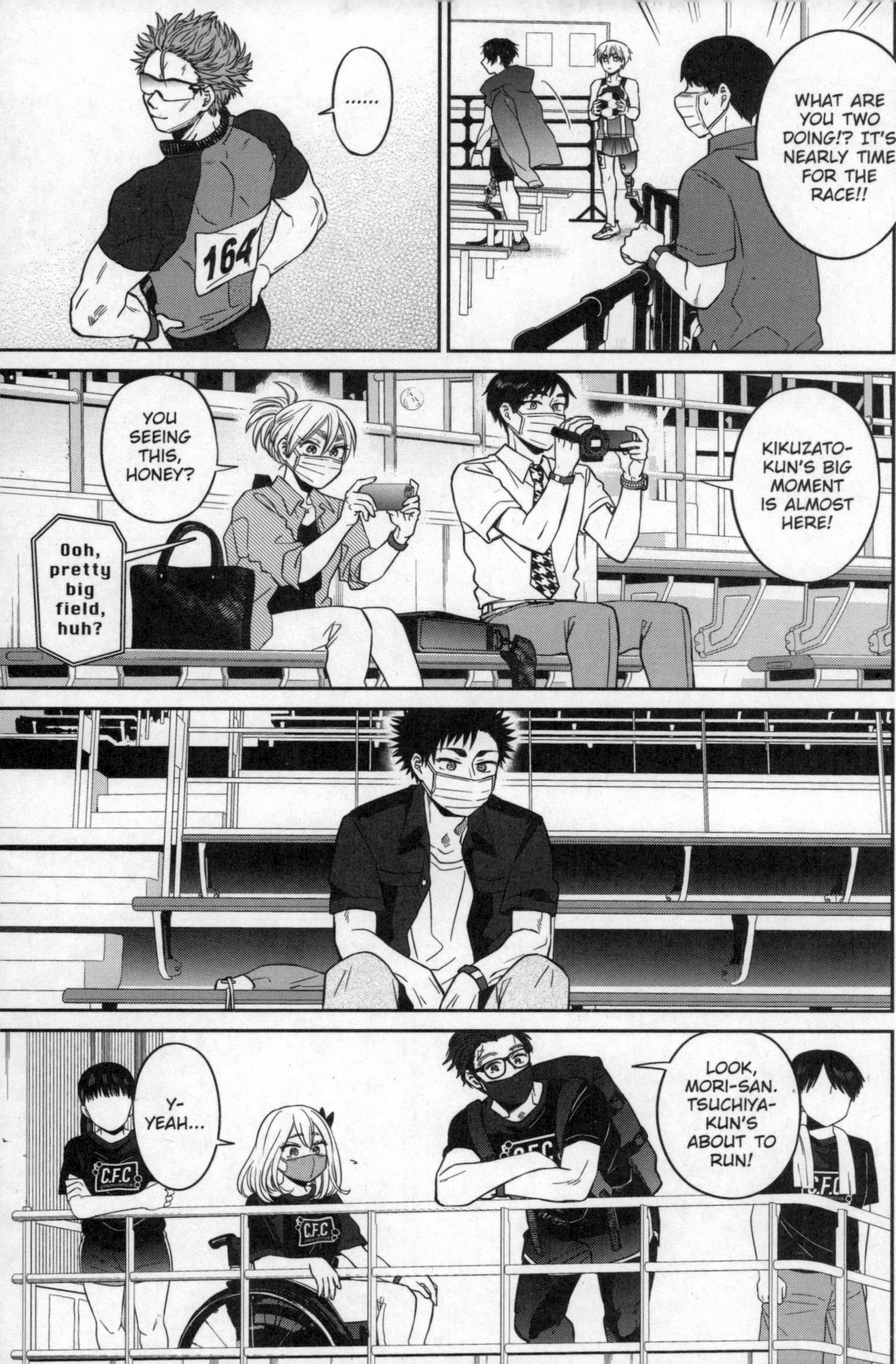
WHAT ARE YOU TWO DOING!? IT'S NEARLY TIME FOR THE RACE!!
......
164
KIKUZATO-KUN'S BIG MOMENT IS ALMOST HERE!
YOU SEEING THIS, HONEY?
Ooh, pretty big field, huh?
LOOK, MORI-SAN. TSUCHIYA-KUN'S ABOUT TO RUN!
Y-YEAH...
C.F.C.

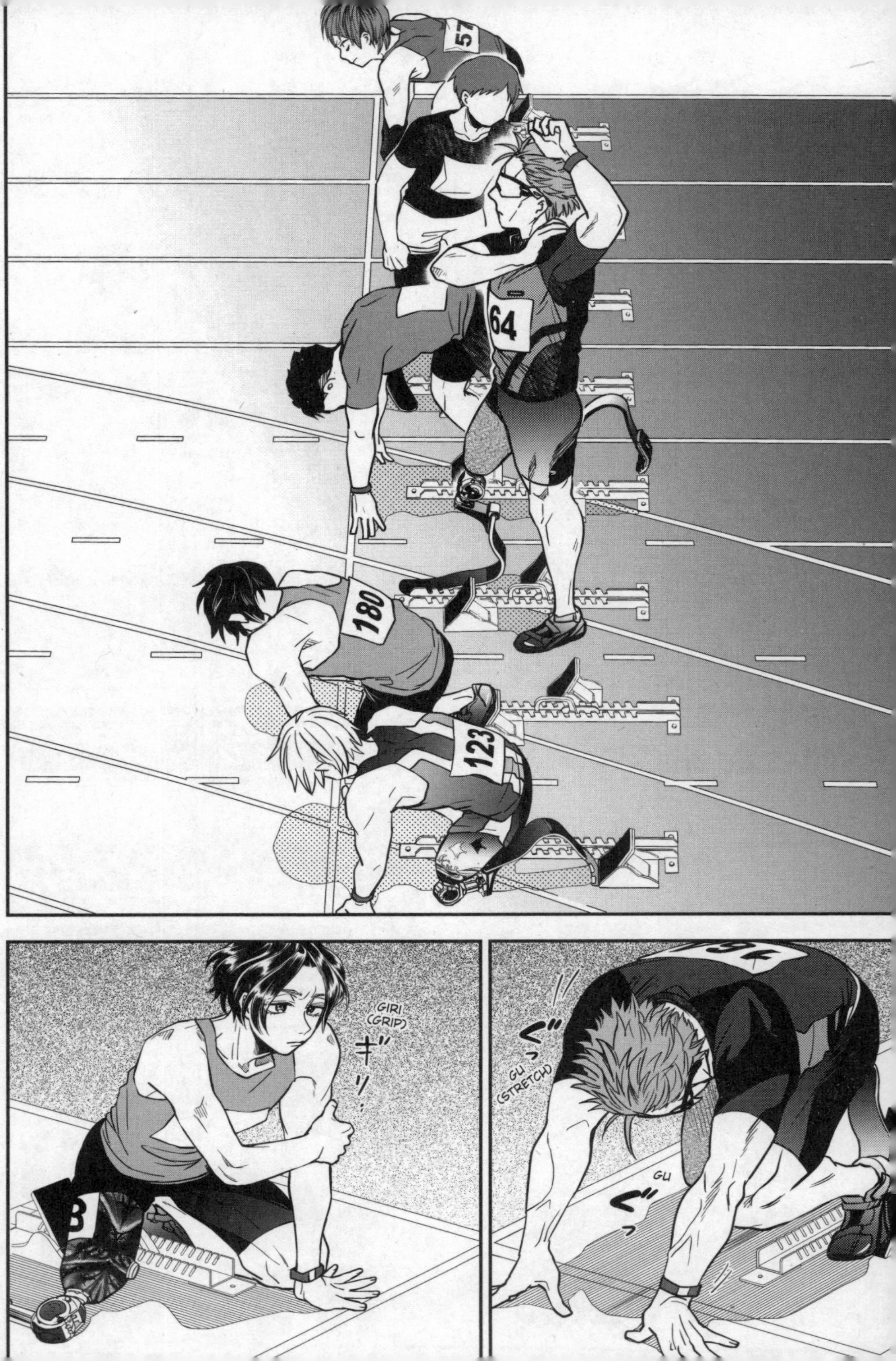

57
64
180
123
ぐっ
GU (STRETCH)
ぐっ
GU
ギリッ
GIRI (GRIP)

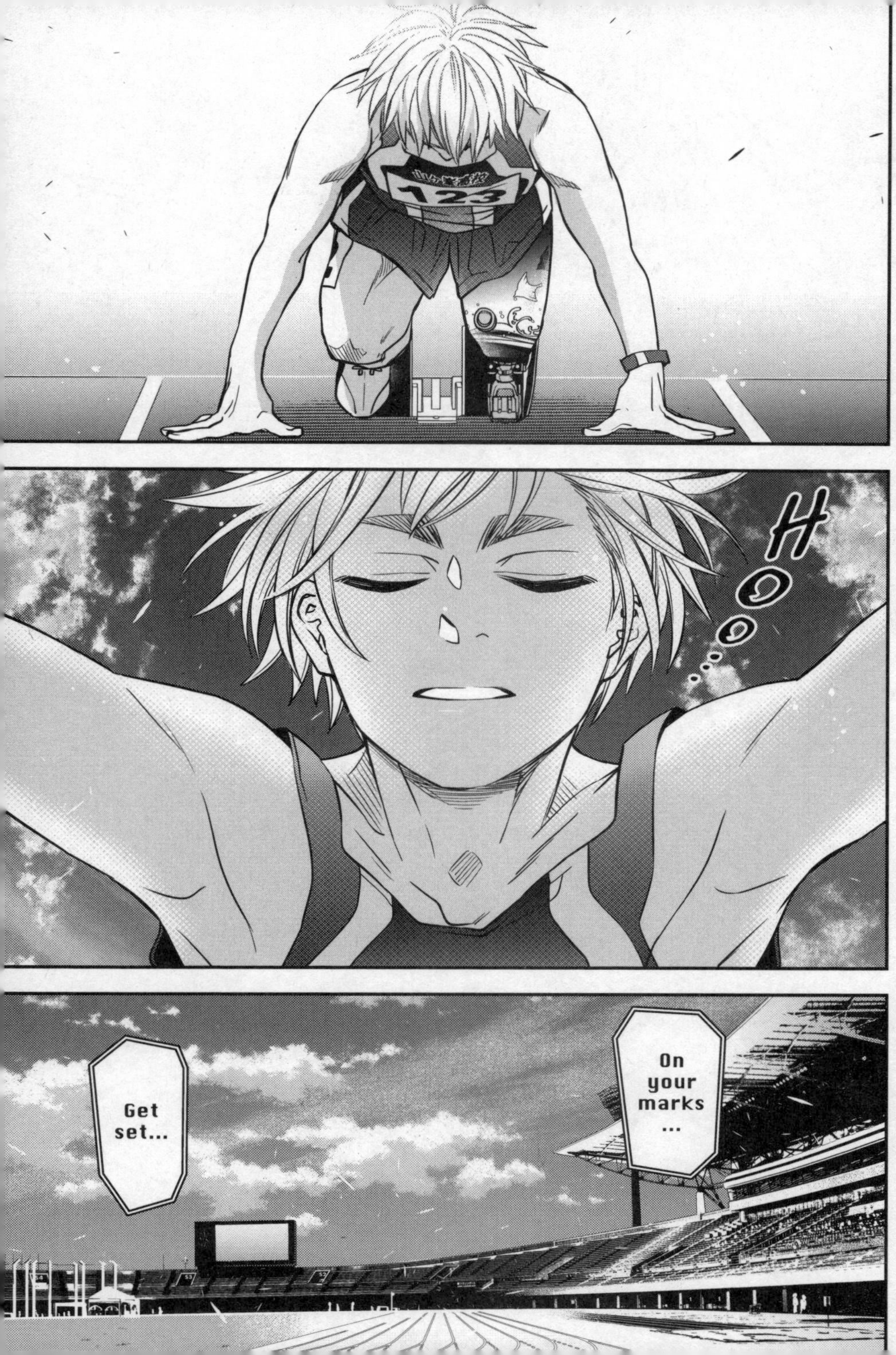
123
Hoo...
On your marks...
Get set...

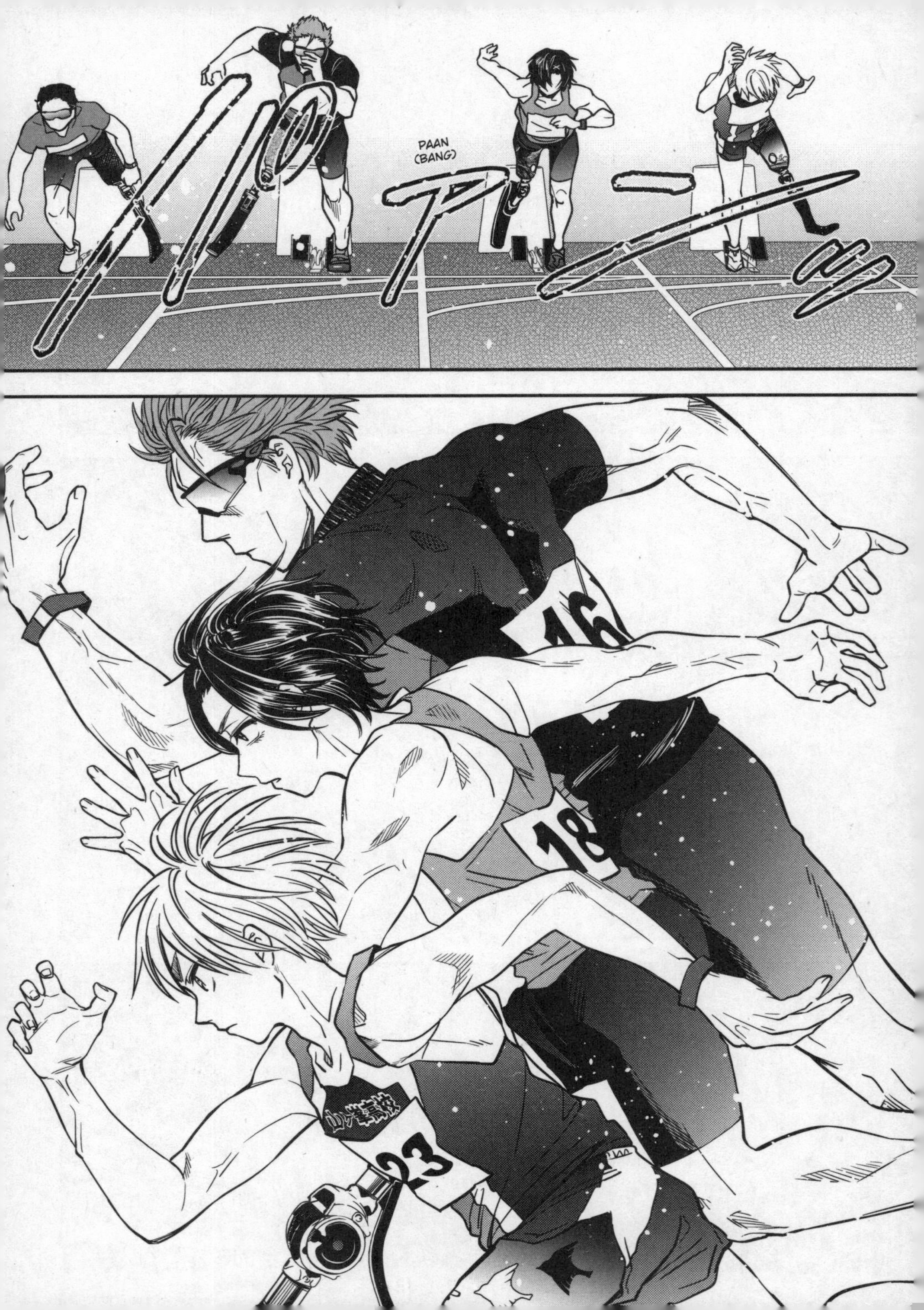
PAAN
(BANG)

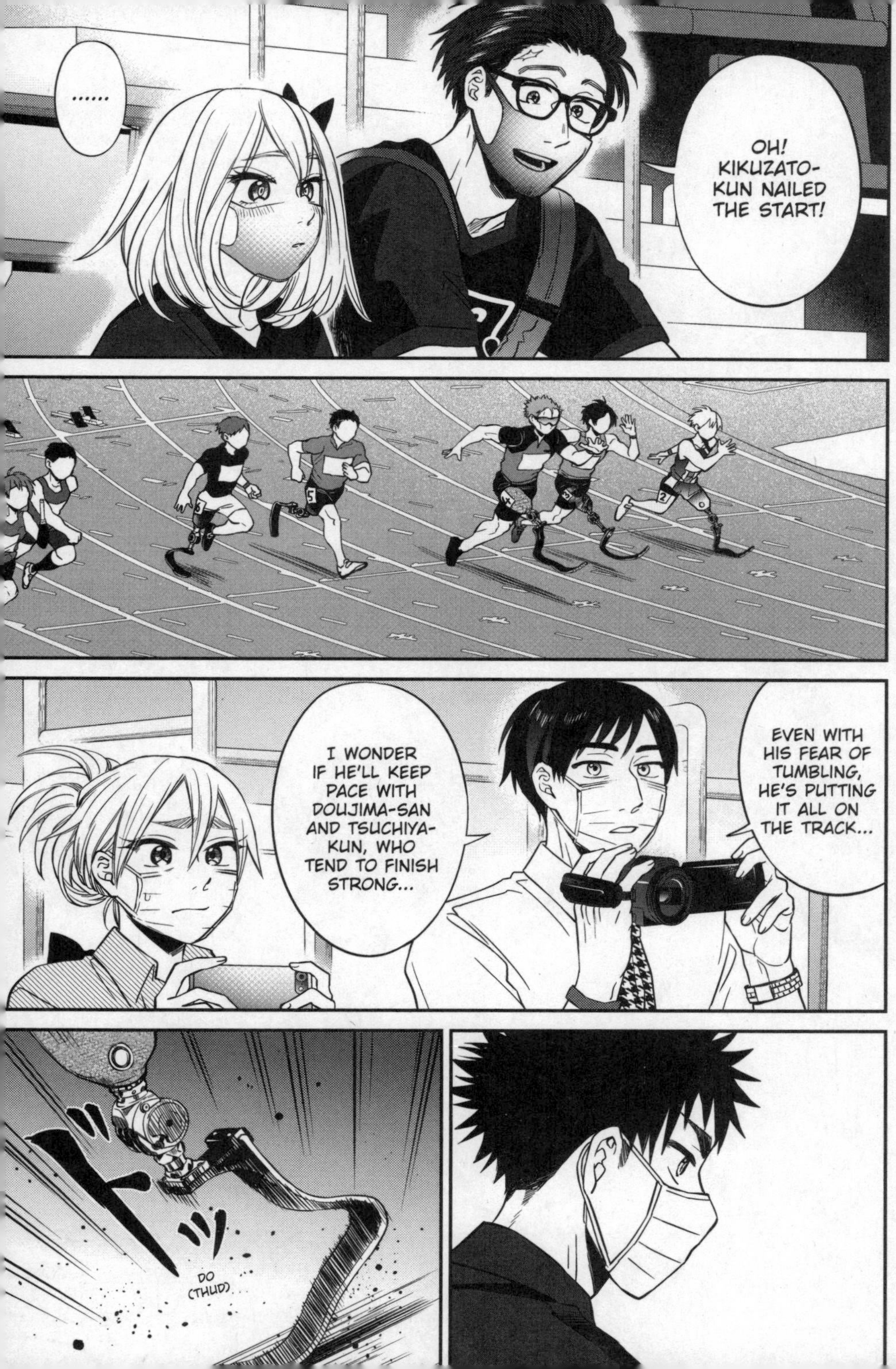
OH! KIKUZATO-KUN NAILED THE START!
......
EVEN WITH HIS FEAR OF TUMBLING, HE'S PUTTING IT ALL ON THE TRACK...
I WONDER IF HE'LL KEEP PACE WITH DOUJIMA-SAN AND TSUCHIYA-KUN, WHO TEND TO FINISH STRONG...
DO (THUD)

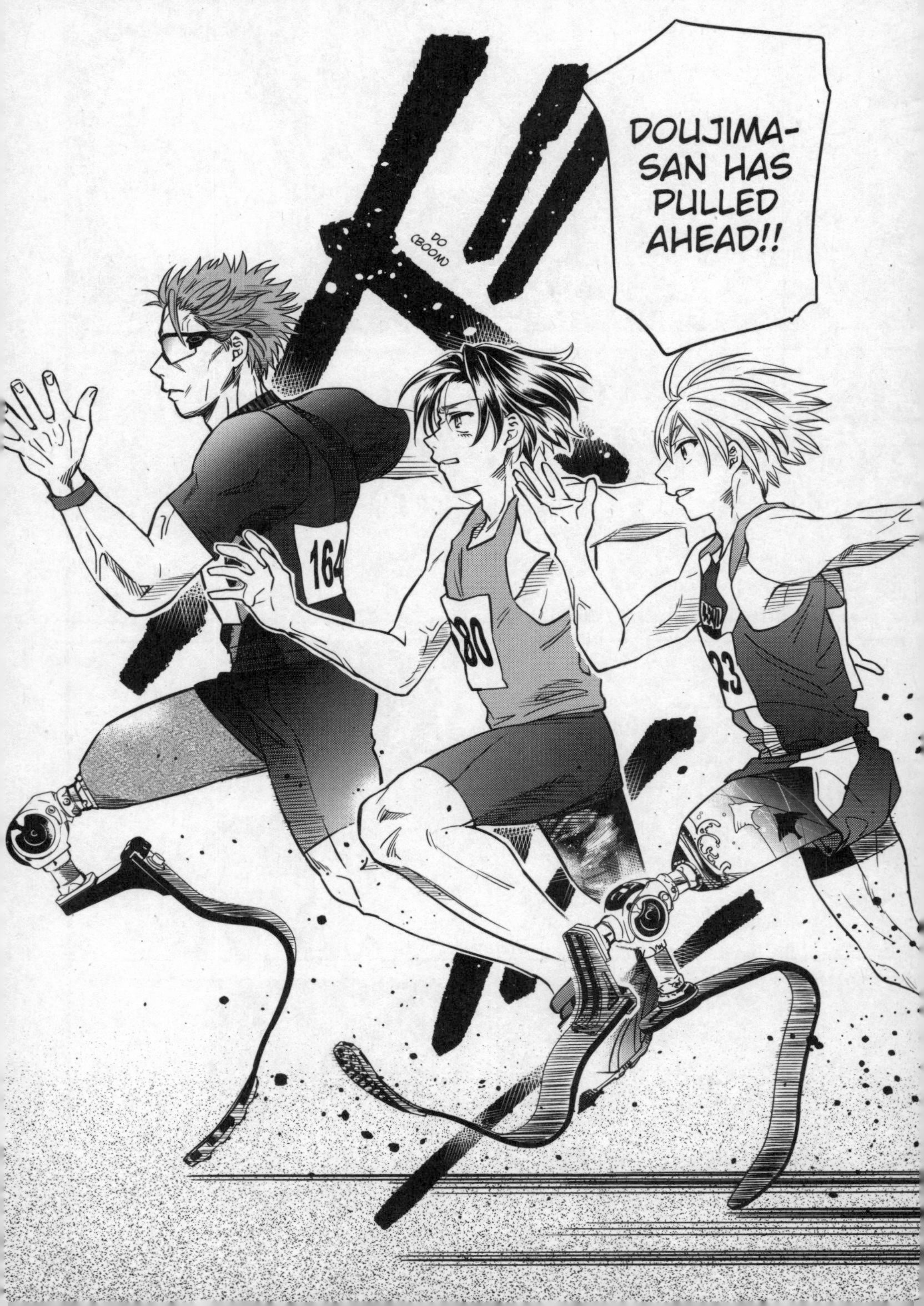
DOUJIMA-SAN HAS PULLED AHEAD!!
DO (BOOM)
164
180
123

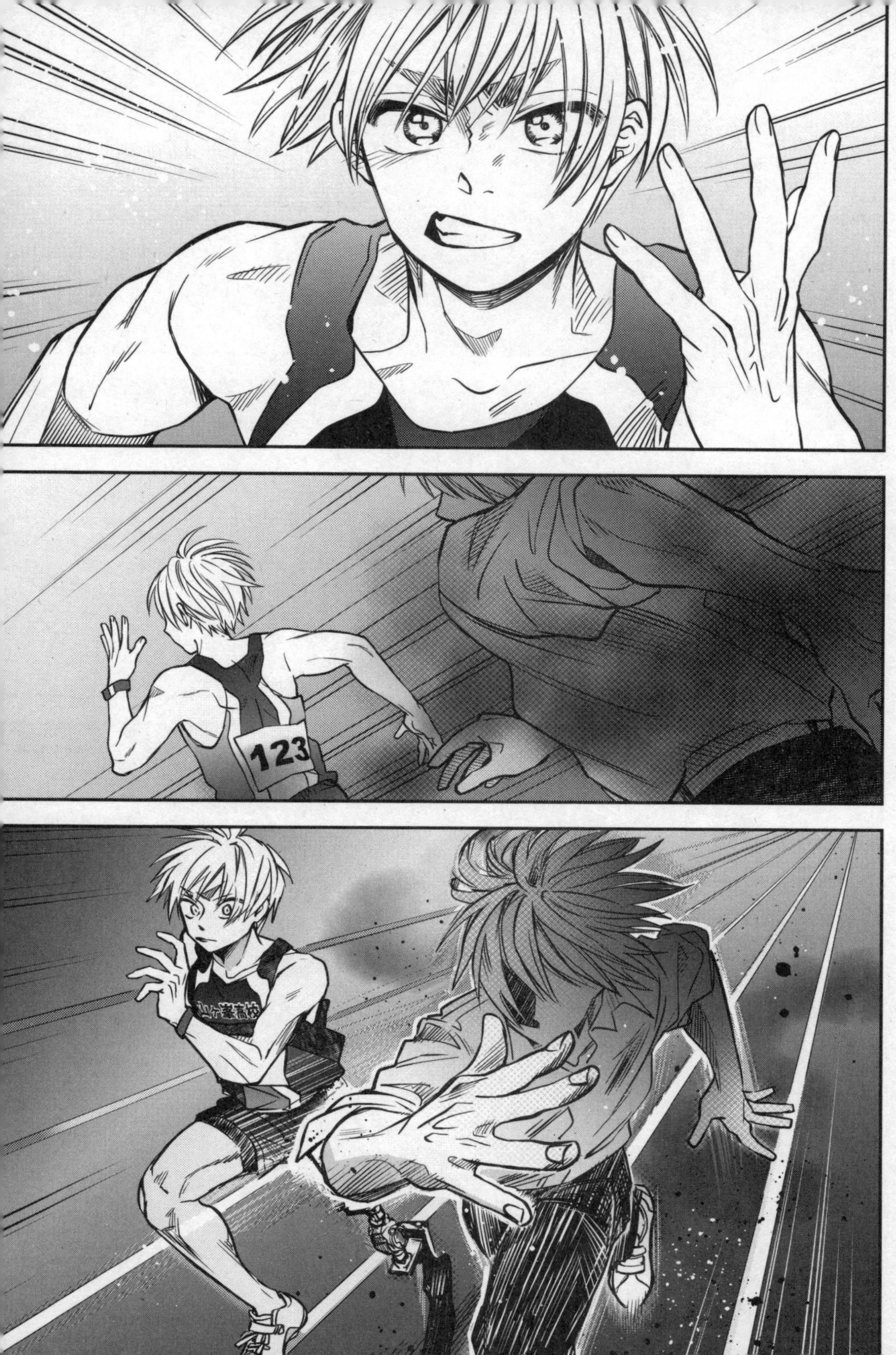
123
ヶ峯高校

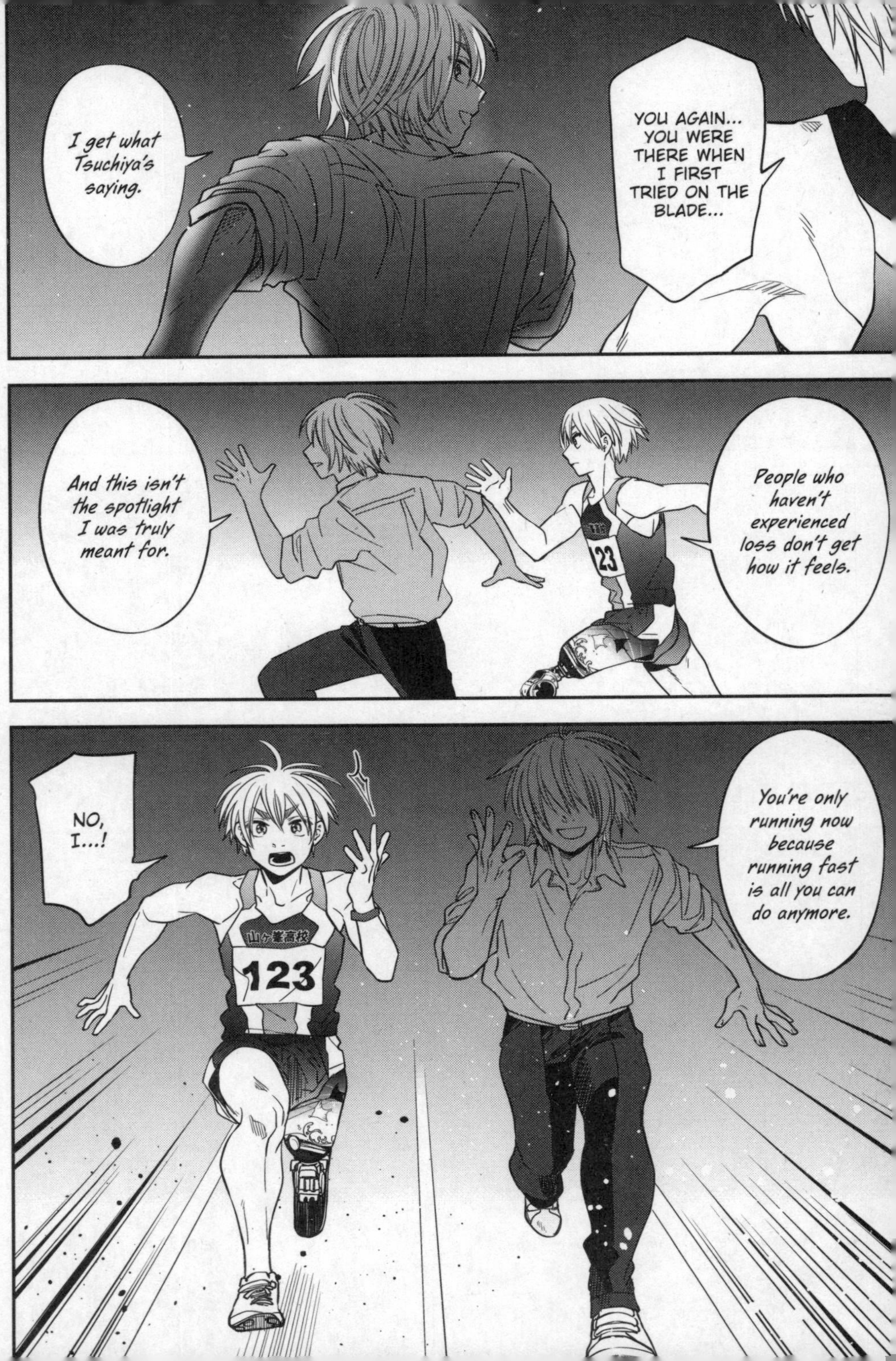
YOU AGAIN... YOU WERE THERE WHEN I FIRST TRIED ON THE BLADE...
I get what Tsuchiya's saying.
People who haven't experienced loss don't get how it feels.
And this isn't the spotlight I was truly meant for.
You're only running now because running fast is all you can do anymore.
NO, I...!
山ヶ峯高校
123

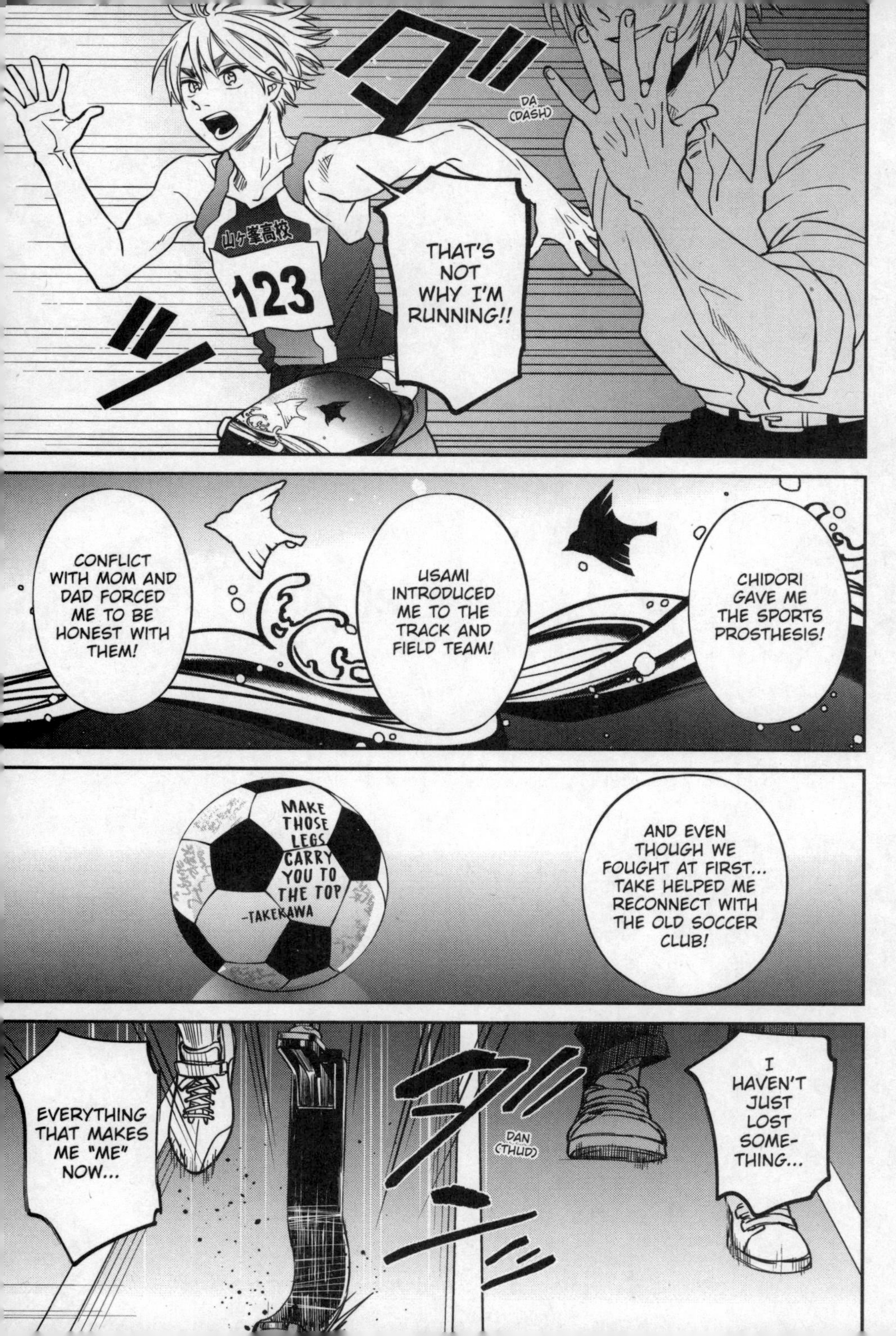
DA (DASH)
山ケ峯高校
123
THAT'S NOT WHY I'M RUNNING!!
CHIDORI GAVE ME THE SPORTS PROSTHESIS!
USAMI INTRODUCED ME TO THE TRACK AND FIELD TEAM!
CONFLICT WITH MOM AND DAD FORCED ME TO BE HONEST WITH THEM!
AND EVEN THOUGH WE FOUGHT AT FIRST... TAKE HELPED ME RECONNECT WITH THE OLD SOCCER CLUB!
MAKE THOSE LEGS CARRY YOU TO THE TOP
-TAKEKAWA
I HAVEN'T JUST LOST SOME-THING...
DAN (THUD)
EVERYTHING THAT MAKES ME "ME" NOW...

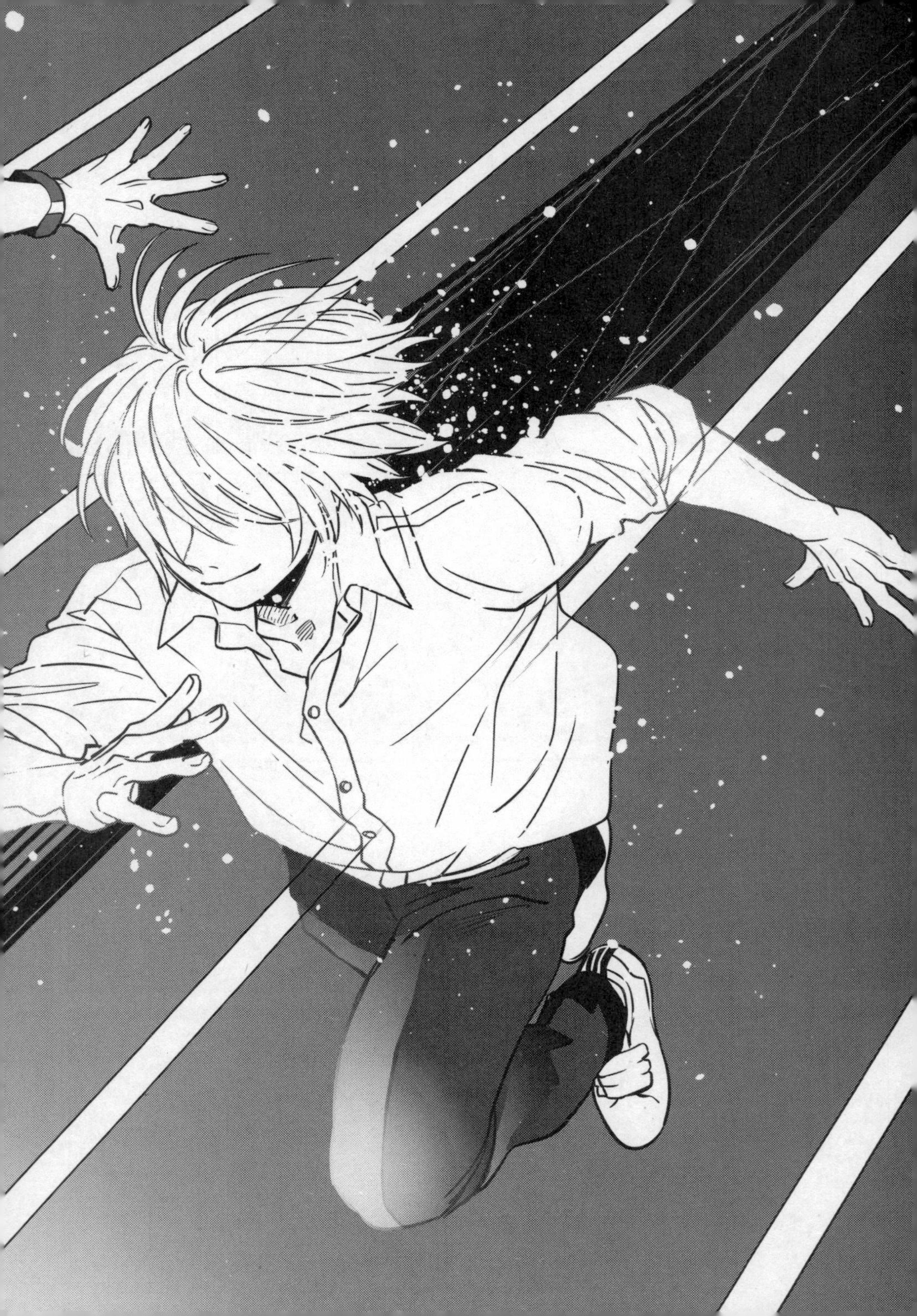

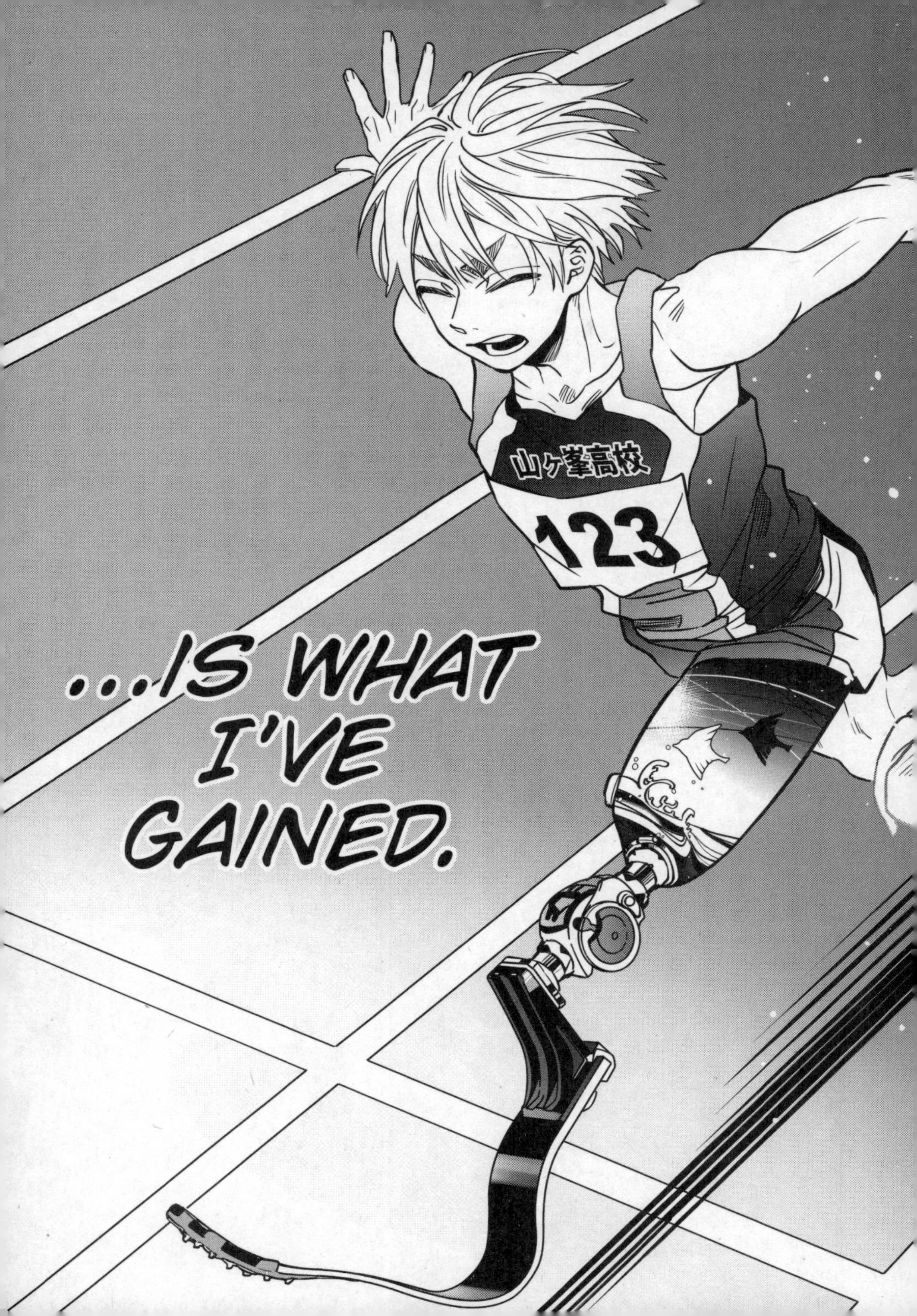
山ヶ峯高校
123
...IS WHAT I'VE GAINED.

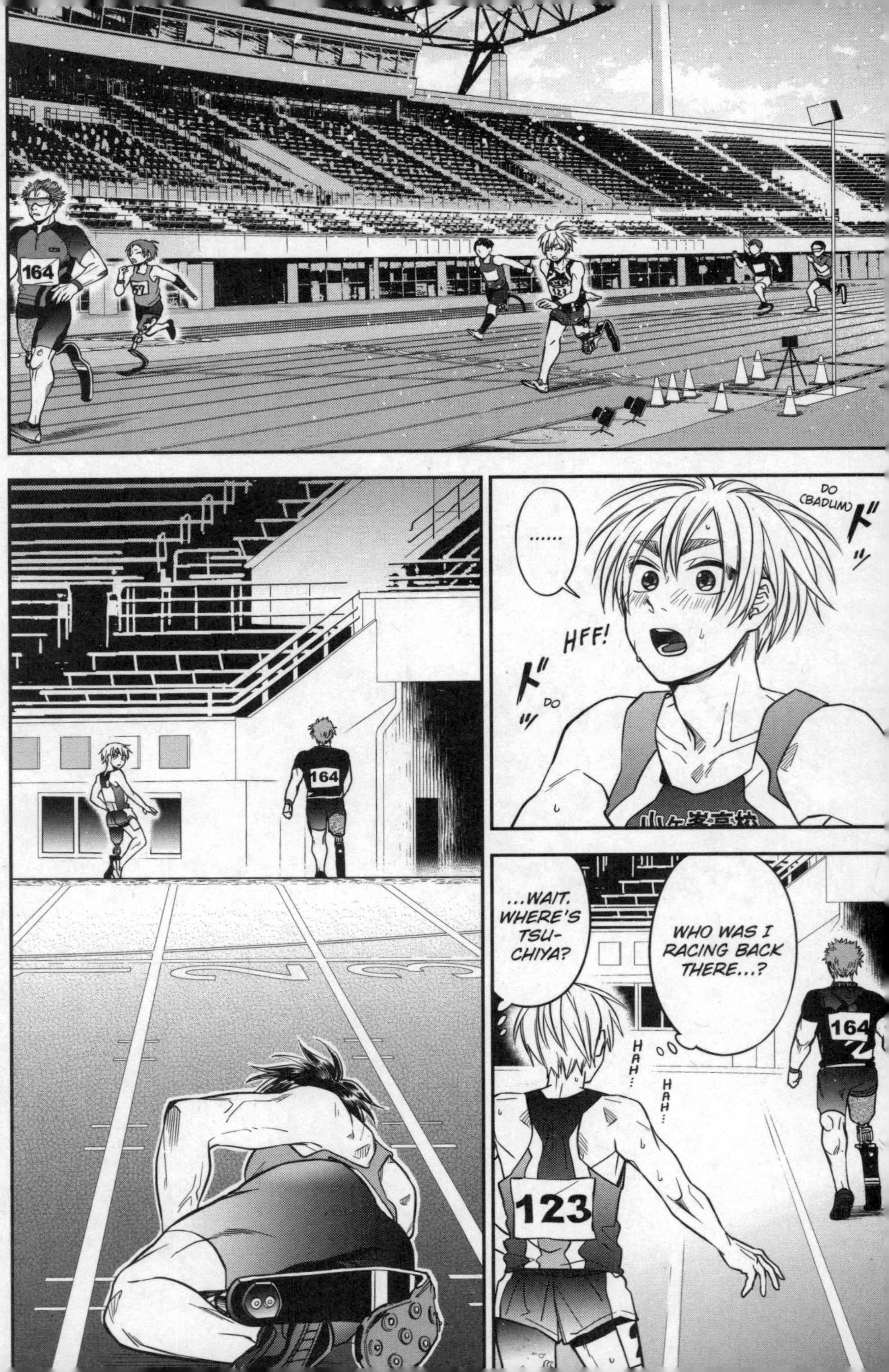

DO (BADUM)
......
HFF!
DO
WHO WAS I RACING BACK THERE...?
...WAIT. WHERE'S TSU-CHIYA?
HAH...
HAH...

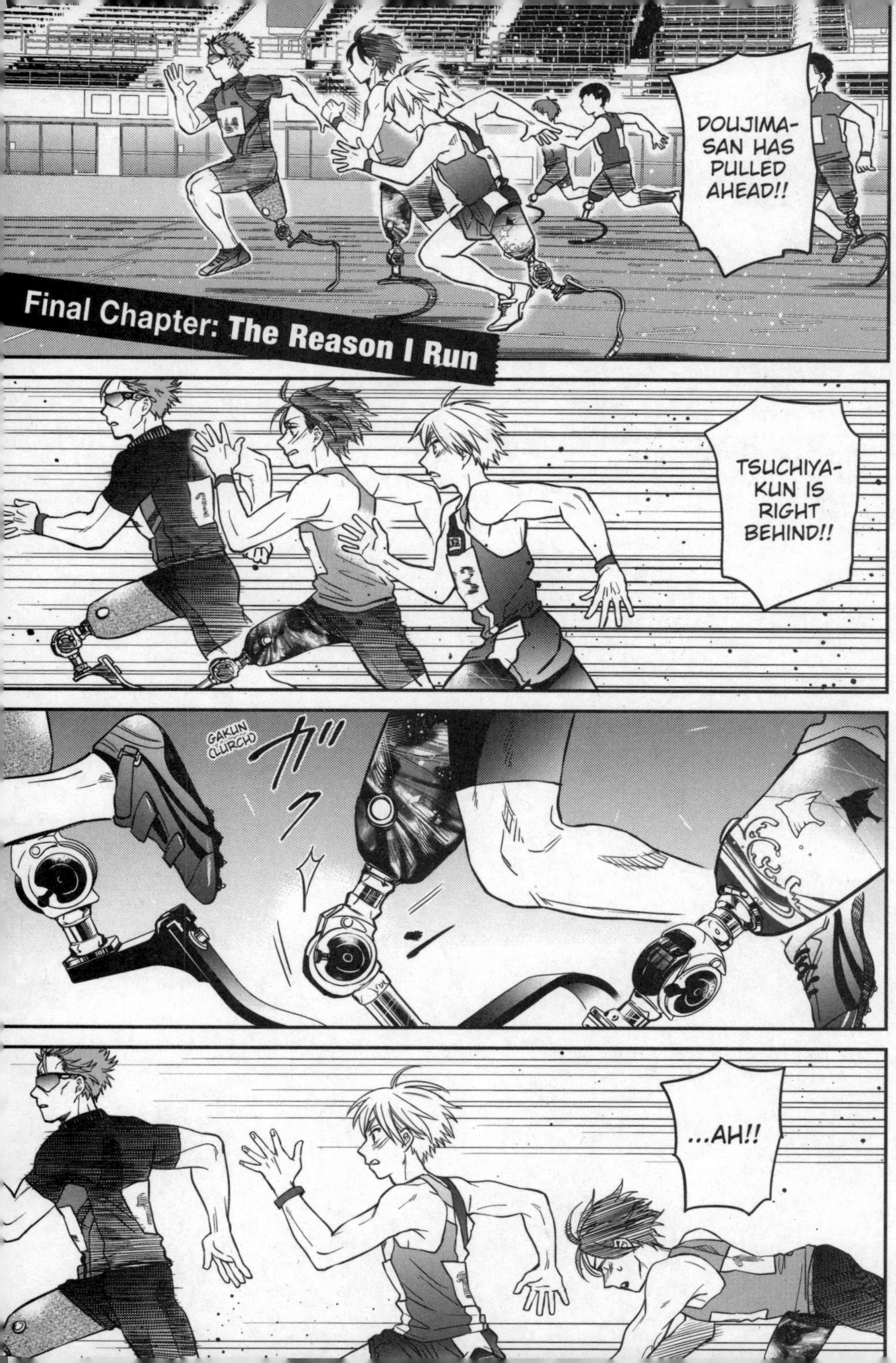
DOUJIMA-SAN HAS PULLED AHEAD!!
Final Chapter: The Reason I Run
TSUCHIYA-KUN IS RIGHT BEHIND!!
GAKUN (LURCH)
...AH!!

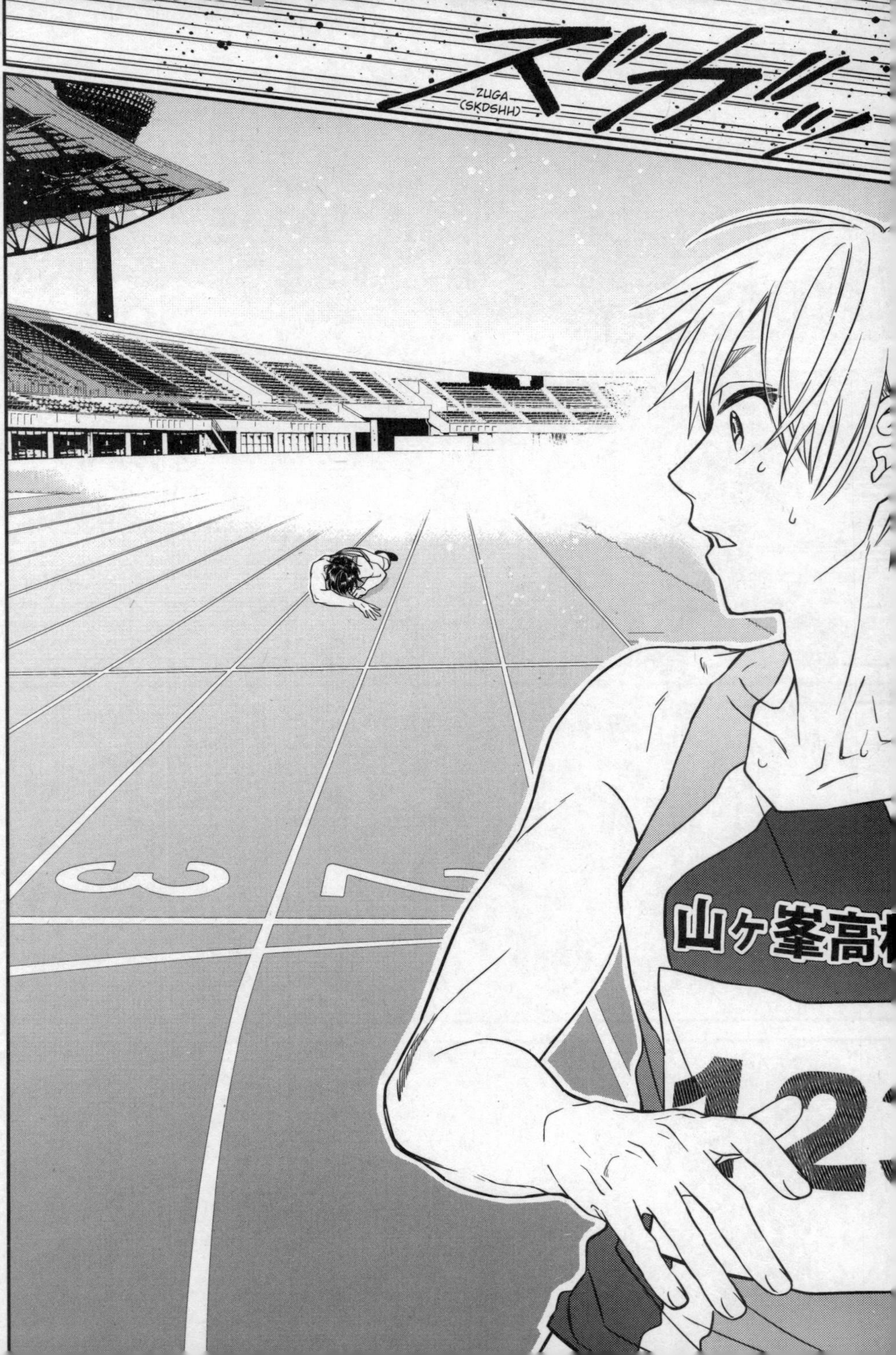
ズガッ
ZUGA
(SKDSHH)

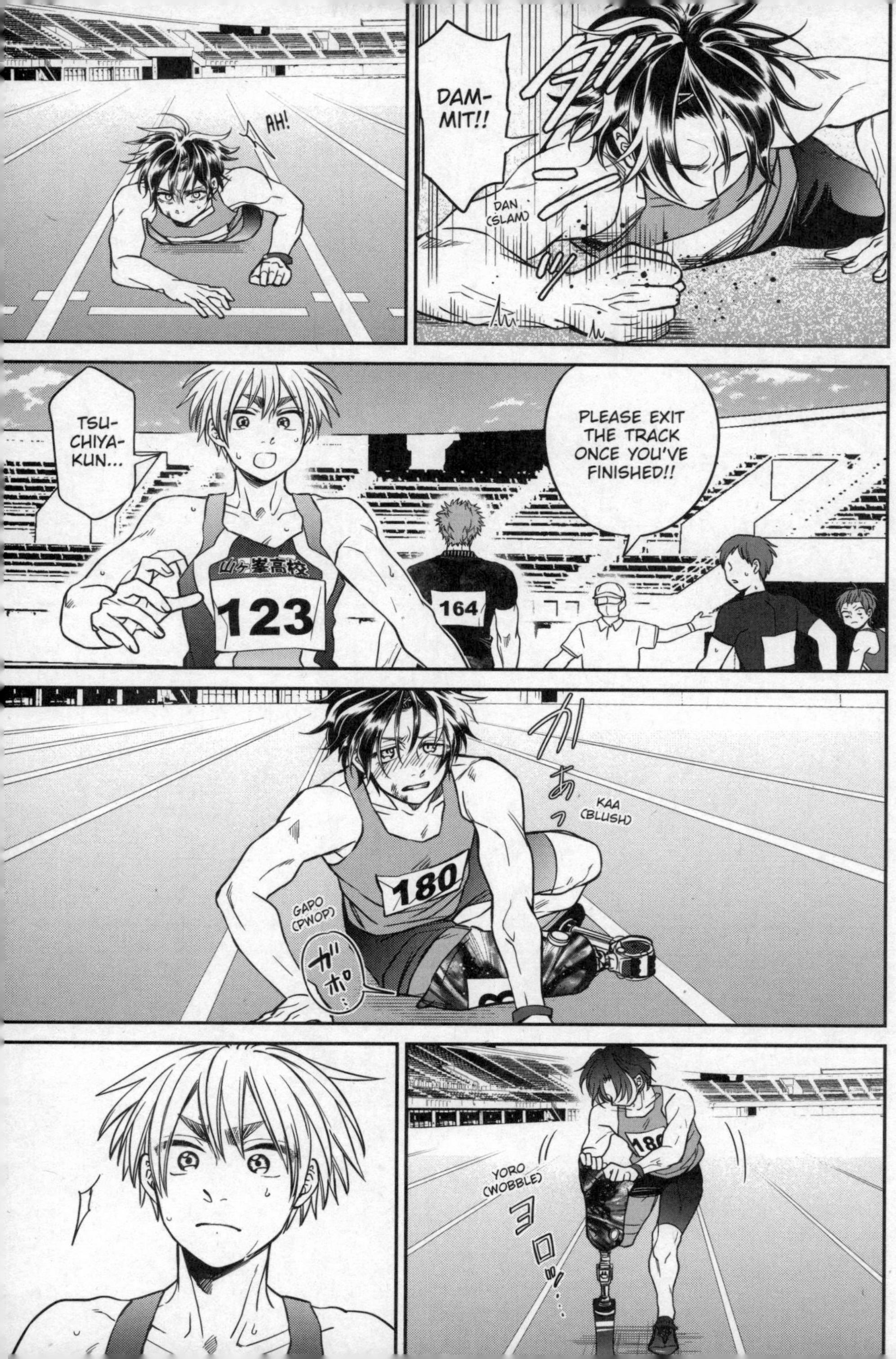
DAM-MIT!!
DAN (SLAM)
AH!
PLEASE EXIT THE TRACK ONCE YOU'VE FINISHED!!
TSU-CHIYA-KUN...
山ヶ峯高校
123
164
かぁっ
KAA (BLUSH)
180
GAPO (PWOP)
ガポ…
YORO (WOBBLE)
ヨロ…

ARE YOU BOWING OUT!?

TSU-CHIYA-KUN!!

FUI
(FWIP)

180

......

"YOU MAY HAVE FALLEN, BUT THE GOAL'S STILL WITHIN REACH!" ISN'T THAT WHAT YOU SAID!?

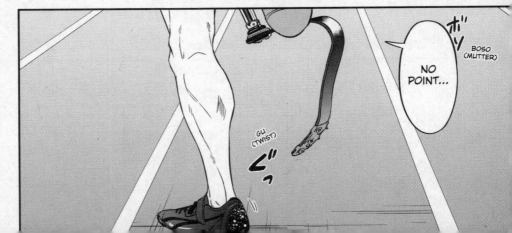

NO POINT...

BOSO
(MUTTER)

GU
(TWIST)

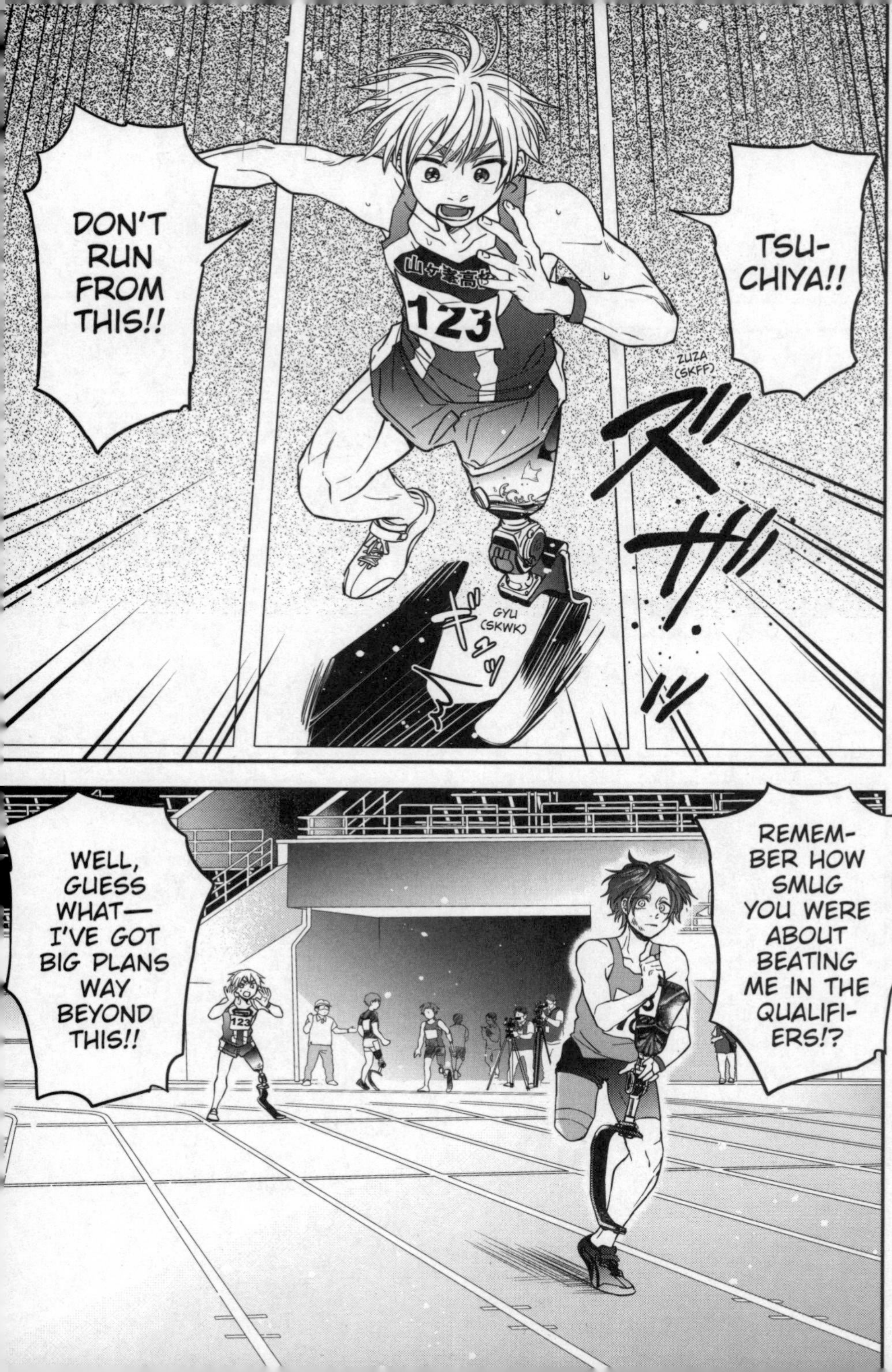
TSU-CHIYA!!
DON'T RUN FROM THIS!!
ZUZA (SKFF)
GYU (SKWK)
123
REMEMBER HOW SMUG YOU WERE ABOUT BEATING ME IN THE QUALIFIERS!?
WELL, GUESS WHAT—I'VE GOT BIG PLANS WAY BEYOND THIS!!

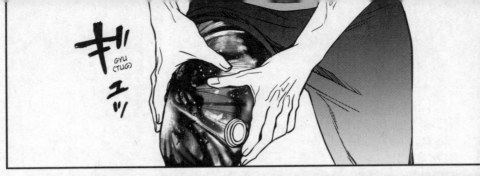

ギュ
GYU
(TUG)

ユッ

ダ
DA
(DASH)

ッ

ME?
SMUG OVER
BEATING
THE LIKES
OF YOU!?
AS IF!!

123

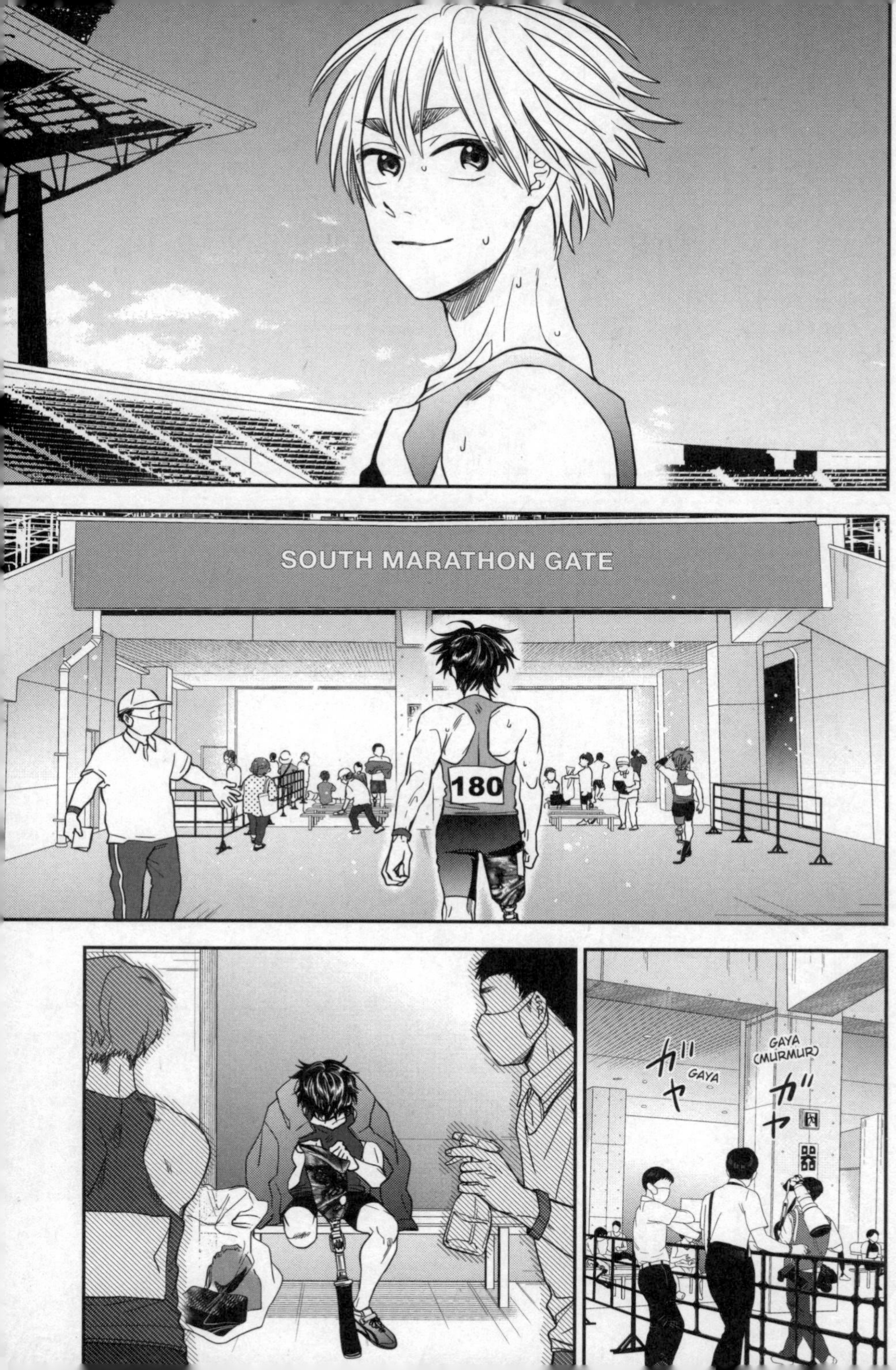
SOUTH MARATHON GATE
180
ガヤ
GAYA (MURMUR)
ガヤ
GAYA

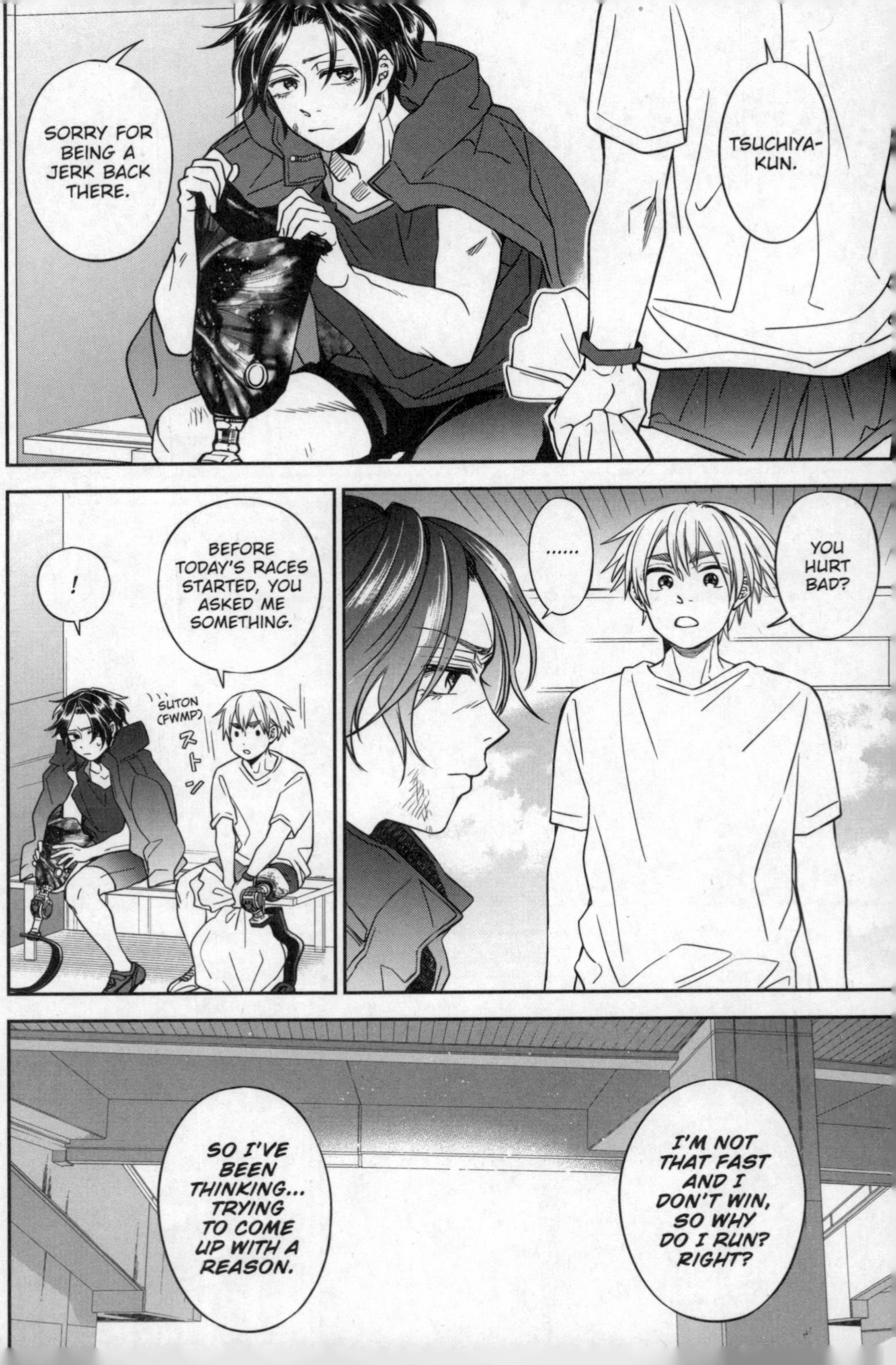
TSUCHIYA-KUN.
SORRY FOR BEING A JERK BACK THERE.
YOU HURT BAD?
......
BEFORE TODAY'S RACES STARTED, YOU ASKED ME SOMETHING.
!
SUTON (FWMP)
ストン
I'M NOT THAT FAST AND I DON'T WIN, SO WHY DO I RUN? RIGHT?
SO I'VE BEEN THINKING... TRYING TO COME UP WITH A REASON.

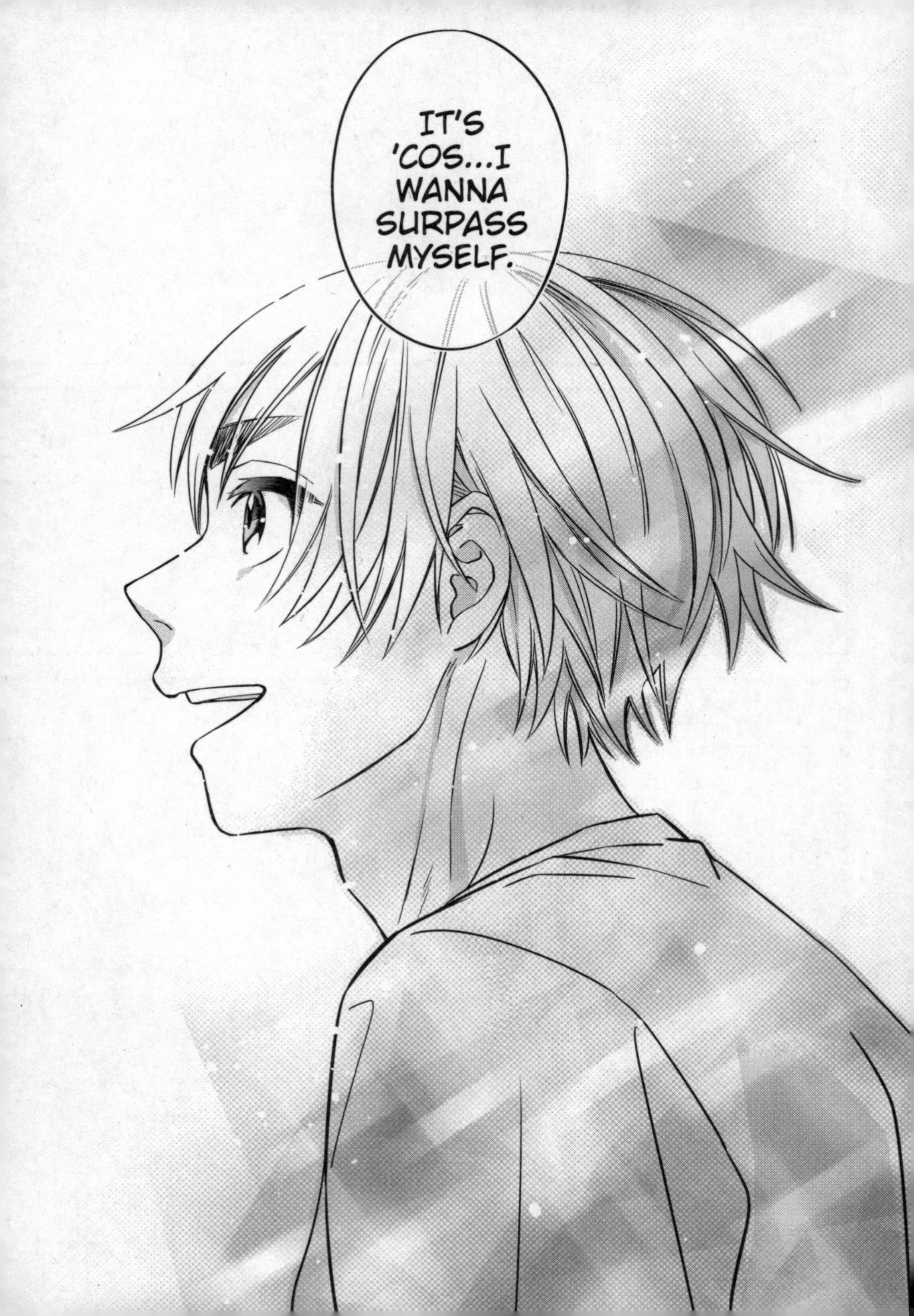
IT'S 'COS...I WANNA SURPASS MYSELF.

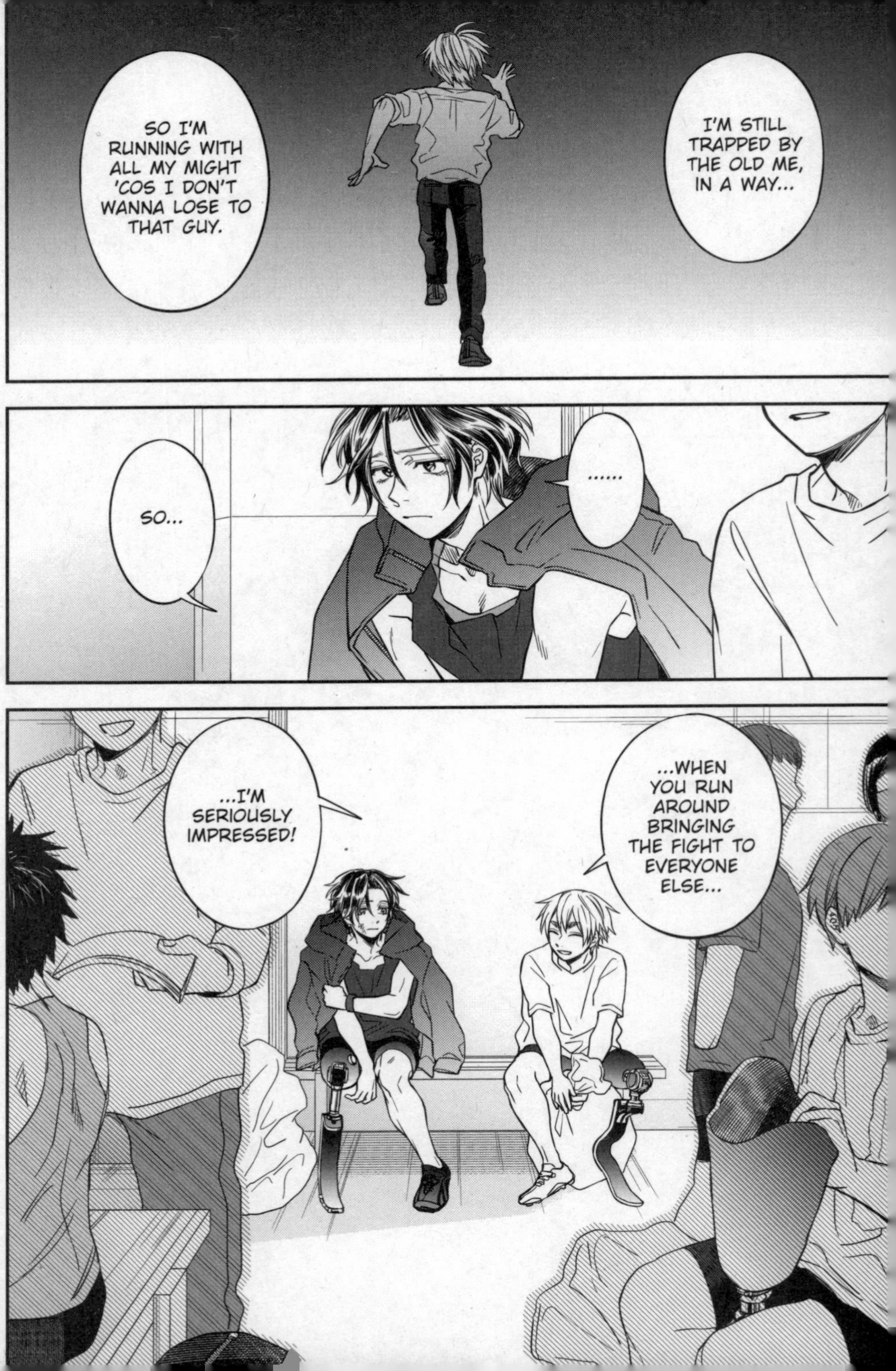
I'M STILL TRAPPED BY THE OLD ME, IN A WAY...
SO I'M RUNNING WITH ALL MY MIGHT 'COS I DON'T WANNA LOSE TO THAT GUY.
......
SO...
...WHEN YOU RUN AROUND BRINGING THE FIGHT TO EVERYONE ELSE...
...I'M SERIOUSLY IMPRESSED!

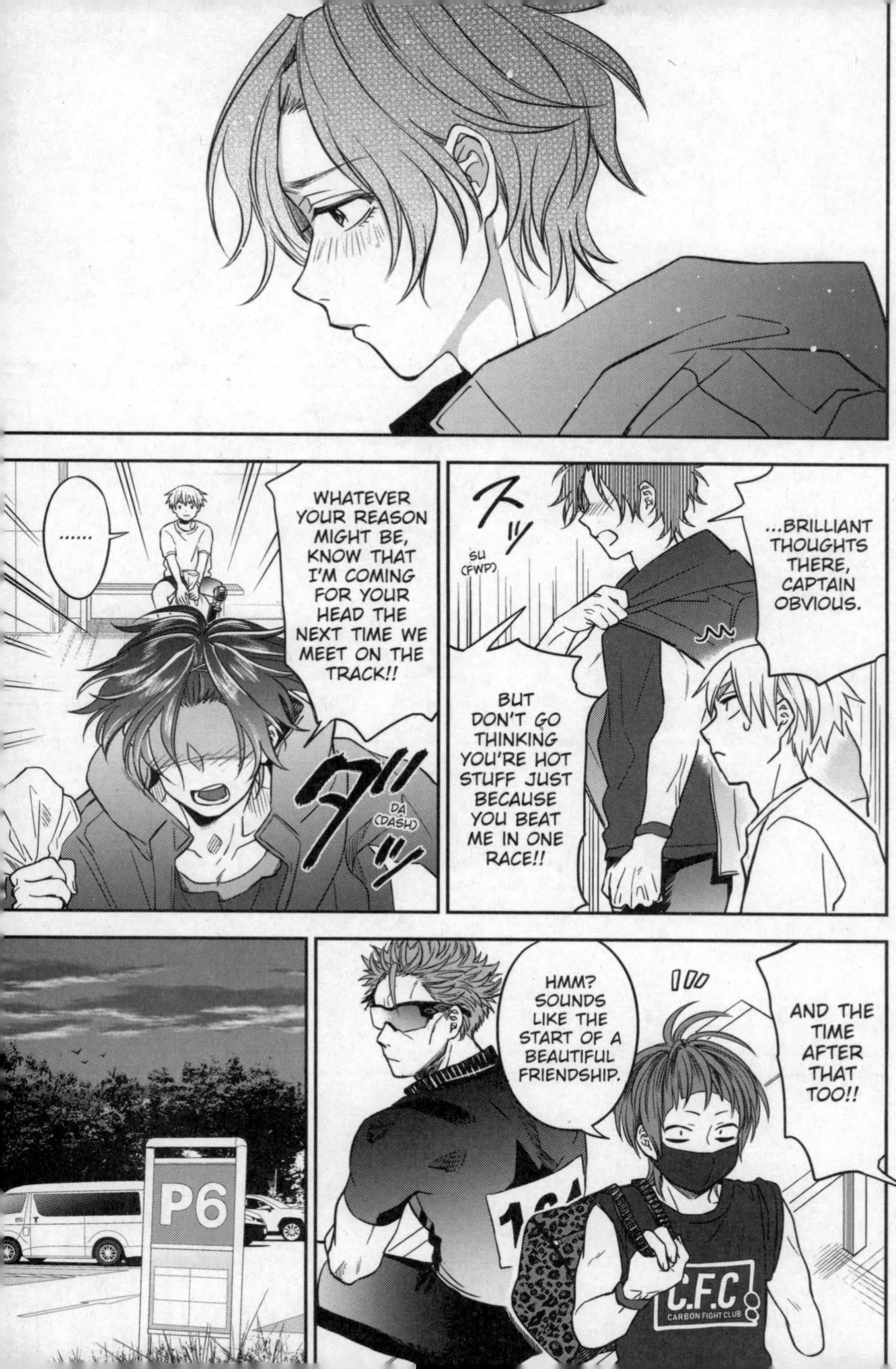
...BRILLIANT THOUGHTS THERE, CAPTAIN OBVIOUS.
スッ
SU (FWP)
BUT DON'T GO THINKING YOU'RE HOT STUFF JUST BECAUSE YOU BEAT ME IN ONE RACE!!
WHATEVER YOUR REASON MIGHT BE, KNOW THAT I'M COMING FOR YOUR HEAD THE NEXT TIME WE MEET ON THE TRACK!!
......
ダッ
DA (DASH)
AND THE TIME AFTER THAT TOO!!
HMM? SOUNDS LIKE THE START OF A BEAUTIFUL FRIENDSHIP.
C.F.C
CARBON FIGHT CLUB
P6

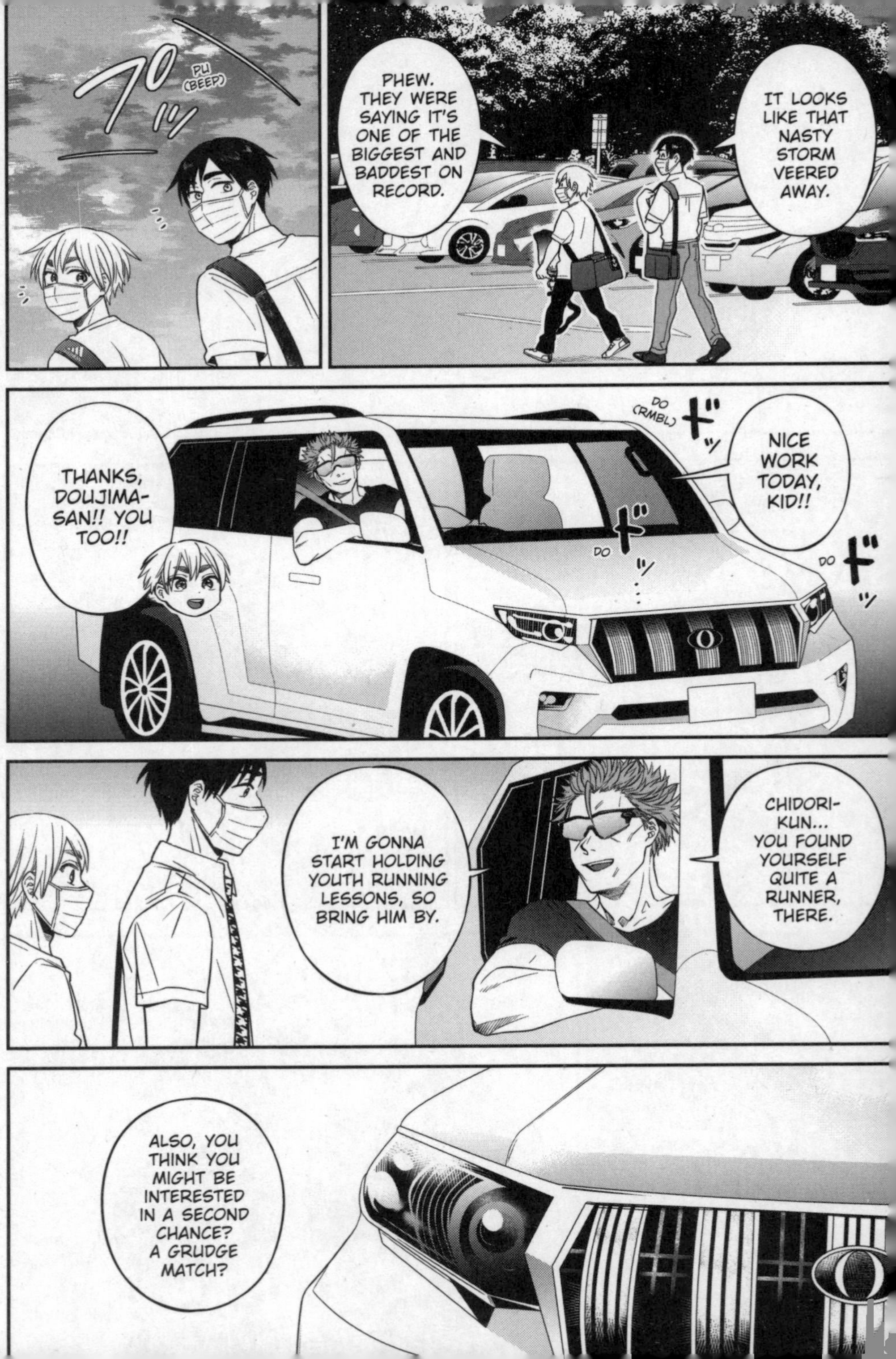
IT LOOKS LIKE THAT NASTY STORM VEERED AWAY.
PHEW. THEY WERE SAYING IT'S ONE OF THE BIGGEST AND BADDEST ON RECORD.
PU (BEEP)
DO (RMBL)
NICE WORK TODAY, KID!!
DO
DO
THANKS, DOUJIMA-SAN!! YOU TOO!!
CHIDORI-KUN... YOU FOUND YOURSELF QUITE A RUNNER, THERE.
I'M GONNA START HOLDING YOUTH RUNNING LESSONS, SO BRING HIM BY.
ALSO, YOU THINK YOU MIGHT BE INTERESTED IN A SECOND CHANCE? A GRUDGE MATCH?

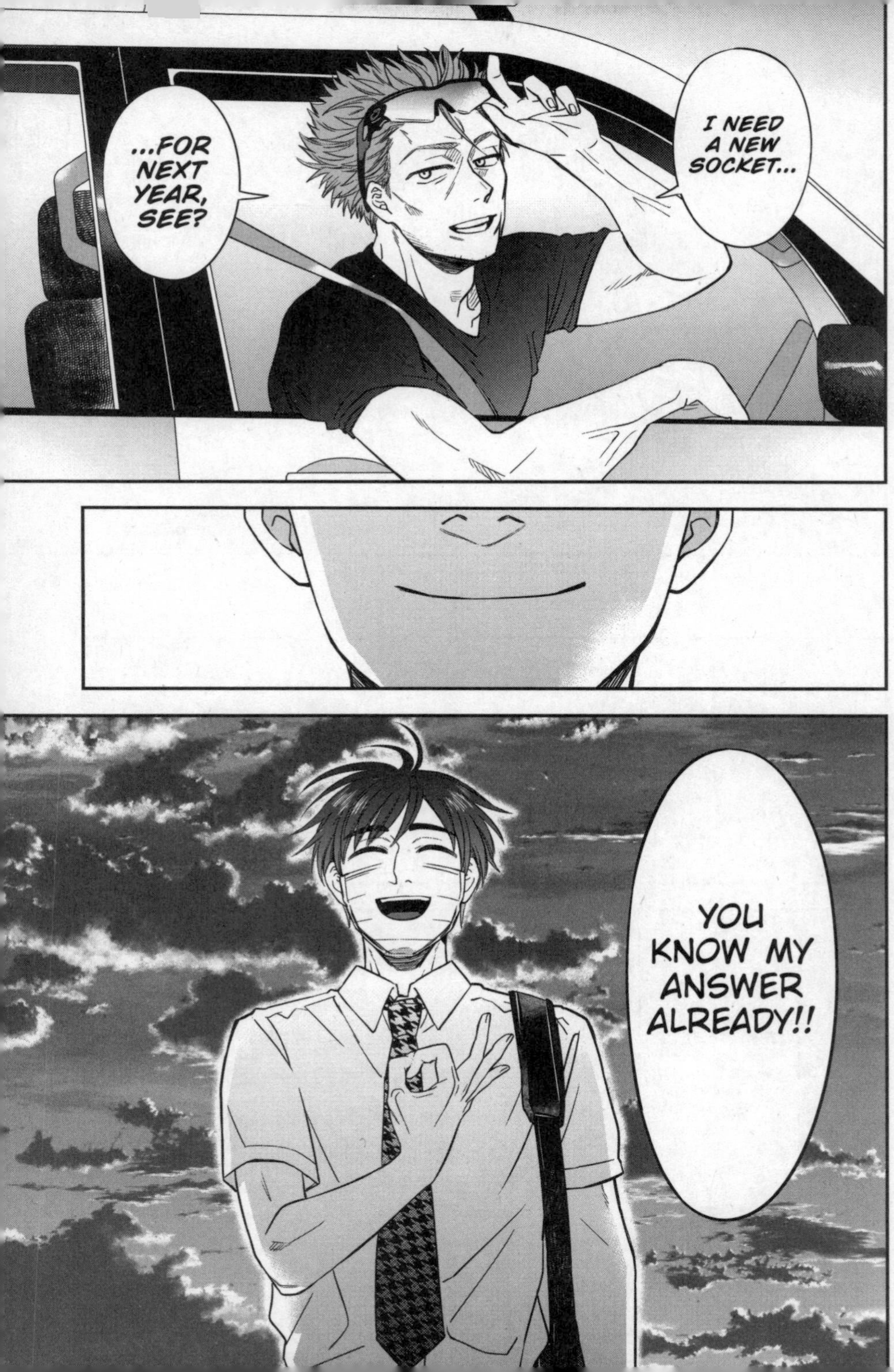
I NEED A NEW SOCKET...
...FOR NEXT YEAR, SEE?
YOU KNOW MY ANSWER ALREADY!!

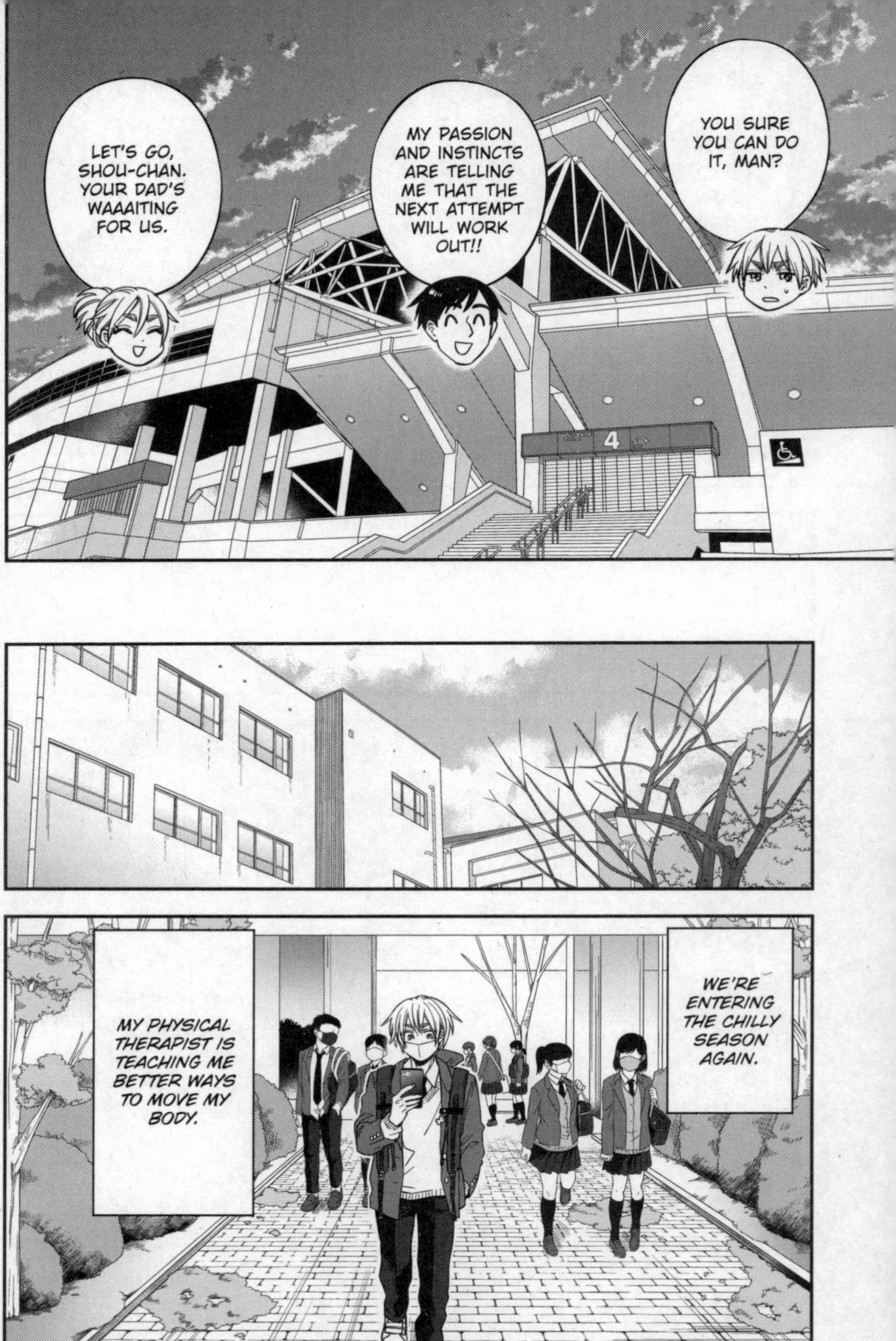
YOU SURE YOU CAN DO IT, MAN?
MY PASSION AND INSTINCTS ARE TELLING ME THAT THE NEXT ATTEMPT WILL WORK OUT!!
LET'S GO, SHOU-CHAN. YOUR DAD'S WAAAITING FOR US.
4
WE'RE ENTERING THE CHILLY SEASON AGAIN.
MY PHYSICAL THERAPIST IS TEACHING ME BETTER WAYS TO MOVE MY BODY.

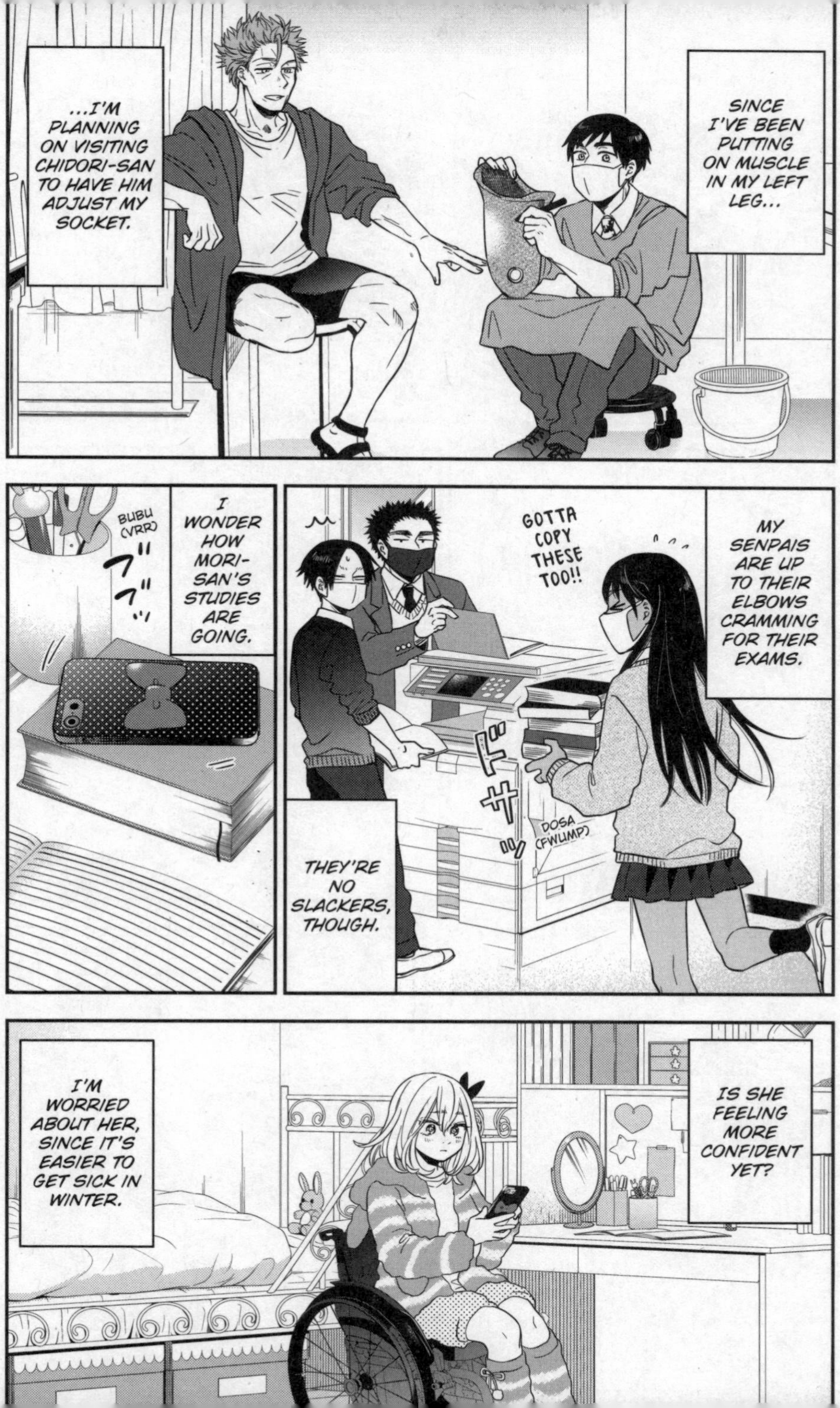
SINCE I'VE BEEN PUTTING ON MUSCLE IN MY LEFT LEG...
...I'M PLANNING ON VISITING CHIDORI-SAN TO HAVE HIM ADJUST MY SOCKET.
MY SENPAIS ARE UP TO THEIR ELBOWS CRAMMING FOR THEIR EXAMS.
GOTTA COPY THESE TOO!!
DOSA (FWUMP)
THEY'RE NO SLACKERS, THOUGH.
I WONDER HOW MORI-SAN'S STUDIES ARE GOING.
BUBU (VRR)
IS SHE FEELING MORE CONFIDENT YET?
I'M WORRIED ABOUT HER, SINCE IT'S EASIER TO GET SICK IN WINTER.

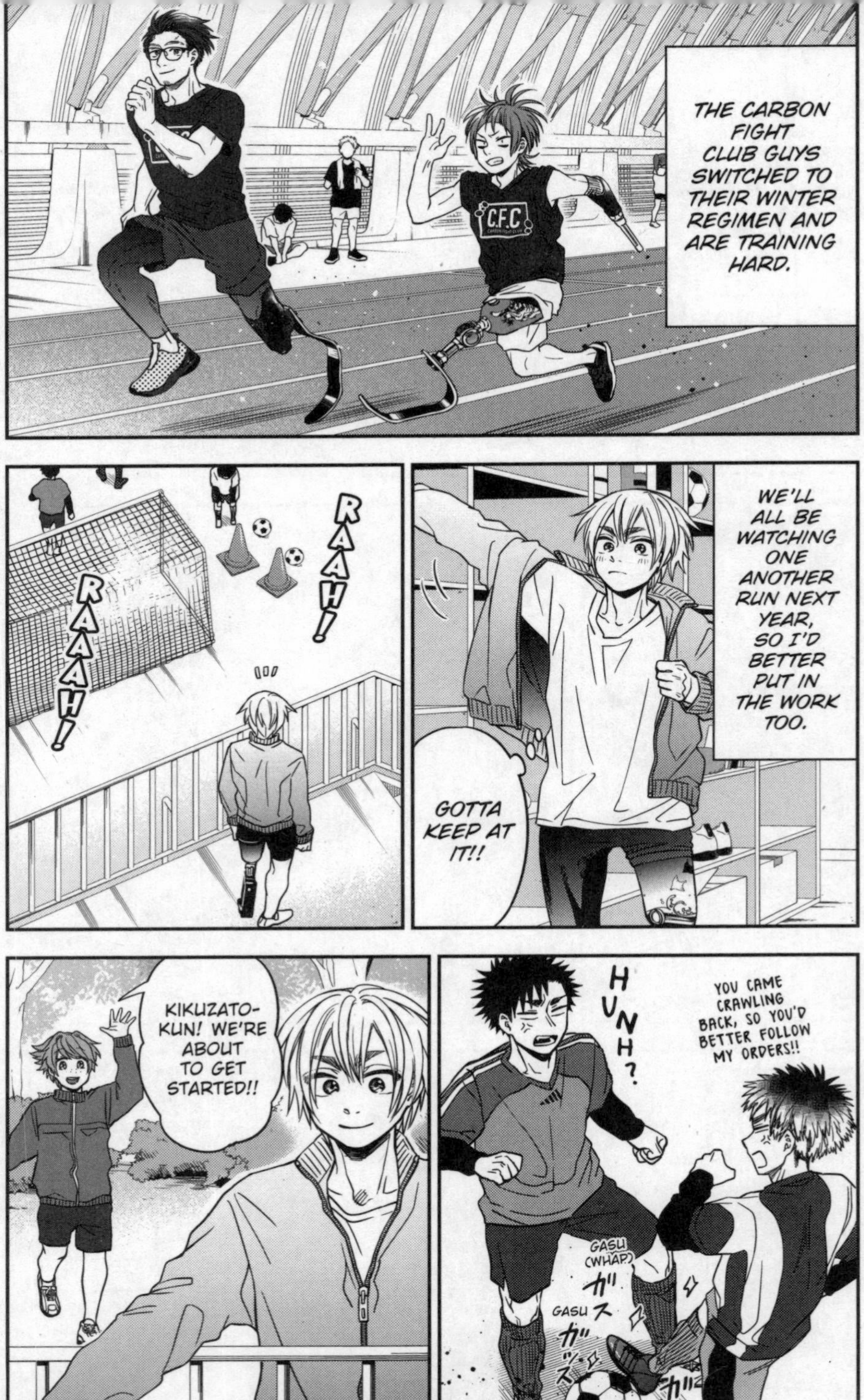
THE CARBON FIGHT CLUB GUYS SWITCHED TO THEIR WINTER REGIMEN AND ARE TRAINING HARD.
C.F.C
WE'LL ALL BE WATCHING ONE ANOTHER RUN NEXT YEAR, SO I'D BETTER PUT IN THE WORK TOO.
GOTTA KEEP AT IT!!
RAAAH!
RAAAAH!
YOU CAME CRAWLING BACK, SO YOU'D BETTER FOLLOW MY ORDERS!!
HUNH?
GASU (WHAP)
ガス
GASU
ガッス
KIKUZATO-KUN! WE'RE ABOUT TO GET STARTED!!

READY TO DO THIS?

YEAH!!

ON YOUR MARK...

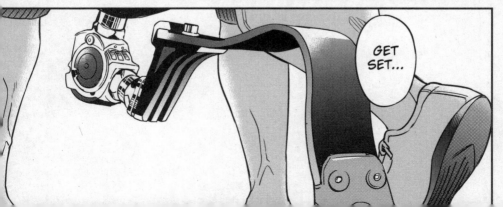

GET SET...

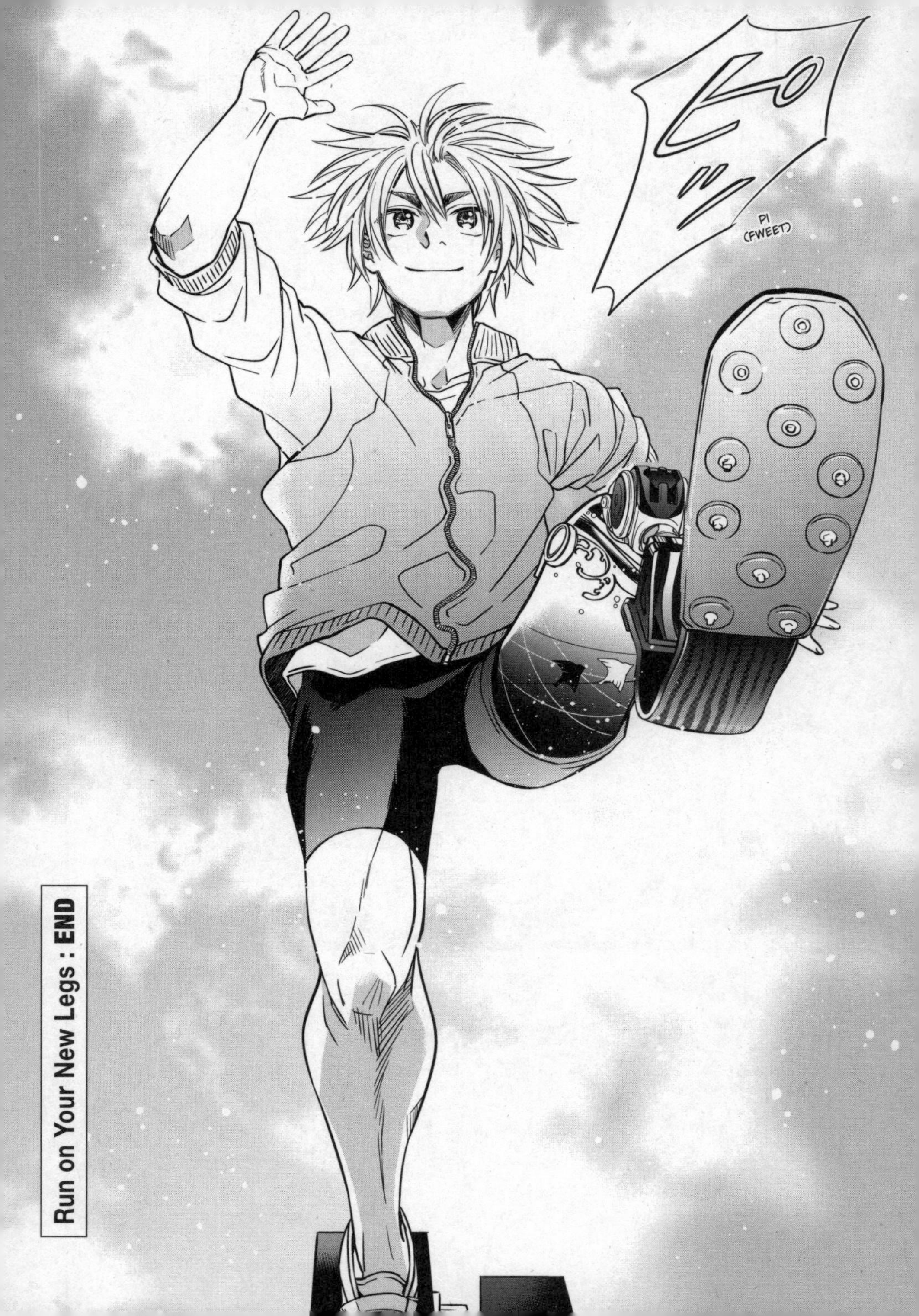
ピーッ
PI (FWEET)
Run on Your New Legs : END

TRANSLATION NOTES

COMMON HONORIFICS

no honorific: Indicates familiarity or closeness; if used without permission or reason, addressing someone in this manner would constitute an insult.

-san: The Japanese equivalent of Mr./Mrs./Ms. This is the fail-safe honorific if politeness is required.

-kun: Used most often when referring to boys, this honorific indicates affection or familiarity. Occasionally used by older men among their peers, but it may also be used by anyone referring to a person of lower standing.

-chan: Affectionate honorific indicating familiarity used mostly in reference to girls; also used in reference to cute persons or animals of any gender.

-senpai: A suffix used when addressing upperclassmen or more senior coworkers.

-sensei: A respectful term for teachers, artists, or high-level professionals.

-sama: An honorific conveying great respect.

CURRENCY CONVERSION

While exchange rates fluctuate daily, a good approximation is ¥100 to 1 USD.

Page 50: A *bento* is a Japanese lunch box, often with partitions like a lunch tray to separate the various dishes.

Page 61: **"Nutmeg"** refers to the act of kicking the soccer ball between the defender's legs. Here, Kikuzato and Takekawa have turned it into a one-on-one game.

Page 92: Hanshin Koshien Stadium is a baseball field near the city of Kobe that hosts national high school baseball tournaments. In media, the name "Koshien" is basically synonymous with high school baseball.

Page 145: In Japanese culture, the **sign Chidori makes with his hand** (touching thumb to tip of pointer finger) is code for "money." While he doesn't openly state his motivation, he is implying it with this gesture.

Page 158: Chidori and Hobara are **exchanging business cards** (held with both hands while bowing slightly), as is the custom in Japan when two professionals are meeting in person for the first time.

Special thanks
to all my consultants

Atsushi Yamamoto (Shin Nihon Jusetsu)
Junta Kosuda (Open House)
Mikio Ikeda (Digital Advertising Consortium)
Tomoki Yoshida

Xiborg
Ottobock Japan
Okino Sports Prosthetics & Orthotics (Atsuo Okino)
D'ACTION (Shuji Miyake)
Naoto Yoshida (Writer)

Cramer Japan: Hideaki Oie/Seiji Nonaka/Everyone Else
National Research and Development Agency
National Institute of Advanced Industrial Science and Technology
Hiroaki Hobara

Yoko Akuta (Graphic Designer)
Osamu Arazeki (Photographer)

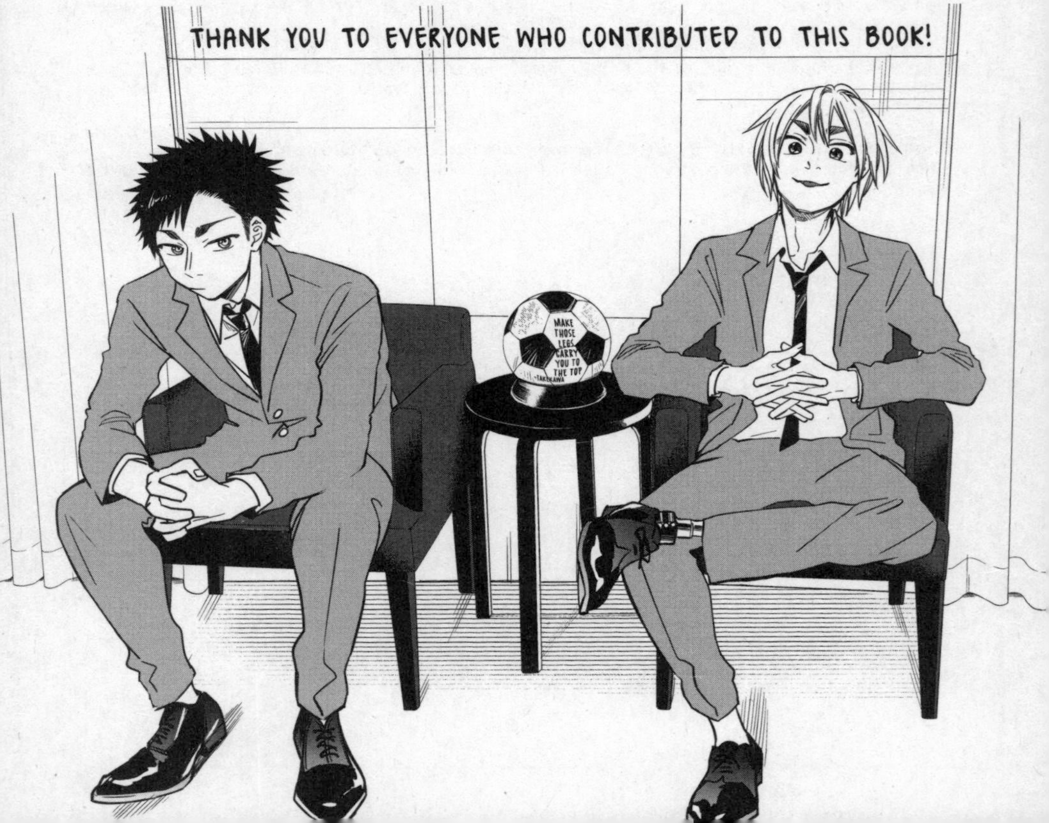
THANK YOU TO EVERYONE WHO CONTRIBUTED TO THIS BOOK!
MAKE THOSE LEGS CARRY YOU TO THE TOP

BONUS

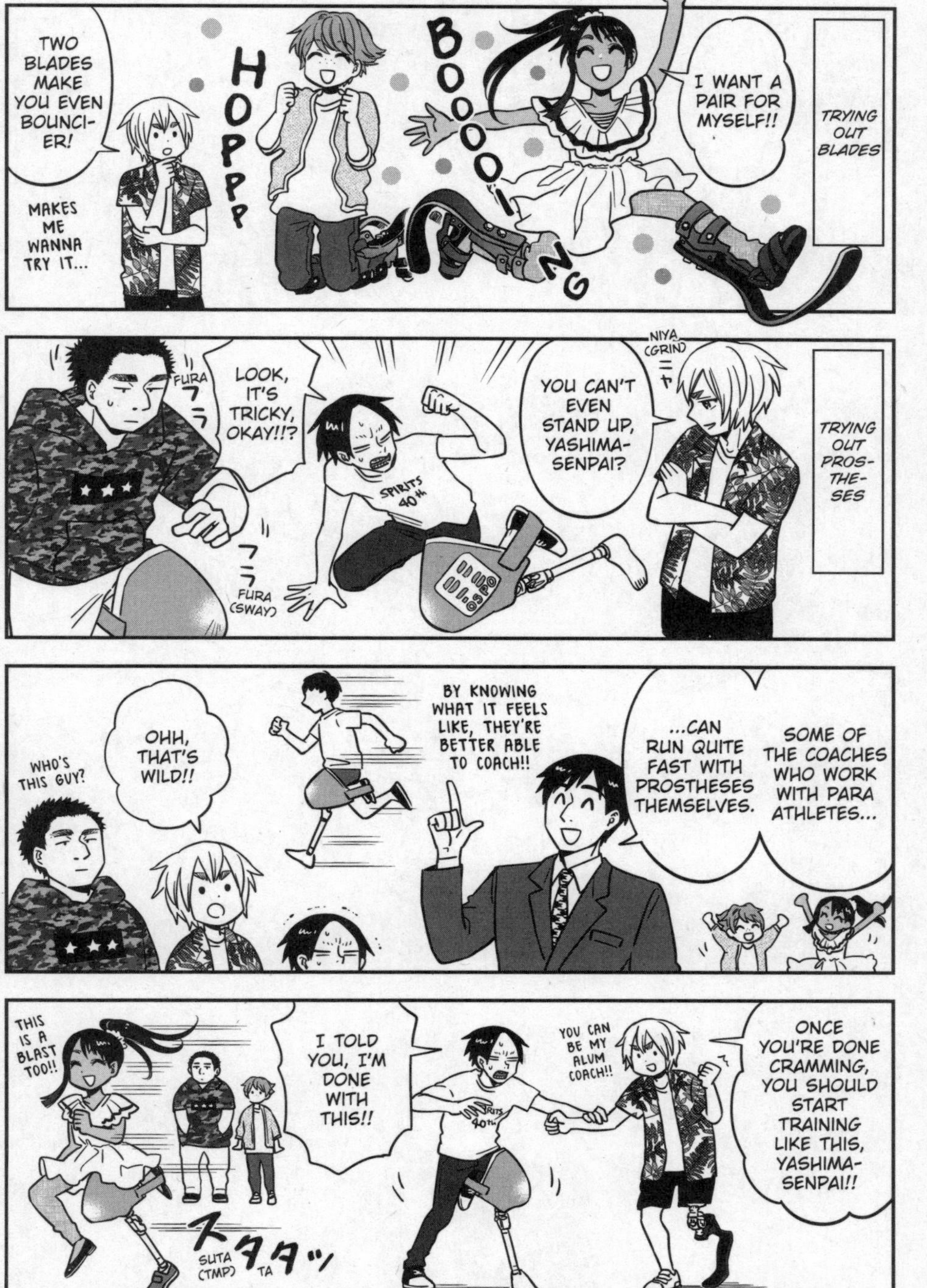
TRYING OUT BLADES
I WANT A PAIR FOR MYSELF!!
BOOOOOOING
HOPPP
TWO BLADES MAKE YOU EVEN BOUNCIER!
MAKES ME WANNA TRY IT...
TRYING OUT PROSTHESES
NIYA (GRIN)
YOU CAN'T EVEN STAND UP, YASHIMA-SENPAI?
LOOK, IT'S TRICKY, OKAY!!?
SPIRITS 40th
FURA
FURA (SWAY)
SOME OF THE COACHES WHO WORK WITH PARA ATHLETES...
...CAN RUN QUITE FAST WITH PROSTHESES THEMSELVES.
BY KNOWING WHAT IT FEELS LIKE, THEY'RE BETTER ABLE TO COACH!!
OHH, THAT'S WILD!!
WHO'S THIS GUY?
ONCE YOU'RE DONE CRAMMING, YOU SHOULD START TRAINING LIKE THIS, YASHIMA-SENPAI!!
YOU CAN BE MY ALUM COACH!!
I TOLD YOU, I'M DONE WITH THIS!!
THIS IS A BLAST TOO!!
SUTA (TMP) TA

STORYBOARD BY: ART BY: NAKAJIMA-SAN (ASSISTANT)

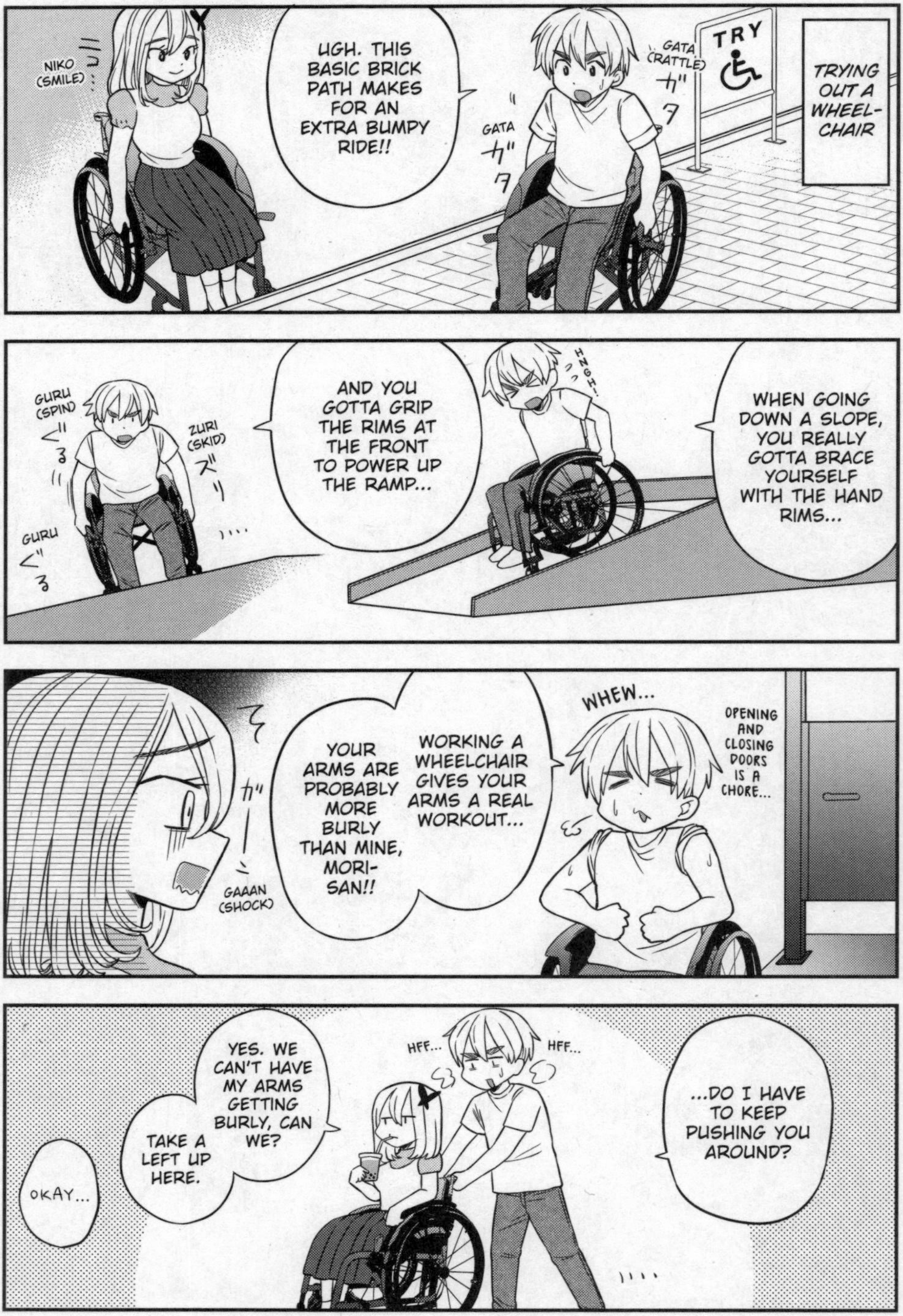
TRYING OUT A WHEEL-CHAIR
TRY
GATA (RATTLE)
ガタ
GATA
ガタ
UGH. THIS BASIC BRICK PATH MAKES FOR AN EXTRA BUMPY RIDE!!
NIKO (SMILE)
ニコ
WHEN GOING DOWN A SLOPE, YOU REALLY GOTTA BRACE YOURSELF WITH THE HAND RIMS...
HNGH!
AND YOU GOTTA GRIP THE RIMS AT THE FRONT TO POWER UP THE RAMP...
ZURI (SKID)
ズリ
GURU (SPIN)
ぐる
....
GURU
ぐる
OPENING AND CLOSING DOORS IS A CHORE...
WHEW...
WORKING A WHEELCHAIR GIVES YOUR ARMS A REAL WORKOUT...
YOUR ARMS ARE PROBABLY MORE BURLY THAN MINE, MORI-SAN!!
GAAAN (SHOCK)
ガーン
...DO I HAVE TO KEEP PUSHING YOU AROUND?
HFF...
HFF...
YES. WE CAN'T HAVE MY ARMS GETTING BURLY, CAN WE?
TAKE A LEFT UP HERE.
OKAY...
....

STORYBOARD BY: ART BY: MORUNGA-SAN (ASSISTANT)

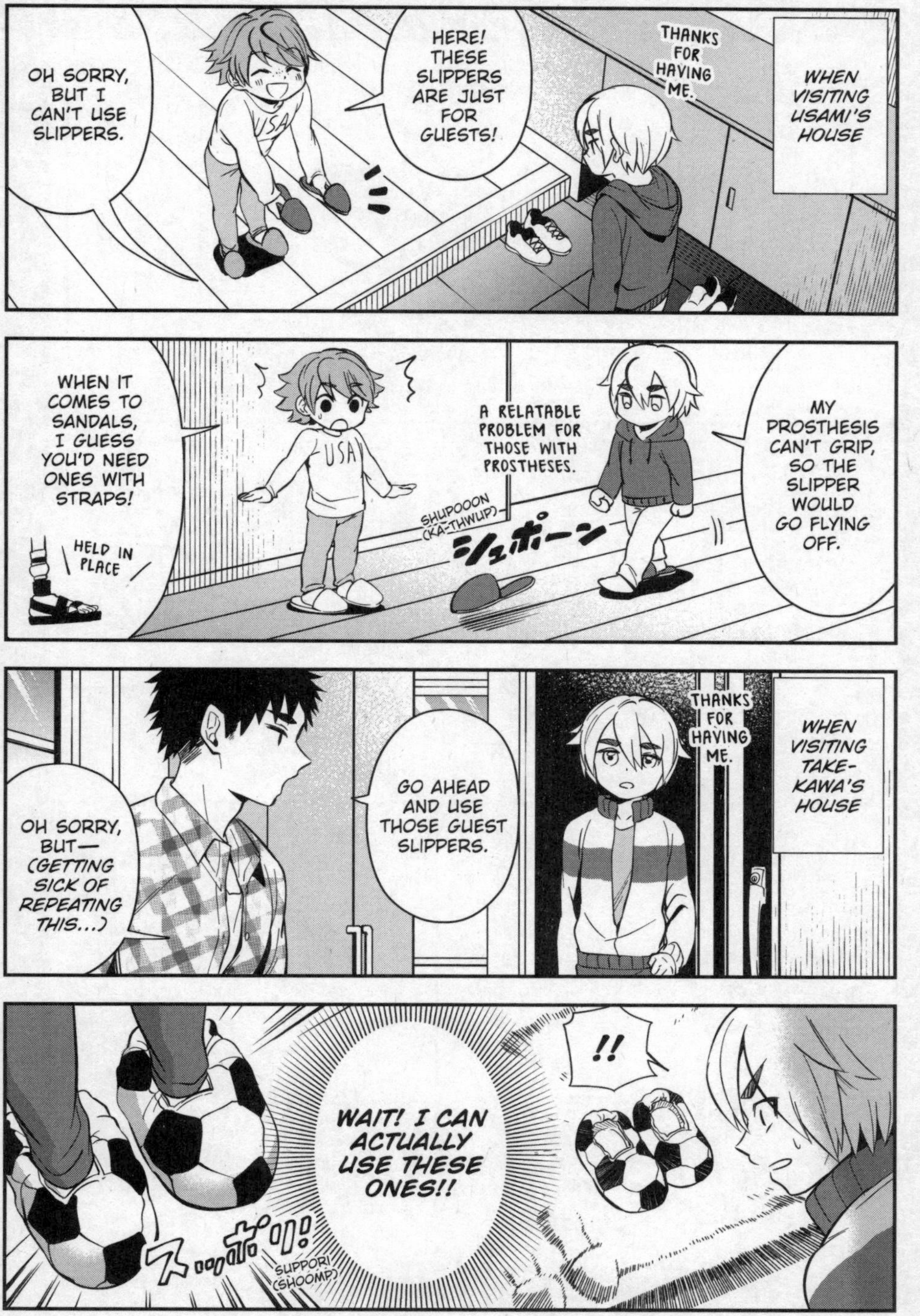
WHEN VISITING USAMI'S HOUSE
THANKS FOR HAVING ME.
HERE! THESE SLIPPERS ARE JUST FOR GUESTS!
OH SORRY, BUT I CAN'T USE SLIPPERS.
MY PROSTHESIS CAN'T GRIP, SO THE SLIPPER WOULD GO FLYING OFF.
A RELATABLE PROBLEM FOR THOSE WITH PROSTHESES.
シュポーン
SHUPOOON (KA-THWUP)
WHEN IT COMES TO SANDALS, I GUESS YOU'D NEED ONES WITH STRAPS!
HELD IN PLACE
WHEN VISITING TAKE-KAWA'S HOUSE
THANKS FOR HAVING ME.
GO AHEAD AND USE THOSE GUEST SLIPPERS.
OH SORRY, BUT— (GETTING SICK OF REPEATING THIS...)
!!
WAIT! I CAN ACTUALLY USE THESE ONES!!
SUPPORI (SHOOMP)

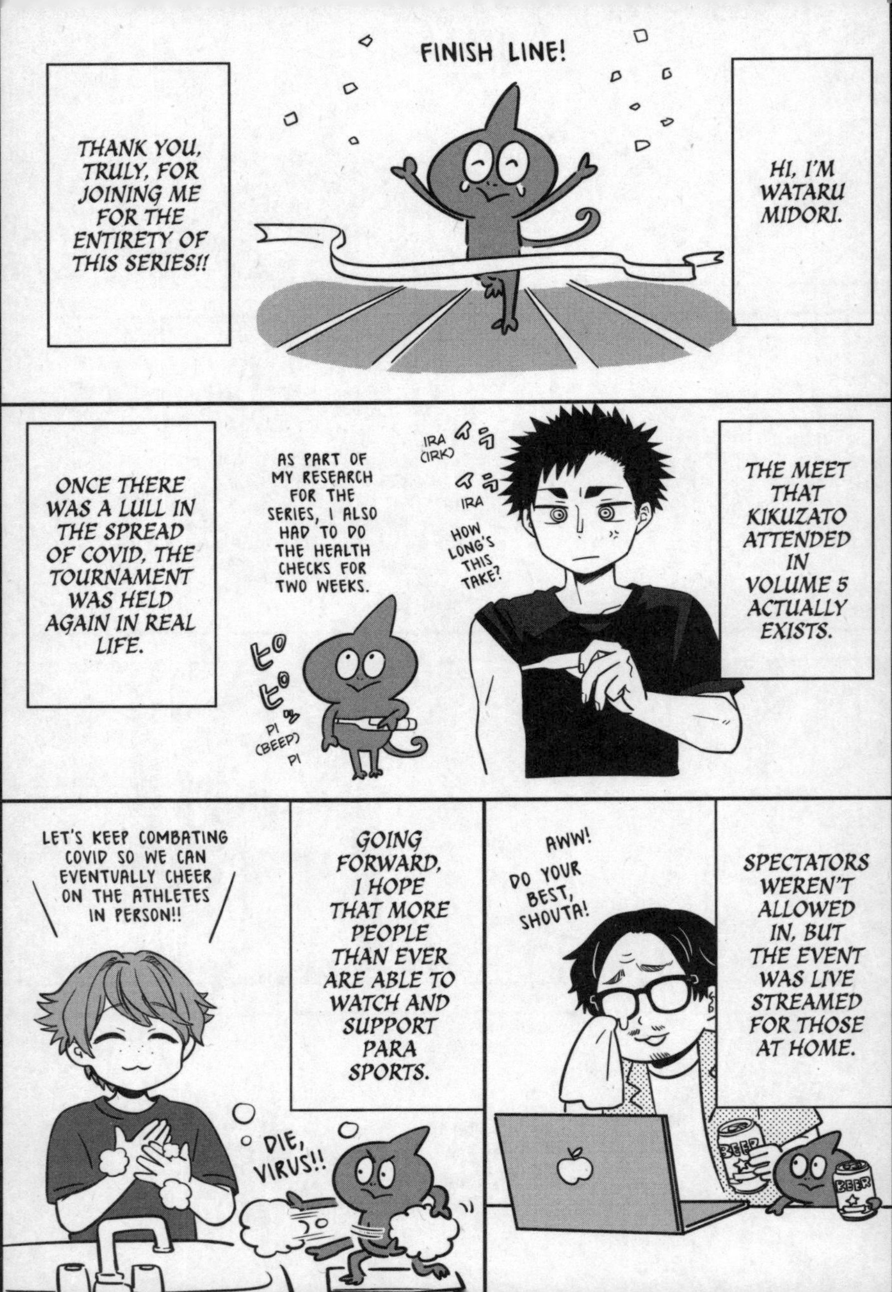
HI, I'M WATARU MIDORI.
FINISH LINE!
THANK YOU, TRULY, FOR JOINING ME FOR THE ENTIRETY OF THIS SERIES!!
THE MEET THAT KIKUZATO ATTENDED IN VOLUME 5 ACTUALLY EXISTS.
IRA (IRK)
IRA
HOW LONG'S THIS TAKE?
AS PART OF MY RESEARCH FOR THE SERIES, I ALSO HAD TO DO THE HEALTH CHECKS FOR TWO WEEKS.
PI (BEEP) PI
ONCE THERE WAS A LULL IN THE SPREAD OF COVID, THE TOURNAMENT WAS HELD AGAIN IN REAL LIFE.
SPECTATORS WEREN'T ALLOWED IN, BUT THE EVENT WAS LIVE STREAMED FOR THOSE AT HOME.
AWW!
DO YOUR BEST, SHOUTA!
BEER
BEER
GOING FORWARD, I HOPE THAT MORE PEOPLE THAN EVER ARE ABLE TO WATCH AND SUPPORT PARA SPORTS.
LET'S KEEP COMBATING COVID SO WE CAN EVENTUALLY CHEER ON THE ATHLETES IN PERSON!!
DIE, VIRUS!!

I'VE SPOKEN OF "MAKING" YOU A PROSTHESIS, BUT IN TRUTH THE PROSTHETIST DOESN'T ACTUALLY CREATE ALL THE COMPONENTS.

ZU (SIP) ズ...

IN VOLUME 4, I MENTIONED THAT I HAD TO CUT SOME DETAILED CONTENT ABOUT PROSTHESES.

THEY'RE WAY TOO EXPENSIVE FOR MOST PEOPLE, BUT THERE ISN'T ENOUGH DEMAND FOR MASS PRODUCTION.

Top Two Athletic Prosthetic Companies	
Ottobock (Germany)	Össur (Iceland)

IT'S ACTUALLY DIFFICULT FOR THESE BUSINESSES TO MAKE MONEY.

THIS IS BECAUSE JAPAN ITSELF HAS A RELATIVELY SMALL NUMBER OF USERS.

A SMALL NUMBER OF OVERSEAS COMPANIES DOMINATE THE MARKET FOR BLADES AND THE OTHER PARTS.

IT TAKES TIME BEFORE NEWER MODELS ARE AVAILABLE FOR JAPANESE USERS, SO JAPAN TENDS TO LAG BEHIND IN THAT RESPECT.

LOOK, I'VE GOT A GROWTH SPURT COMING, OKAY?

THESE FOREIGN COMPANIES USE LOCAL ATHLETES AS THEIR STANDARD, SO THE PRODUCTS OFTEN AREN'T SIZED PROPERLY FOR JAPANESE PEOPLE.

UP NEXT IS A REPORT FROM MY FACT-FINDING VISIT TO ONE OF THOSE RESEARCH ORGS.

EACH ORGANIZATION CAN SHARE THE FRUITS OF ITS SPECIALTY WITH THE OTHERS.

THAT SAID, THERE ARE MORE AND MORE OPPORTUNITIES IN JAPAN FOR COLLABORATION BETWEEN INDEPENDENT MANUFACTURERS OF ATHLETIC PROSTHESES, SPORTS-GEAR COMPANIES, AND RESEARCH ORGANIZATIONS.

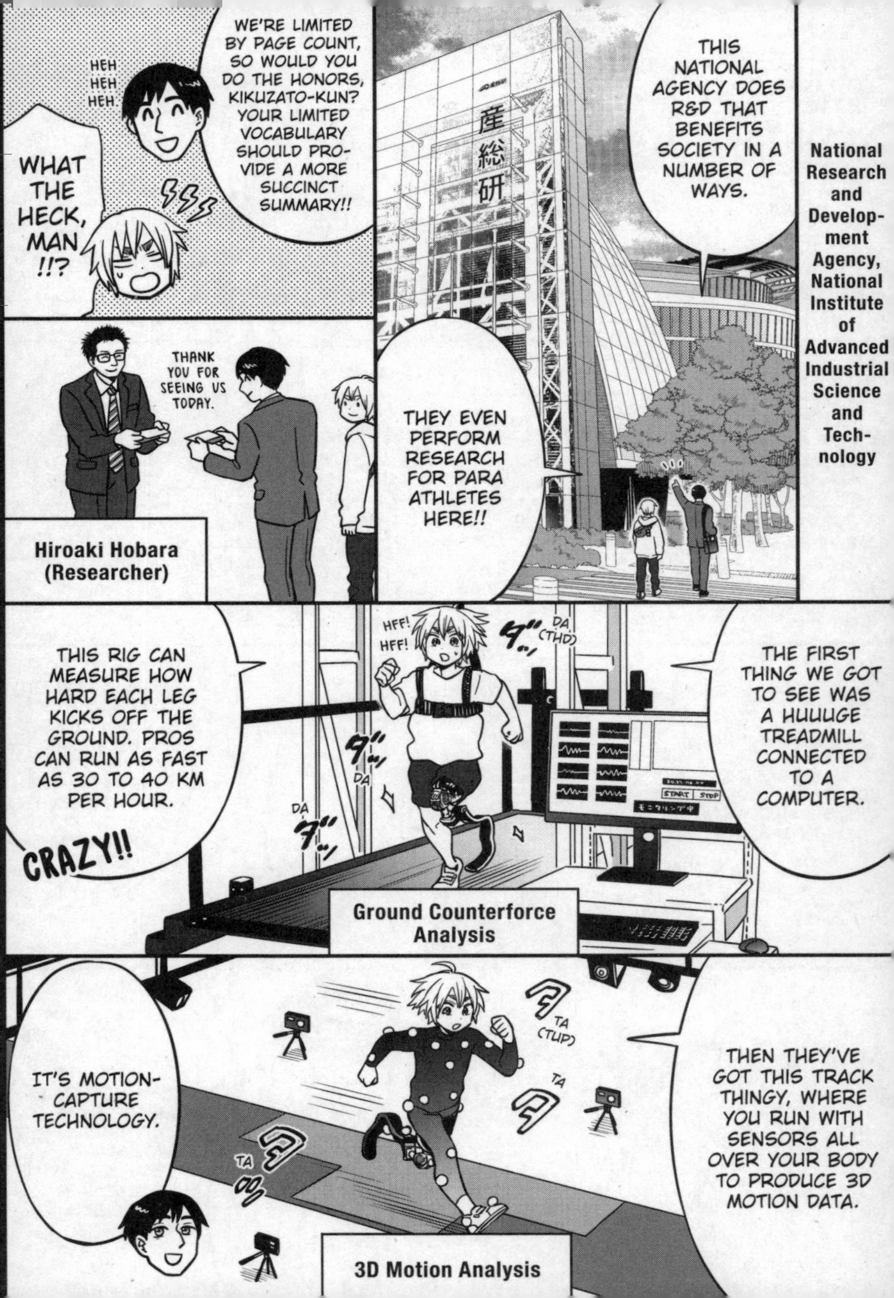
National Research and Development Agency, National Institute of Advanced Industrial Science and Technology
産総研
THIS NATIONAL AGENCY DOES R&D THAT BENEFITS SOCIETY IN A NUMBER OF WAYS.
THEY EVEN PERFORM RESEARCH FOR PARA ATHLETES HERE!!
WE'RE LIMITED BY PAGE COUNT, SO WOULD YOU DO THE HONORS, KIKUZATO-KUN? YOUR LIMITED VOCABULARY SHOULD PROVIDE A MORE SUCCINCT SUMMARY!!
HEH HEH HEH
WHAT THE HECK, MAN!!?
THANK YOU FOR SEEING US TODAY.
Hiroaki Hobara (Researcher)
THE FIRST THING WE GOT TO SEE WAS A HUUUGE TREADMILL CONNECTED TO A COMPUTER.
DA (THD)
HFF! HFF!
START STOP
THIS RIG CAN MEASURE HOW HARD EACH LEG KICKS OFF THE GROUND. PROS CAN RUN AS FAST AS 30 TO 40 KM PER HOUR.
DA
DA
CRAZY!!
Ground Counterforce Analysis
THEN THEY'VE GOT THIS TRACK THINGY, WHERE YOU RUN WITH SENSORS ALL OVER YOUR BODY TO PRODUCE 3D MOTION DATA.
TA (TUP)
TA
TA
IT'S MOTION-CAPTURE TECHNOLOGY.
3D Motion Analysis

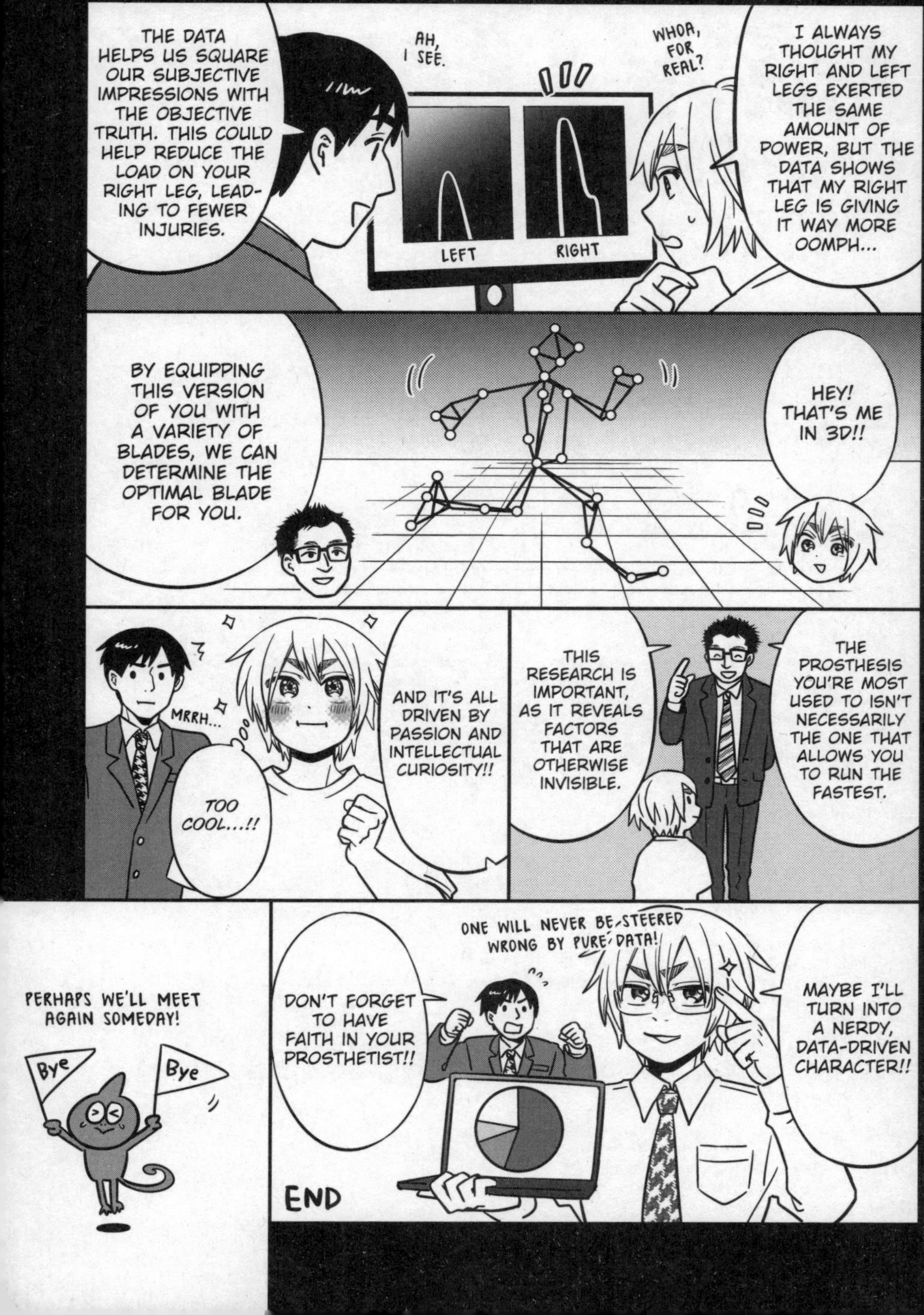
I ALWAYS THOUGHT MY RIGHT AND LEFT LEGS EXERTED THE SAME AMOUNT OF POWER, BUT THE DATA SHOWS THAT MY RIGHT LEG IS GIVING IT WAY MORE OOMPH...
WHOA, FOR REAL?
AH, I SEE.
THE DATA HELPS US SQUARE OUR SUBJECTIVE IMPRESSIONS WITH THE OBJECTIVE TRUTH. THIS COULD HELP REDUCE THE LOAD ON YOUR RIGHT LEG, LEADING TO FEWER INJURIES.
RIGHT
LEFT
HEY! THAT'S ME IN 3D!!
BY EQUIPPING THIS VERSION OF YOU WITH A VARIETY OF BLADES, WE CAN DETERMINE THE OPTIMAL BLADE FOR YOU.
THE PROSTHESIS YOU'RE MOST USED TO ISN'T NECESSARILY THE ONE THAT ALLOWS YOU TO RUN THE FASTEST.
THIS RESEARCH IS IMPORTANT, AS IT REVEALS FACTORS THAT ARE OTHERWISE INVISIBLE.
AND IT'S ALL DRIVEN BY PASSION AND INTELLECTUAL CURIOSITY!!
MRRH...
TOO COOL...!!
MAYBE I'LL TURN INTO A NERDY, DATA-DRIVEN CHARACTER!!
ONE WILL NEVER BE STEERED WRONG BY PURE DATA!
DON'T FORGET TO HAVE FAITH IN YOUR PROSTHETIST!!
END
PERHAPS WE'LL MEET AGAIN SOMEDAY!
Bye
Bye

RUN ON YOUR NEW LEGS 5

WATARU MIDORI

TRANSLATION: Caleb Cook • **LETTERING:** Abigail Blackman

ATARASHII ASHI DE KAKENUKERO. Vol. 5
by Wataru MIDORI
© 2020 Wataru MIDORI
All rights reserved.
Original Japanese edition published by SHOGAKUKAN.
English translation rights in the United States of America, Canada, the United Kingdom, Ireland, Australia and New Zealand arranged with SHOGAKUKAN through Tuttle-Mori Agency, Inc.

Original Cover Design: Yoko AKUTA

English translation © 2023 by Yen Press, LLC

Yen Press
150 West 30th Street, 19th Floor
New York, NY 10001

Visit us at yenpress.com
facebook.com/yenpress
twitter.com/yenpress
yenpress.tumblr.com
instagram.com/yenpress

First Yen Press Edition: July 2023
Edited by Abigail Blackman & Yen Press Editorial: Carl Li
Designed by Yen Press Design: Liz Parlett, Wendy Chan

Yen Press is an imprint of Yen Press, LLC.
The Yen Press name and logo are trademarks of Yen Press, LLC.

Library of Congress Control Number: 2021951359

ISBNs: 978-1-9753-3904-3 (paperback)
       978-1-9753-4573-0 (ebook)

10 9 8 7 6 5 4 3 2 1

WOR

Printed in the United States of America